F. A. JENNEIS
1980

The Structure of Action

The Structure of Action

Edited by Michael Brenner

BASIL BLACKWELL · OXFORD

©Basil Blackwell Publisher 1980
5 Alfred St
Oxford OX1 4HB

British Library Cataloguing in Publication Data

The structure of action.
  1. Social psychology
  I. Brenner, Michael
  301.1   HM251

  ISBN 0-631-19700-1

Filmset by Vantage Photosetting Co. Ltd,
Southampton and London
Printed by Billing and Sons Ltd,
Guildford, London, Oxford, Worcester

Contents

Preface

This book originated partly from an informal symposium 'The Structure of Action' held at Wolfson College, Oxford. I wish to thank Michael Argyle and Rom Harré without whose guidance, encouragement and inspiration this project would not have been possible. I thank my wife Marylin for her help in editing the papers and Maureen Molyneaux for her excellent typing.

Michael Brenner,
Oxford, April 1979

The Structure of Action:
Introduction

MICHAEL BRENNER   *Oxford Polytechnic*

---

1   *The New Social Psychology*

Social psychology has undergone dramatic changes in recent times. So much so that it has become a standard rhetorical gesture to draw a picture of the current state of the subject as being 'in turmoil' (see, for example, Tajfel and Fraser 1978, p. 11). What has happened? Social psychologists have become increasingly dissatisfied with much of what once passed as scientific social psychology. Armistead (1974, p. 7), for example, noted the lack of realism of traditional social psychology: 'We feel that social psychology should be making some sense of our experience and that it doesn't: we feel disappointed.' Mann (1967, p. 7) complained on similar lines about the practical irrelevance of small group research:

Ask a group therapist, a trainer, or a teacher what use he can make of the voluminous outpouring of empirical research on small groups. The unhappy fact is that many, if not most, of the potential consumers of such work feel that such research is constantly asking the wrong questions in the wrong ways and that it is at best irrelevant and at worst inaccurate and misleading.

So far, numerous blueprints for a new science of social

psychology have been developed (see, for example, Argyle 1969; Harré and Secord 1972; Armistead 1974; Shotter 1975; Strickland, Aboud and Gergen 1976; Gauld and Shotter 1977; Collett 1977; Ginsburg 1979; Harré 1979). As differentiated as the new social psychology actually is, there are some unifying characteristics which are worth pointing out.

First, I think that the new social psychology involves just one fundamental theoretical position. This position has been expressed by Duncan and Fiske (1977, p. 10–11):

We believe that any adequate description of face-to-face interaction must take into account both the *structure*, that is, the social forms for that interaction, and the individual *operating within that structure*. Any social action may be seen as shaped by *both these elements*. (My italics)

Duncan and Fiske point out, in other words, that an adequate understanding of human action necessitates, first of all, a consideration of the *natural social context* in which it occurs. Just as we cannot conceive of the flow of a river without paying attention to, among other factors, its bed, it would be wrong to treat human action as if it were context-free, unconstrained by particular natural 'social forms'. Duncan and Fiske then stress that an adequate understanding of action must take into account the *actor as operator*, as constructor of his paths of action. Just as it would be unreasonable to assume, for example, that the river's bed *fully* determines the flow of the river, as this may be dependent on the quantity of the water generated by the river's source and so on, it would be misleading to assume that people act only *reactively*. Thus, as Duncan and Fiske finally indicate, a sufficient explanation of human action involves *both* a consideration of the natural social context by which it is shaped and of the actor as an active agent or operator.

Secondly, I think that the new social psychology involves just one fundamental methodological position. This has emerged in critical contrast to the traditional experimentation-

and-experimentation-only methodology in social psychology (see, for example, Argyle 1969, pp. 17–20; Harré and Secord 1972, pp. 44–64). It was noted that the social psychology experiment may involve a transformation of human action into a kind of being which is unrecognisably alien to the natural structure and experience of action. Whilst in our ordinary lives we experience our actions as contextually specific and as originating from *us*, the experimental social psychologist may view people 'as objects which are passively affected by events in their environment' (Harré and Secord 1972, p. 30). As David Clarke argues in this book, the experimental study of human action, when involving the search of externally manipulable causes of behaviour, may be wholly inappropriate, as it fails to take into account the actual *human* characteristics of the process within which action is generated:

The idea that action is causally determined is an assumption which may be untrue or at least unhelpful, especially if it leads us to overlook the crucial role of *meaning and interpretation* in human affairs. It is not so much the physical properties of our environment which influence our reactions, as the significance they hold for us. (My italics)

Whilst the traditional experimental methodology in social psychology has frequently been found to distort and to mis-represent the actual structure of action processes, the methodology of the new social psychology may be funda-mentally characterized by attempts at adequate *reconstruction* of the components involved in the natural genesis of action. The quest for adequate reconstruction of action processes has brought about the application of a great variety of particular methods and also a critical and reflective sense of the uses to which methods can and should be put (see, for example, Brenner, Marsh and Brenner 1978).

Whilst there are fundamental points of convergence in the new social psychology, the actual research interests and prac-tices displayed are, however, very varied. There is a strong reliance on an anthropomorphic model of man, on a view of people '*as if they were human beings*' (Harré and Secord 1972, p. 87) operating in specific social worlds, yet there is no agreement about which components of human action to study in which ways. Given this situation, some observers have come to diagnose a 'rapid flux of fads and fashions, some of them come and gone at bewildering speed' (Tajfel and Fraser 1978, p. 11) in the development of the new social psychology. I believe that the extraordinary differentiation of theory and practice in the new social psychology is both necessary and healthy. It is only through radical trial and error that more lasting novel perspectives in social psychology may be established. The present highly differentiated and highly personalised state of the new social psychology is reflected in the contributions to this volume. This will become apparent in the summary of the substantive and methodological lines of argument proposed in the papers.

2   The Structure of Action: Substantive Issues

John Shotter suggests that our social psychological enquiries must be grounded in a full understanding of *human agency* in action processes. As he points out:

Human behaviour would seem to be unique not because, from an external observer's point of view, no other behaviour is quite like it, but it is only about human behaviour that we are able to make *and sustain* certain assumptions. Observing a projectile now (as beneficiaries of Cartesian metaphysics and modern science) we ascribe the pattern of its trajectory to the operation of impersonal general laws, but in observing people's motions we still ascribe their trajectories *to them*; we still think of them as controlling their own movements in relation to their own thoughts and feelings.

How do people come to construct their paths of action? Shotter regards intentionality as the key generative mechanism here: 'intentionality is a fundamental and irreducible feature, a pre-supposition of all thought, all conceptual activity, and all action.' Intentionality works not only within the specific here–and–nows of action processes; it is embedded in particular time structures. Action processes have a meaningful continuity for the actors: not only is the present under conscious control, but the past is also revocable, just as the horizon of future action can be taken into account.

While intentionality is seen as 'an inner *forming activity*, which is the cause of the growth of things, and of the development and differentiation of their various essential forms', it is not *wholly* responsible for the outcomes of action. Shotter provides the following analogy:

In the same way that an intention is said to 'contain' or 'point to' its object, so an acorn may be said to 'contain' or 'point to' an oak tree. But an acorn certainly does not contain an oak tree, or anything like it, even in miniature. It is best seen as the *structured medium or means* through which, in interaction with its surroundings, an oak tree forms, developing itself as the structured means for its own further development or growth. Furthermore, although an acorn specifies the production of an oak tree from it, and not any other kind of tree, it does not specify the tree that grows from it exactly (number of branches, twigs, leaves, and so on), for the tree grows in unpredictable interaction with its surroundings.

While intentionality provides a differentiating criterion between action and mere behaviour, 'between things people *do* and things which merely happen to them', Shotter stresses also that action is constrained by contextual and other characteristics. For example, people may fail to realise intentions because of lack of skill or lack of opportunity for action.

The consideration of contextual and other constraints on action, besides intentionality, is particularly important when we deal with joint action, 'such activities as discussions, industrial negotiations, football matches, tutorials, greetings, insults', and so on. Here, personal intentionality is constrained by the acting presence of others: 'men must often interlace their actions in with those of others, hence, what they as individuals desire and what actually happens *are often two quite different things.*' Personal intentionality is also guided by the particular *style* (or definition) of the interaction situation: 'people know in which activity they are engaged and conduct themselves accordingly.' Furthermore, Shotter argues that interaction situations involve *moral* commitment on the part of the participants, more, interaction situations may be seen as *morally coercive*: 'they provide a world in terms of which a person who inhabits it *must* determine his action'. Yet a person's action is never just situationally reactive; it is intentional, all the time. This implies that intentionality is both a person characteristic and is socially constructed. The social reality dependence of intentionality provides an ultimate boundary for the degrees of freedom people's particular actions can have: 'there is no way in which their actions can lead to results *beyond* that reality; it is reflexive in the sense that, no matter what happens, it is understood and dealt with in terms that the reality provides.'

Shotter, complex and meta-theoretical, if not metaphysical, as his arguments may frequently be, provides an ultimate horizon for the study of human action. It should be clear by the end of his paper that an adequate explanation of action must take into account both human agency, particularly intentionality, as a generative source for action and also the social context of its occurrence, by which action is moulded and constrained. Shotter does not, however, outline any *specific* aspects or components of the relationships between people as actors and social contexts in the genesis of action.

In a sense, Michael Argyle's paper may be seen as contributing both a continuation and a development of Shotter's framework for the study of action. Argyle stresses that social psychological enquiry must consider action as specific for particular social situations: 'If we want to explain social behaviour we must explain how social situations influence it.' He proposes using games as models of action in social situations. He points out that in using the game analogy, 'game' is understood in a rather general sense so that the element of competition which is often absent from social situations is underplayed.

Argyle suggests that we consider, for various purposes of enquiry, eight aspects or components of action in social situations:

a. *Goal structure.* 'Why do people enter social situations, indeed why do they engage in social behaviour at all? A functional account would suppose that they are motivated to do so, i.e., they expect that certain needs will be satisfied, certain goals obtained.' Goals refer, thus, to certain physical needs or drives of a person or to certain socio-cultural characteristics, such as the desire to learn at university. Goals may form a structure 'if a person is pursuing more than one goal, or if there is more than one person there.'

b. *Repertoire of elements.* 'The hypothesis I want to develop is that each basic kind of social situation has a characteristic repertoire of elements. To some extent these elements follow from, and could be deduced from, the goals of the situation; the elements are the moves which are needed to attain the goals. Thus problem-solving requires moves like "makes suggestion", "asks question", "disagrees", and so on.'

c. *Rules.* 'Continuing our analogy between social situations and games, I want to propose that all social situations are rule-governed.' Rules are seen as the ultimate 'regulations about how the game is to be played, which must be agreed to and followed by all players.'

d. *Sequences of behaviour.* 'Just as situations have characteristic repertoires of elements, so also do they have characteristic sequences of these elements. The sequences of acts form the route to the goals of the interactions.' There are simple sequences, as in greetings, and more complex ones, as in doctor-patient interaction or interviewing.

e. *Concepts.* 'In order to deal with complex stimuli or problems or to perform skills, it is necessary to possess the relevant concepts. In order to play cricket it is necessary to be familiar with such concepts as "out", "declare", "no-ball", "l.b.w.", and so on. In addition, the higher levels of skill may depend on the acquisition of additional concepts. In chess, for example, it soon becomes necessary to know about "check by discovery", "fork", and so on.'

f. *Environmental setting.* This refers to the influence of the physical setting of a situation on the interaction; 'environment causes behaviour, as is shown by studies of the effects of over-crowding, for example.' And 'someone who, for example, arranges the furniture in a room, does so in the expectation that this will affect interaction in some way.'

g. *Roles.* 'Most situations contain a number of different roles, i.e., there are positions for which there are different patterns of behaviour and different rules.'

h. *Skills and difficulties.* 'Every social situation presents certain difficulties, and these need certain social skills in order to deal with them.'

While Argyle's approach provides a range of important dimensions to be considered in the analysis of action, a number of problems may arise in its application. For example, it is possible to argue that the game analogy will not apply to *all* social situations, for one can imagine social situations which do not require action as definitely structured by particular goals, rules, behaviour sequences, roles, and so on. Wittgenstein (1968, § 83) has provided a relevant example of social interaction in this context:

We can easily imagine people amusing themselves in a field by playing with a ball so as to start various existing games, but playing many without finishing them and in between throwing the ball aimlessly into the air, chasing one another with the ball and bombarding one another for a joke and so on.

Ragnar Rommetveit, in his paper, points out a further problem that we may need to consider when using Argyle's game analogy. This may arise when there is a reason to believe that people, in some interaction, do not fully, but only partially, share the meaning of the social situation. Action, if this is the case, must then be studied from an actor's-meaning-point-of-view. As Rommetveit indicates, *interaction* and the *mutual* understanding of each other's actions can become problematic when participants do not fully share the meaning of the 'game':

Mutual understanding can then no longer be accounted for in terms of either unequivocally shared knowledge of the world or linguistically mediated literal meaning. It becomes to a considerable extent a matter of, for example, actual and reciprocally assumed control of what is meant by what is said and of, in some sense, a self-fulfilling *faith* in a shared world. Also, the study of human communication becomes an enquiry into a hitherto largely unexplored range of possible, sustained and/or only temporarily established states of partially shared social realities.

On the lines of Rommeveit's perspective, one would often need to conceptualize action in more than one way, as it would be fallacious to insist that an action must always involve *a* particular meaning for all participants. The various meanings of an action may be discovered in a number of ways. We may consider the meanings of an action for the performer on the level of his intentions and motives and the various other understandings he is able to produce of what he is, or was, doing. We may also invite the understandings of other participants and bystanders which may explain an action in other ways. It is only at the intersection of all understandings that there is *mutual consensus* about what an action means. This may just be a trivial minimum, as is the case when people agree that an act of mowing the lawn is performed by various actions,

without, however, thereby *further* explicating what these actions *fully* mean for the performer, for other participants and
for bystanders. These further action meanings are accordingly, as they do not intersect, 'private', contingent upon particular personal positions from which action is experienced and
made sense of. 'Having a particular position in understanding'
implies thus that the meanings of an action are not independent of the understander, it 'implies a definite perspective and
hence necessarily a restricted range of possible alternatives
against which only specific aspects of the event acquires
significance and salience.' Rommetveit illustrates this issue
thus:

Consider, for instance, at trivial minimum of *holding hands and
singing lullabies at the bedside of a small child.* What is implied by such an
act to the middle-aged father engaged in the act, to the child, to
observers in different positions? Is the father merely doing his
parental duty? Is he comforting the child? Is he spoiling it? Which
potential aspects become salient when the act is viewed from the
position of the child's teenage brother? Which aspects acquire significance within grandfather's private world of memories and retrospective wisdom?

What is going on in the bedroom in such a case 'means' obviously
different things to *the child* and to *the father.* But what? The teenage
brother may maintain that his small sister is being overprotected and
spoiled, whereas the holding of hands when viewed from *the old
man's position* perhaps is transformed into an enigmatic existential
bridge between two generations of human life: A middle-aged man
consoling an anxious child while actually, though unknowingly,
himself seeking comfort and courage in the young hand. Is the
'meaning' of the act *sub specie aeternitatis* thus perhaps embedded in
the refrain of the lullaby, though in such a way that it cannot be fully
revealed *to the agents* until a late stage of life? Let us listen:

> . . . so sullelee – lullelee – loo
> our boat is drifting ashore
> where one and one don't make two
> but something mysteriously more . . .

The papers considered so far have dealt with the structure of action in quite general terms. Actions, however, from a performance perspective, are always behaviourally specific. They appear in non-verbal and/or linguistic form. The study of non-verbal actions may pose particular problems, as Peter Collett points out in his paper:

Suppose I move my arm through the air. There is a sense in which it would be impossible to offer an objective description of the separate actions that I have performed. Any attempt to identify the constituents, let alone the boundaries of the actual movement itself, would necessarily arise out of a set of assumptions that I entertain about the nature of such action. In other words, the stream of behaviour is, for all practical purposes, homogeneous in time. It is seamless, and it is only by virtue of the segmentations that I impose on it, and the way in which these segments are seen as relating to each other, that it can have any meaning or significance for me.

The study of linguistic action is not less troublesome when we become interested in its communication aspect. We may then ask, for example: How is linguistic communication achieved and sustained in interaction? What are its functions as action and in interaction? Why and when does linguistic communication fail in interaction? These questions are addressed in the papers by Jens Allwood, Marga Kreckel and Rolv Blakar.

Allwood argues that an understanding of linguistic communication involves a reconstruction of speech activity in terms of action. Before speech can become significant as communicative action, it should comply with a range of particular 'felicity conditions', or as Allwood puts it:

In order to investigate the factors which are relevant for our conception of a certain type of action, it is often helpful to study the 'felicity conditions' of the action concerned; that is to say those conditions which have to be met so that the action may be considered ideally felicitous.

Which kinds of 'felicity conditions' should we consider in attempts to identify the fundamental dimensions which underlie, and make up, communicative action? Allwood suggests:

a. Communicative action should be *voluntary and intentional*. 'Intentional' means here that the speech activity should be 'directed towards a certain goal. Behaviour which is not intentional, as, for example, patellar reflexes or breathing, is therefore not viewed as action.'

b. Communicative action should be *rational*, that is, 'adequate' and 'competent', 'as effective and efficient as possible'. It 'should only be performed if there is a likelihood of success. Actions which are not intentional and rational in the sense intended here are likely to be seen as irrational or even irresponsible, and can be subject to social sanctions . . .'

c. Communicative action must meet certain *ethical require-ments*. Besides politeness and other issues, perhaps 'the most important ethical requirement of communication is genuine-ness. Senders should possess those feelings, attitudes or inten-tions which are usually connected with the behaviour of the sender on natural or conventional grounds by a receiver. For example, my questions should express my desire for informa-tion and my statements should express what I believe to be true.'

d. Communicative action implies specific *forms of linguistic behaviour*. Besides possessing 'a certain speed or strength of movement', communicative action 'should be conventionally correct with regard to (a) the correspondence between units of expression and desired content (lexical conventions) and (b) the joining together of units of expression to form bigger units (syntax).'

e. Communicative action should be *contextually specific*. 'Cer-tain contents can only be expressed in certain contexts.'

f. Communicative action should be *success-oriented*. 'In order to be felicitous the purpose of an action must be achieved. For a communication action this usually means that a sender, by transferring information to a receiver, is able to effect the receiver in the way he had intended.'

Kreckel proposes studying communicative action on very similar lines. She starts from Grice's (1975) four maxims of communicative co-operation:

a. Communicative action should be *informative*, but not over-informative.

b. Communicative action should be *genuine*. 'That is, do not say anything you believe to be false or for which you lack adequate evidence.'

c. Communicative action should be *contextually relevant*.

d. Communicative action should be *clear*. 'Try to avoid ob-scurity, ambiguity, wordiness, and disorderliness in your use of language.'

How are these maxims realised in interaction? In order to determine the empirical forms which the maxims take in any specific communicative situation, she suggests taking into account the degrees of *shared knowledge* between participants. She argues:

first, that a high degree of shared knowledge is a necessary precondi-tion for relatively unambiguous understanding, and, secondly, that shared knowledge increases the likelihood of communicants relying on the same cues when they encode and decode communicative behaviour.

Thus, Kreckel makes us aware of the fact that an adequate reconstruction of communicative action processes needs to involve the actors' perspective, that is, an empirical analysis of the actual means used by participants 'in the process of encoding and decoding knowledge about the world.' Encoding and decoding relies, first, on the specific ways in which signs are, and can be, understood by participants, and, secondly, on the specific uses to which signs are put by the speaker in communicative action. As she points out, considering the implications of various focal stresses for the same utterance:

. . . one might interpret //*John* flew to Paris// as 'accusation' (implying, for example, John flew to Paris without Jill), //John *flew* to Paris// as 'reproach' (he spent much more money flying than if he had taken a train), and //John flew to Paris// as 'affirmation' (John flew to Paris and not to Stockholm).

Blakar, in his report of the Oslo research on psychopathology and familial communication, starts from an understanding of communicative action which is close to Allwood's and Kreckel's positions:

The most essential characteristic of communication is that something is being made known to somebody. It follows from this that an act of communication is *social* and *directional* (from a sender to a receiver). A crucial characteristic distinguishing communication from the general flow of information is that the sender has an intention to make something known to the (particular) receiver.

While Allwood and Kreckel are concerned with the prerequisites for successful communication, that is, with outlining the conditions under which a speaker will succeed in making something known to somebody, Blakar takes a clinical perspective. He asks: 'Which of the pre–conditions have *not* been satisfied when communication fails?' To answer this question, he and his collaborators suggested a specific experimental situation:

An ideal experimental situation would thus be one where two (or more) participants communicate with each other *under the belief* that they are 'in the same situation' (i.e., have a common definition of the situation's 'here' and 'now'), but where they are in fact in different situations.'

This idea was developed in the following way:

Two persons, A and B, are each given a map of a relatively complicated network of roads and streets in a town centre. On A's map two routes are marked with arrows, one short and straight-forward (the practice route), and another longer and more compli-cated (the experimental route). On B's map no route is marked. A's task is then to explain to B the two routes, first the simple one, then the longer and more complicated one. B will then, with the help of A's explanations, try to find the way through town to the pre-determined end-point. B may ask questions, for example, ask A to repeat the explanations, or to explain in other ways, and so on. The experimental manipulation is simply that the two maps are not identical. An extra street is added on B's map. So, no matter how adequately A explains, no matter how carefully B carries out his instructions, B is bound to go wrong. The difference between the two maps has implication only for the complicated route, however; the practice route is straightforward for both.

The method was then used 'to illuminate communication deficiences in families with schizophrenic members.' It was discovered that couples with schizophrenic children (Group S) were mostly unable to cope with the induced communication problem, while couples with normal children (Group N) could. This result, among other factors, was related to differ-ences in the communicative practices of the two groups. The communication of the Group S couples, when compared with the Group N couples, was characterized

. . . by more rigidity (in explanation strategy, in role distribution, and so on), by less ability and/or willingness to listen to, and take into account, what the other said, by a more imprecise and diffuse use of language (imprecise definitions, concepts, and so on) and by more 'pleasing' and/or pseudo-agreement in situations in which the erroneous maps had produced interaction problems.

The research reported by Blakar is, of course, confined to just one communicative situation. The evidence generated by the Oslo work is, thus, both restricted and, in a sense, just correlational as the natural patterns of communication in the family which are thought to play a role in the ontogenesis of schizophrenia (see, for example, Watzlawick, Beavin and Jackson 1967) still remain to be researched. Nonetheless, Blakar and his collaborators have succeeded in demonstrating that it is possible to research the natural structures of communicative action within a controlled and standardized experimental design.

So far, explanations of action processes have been offered in terms of specific components of action, such as intentions, goals, rules, roles, skills, environmental factors, actors' meanings of actions and various aspects of effective or deficient communication. David Clarke suggests, in contrast to these specific strategies, a different approach to an explanation of action processes:

By explanation I mean the discovery of the underlying mechanism or generative process by which observed events are called into being. Since the process is not directly accessible, this usually amounts to the proposal of imaginary mechanisms and then a demonstration, part rational and part empirical, that they could reproduce the facts as we observe them . . .

Which kind of generative mechanism shall we imagine for an explanation of action processes? Clarke proposes a syntactic approach in analogy to the use of generative syntax in the explanation of sentence structure in linguistics:

An attractive feature of a structural approach, found particularly in modern linguistics, is the use of generative models. The domain, in this case a language, is captured not merely by a passive description of organisational features but by an active model, a generative grammar consisting of rules which, after the fashion of a formal theorem-proving system, can derive all sentences from a simple axiom S.

Ideally, Clarke points out, a syntax of action could be produced thus:

Working at first from native actors' intuitions of a familiar behavioural structure we should propose a set of formal generative rules. A grammar is said to have no discovery procedure, only an elevation procedure. The rules would then be tested for their adequacy, that is their capacity to produce all well-formed *wholes* in the *domain*, and possibly provide other information correctly about each one as well.

There are, however, a number of practical problems which, at present, stand in the way of devising an empirically satisfactory syntactic approach to action processes. The first has to do with problems of description, that is, it may be difficult to say precisely what kinds of action are actually involved in a set of activity sequences. As Clarke points out:

Unlike a grammar for a natural language, a syntax of action has to deal with the ordering of a set of *parts* which is indefinitely large and possibly infinite. There are no direct counterparts of the morpheme set which can be used as the vocabulary in which *wholes* are to be created and described. Speech act or action taxonomies . . . are a help but in themselves are insufficient as a set of descriptions for activity *parts*. Consequently the rules which specify how *parts* may combine into *wholes* cannot be written until there is a descriptive language for *parts* which is concrete enough to be governed by a formal generative system (or a computer simulation) while at the same time being rich and human enough that a string of such descriptions will provide a satisfactory representation of the activity sequence under study.

Another problem arises from the fact that action processes, unlike language, cannot be analysed by considering only just one plane of action, for activity sequences usually involve various verbal and nonverbal 'channels' of action simultaneously. By 'channels' I mean that action is frequently not just verbal, but involves paralinguistic, proxemic, kinesic and chronemic aspects as well. For any particular activity sequence we then have to establish which aspects or channels of action have prominence for the participants. This may imply that we need to search for more than just one social syntax, as each salient channel of action may need specific attention. In order to be empirically adequate these syntaxes would have to be interrelated in such a way as to represent accurately the participants' actual encoding and decoding of actions for all verbal and nonverbal channels under consideration. As Rommetveit has pointed out, these encoding and decoding processes may involve different realms of meaning and social experience for participants so that we may even need to consider a specific set of social syntaxes for each participant in order to account for *his* specific genesis of action. As Clarke's idea of a social syntax is mostly programmatic at this stage, it remains to be seen whether it will generate fruitful empirical research.

Rom Harré, finally, concerns himself with the question of how social psychological knowledge may be used within, and for the purposes of generating, social change. This project implies, for a start, an understanding of naturally occurring change. As regards natural social change occurring on the level of small-scale social interactions, Harré points out that we may encounter the appearance of new conventions 'associating a different action with the same act.' The performance meaning of actions may also change, and altogether novel act/action structures may appear.

Harré then proceeds to outline a spectrum of evolutionary theories, as natural social change 'has to be understood by graphing the theory of social change on a general layout of all possible evolutionary theories.' On the basis of this discussion, he then looks at the possibilities for contriving social change by 'exploiting the knowledge we have acquired'. To which areas of social change could social psychology contribute? Harré suggests that new rules to guide action may be developed when existing rules come to obstruct certain action projects. Social psychologists could further provide new techniques for accounting which people could use to make their activities more intelligible and warrantable for themselves.

There are, however, certain natural limits to induced social change. As not all 'possibilities of transformation of the social world by the exploitation of social psychological knowledge' are equally well realizable, as people may resist change or certain invented social practices may prove impractical, some 'pre-testing' of projects of social change should occur. This may be done, for example, in the form of experimental theatre where a 'fragment of a new life' could be tried out under realistic conditions.

3   The Structure of Action: Methodological Issues

I noted at the beginning of this chapter that the methodology of the new social psychology may be characterized by attempts at adequate *reconstruction* of the components involved in the natural genesis of action. Broadly, these components, as proposed by the contributors to this volume, may be ordered in the following form:

a. Action occurs in a *specific context*. It involves a physical environment, roles and rules.

b. Action involves *agency*. A person acts according to goals and intentions and with reference to concepts of what to do. Action also requires certain skills.

c. Action involves specific *behavioural forms*. It is performed verbally and/or nonverbally.

d. Action is *meaningful*. The meanings of action may vary among performers, participants and bystanders.

e. Action occurs in *real time*. It appears as process which may have a specific sequential or syntactic structure.

As we have seen, none of the contributors takes into account all these aspects of action. Only *particular* components of action are considered, and, consequently, only *particular* methodological strategies are proposed.

John Shotter is particularly concerned with the aspect of *agency*. Action, Shotter argues, involves *reason*. If we want to explain why a person is acting in a certain way then we must attempt to discover what he was trying to do. This may be done by asking the person to give us an *account* of why he acted in a certain manner. As Shotter points out:

Thus, instead of people being treated as mechanisms caused to behave like mindless billiard-balls by they-know-not-what forces acting upon them externally, people are to be treated as entities able to explain themselves by giving, or at least by negotiating with those who are investigating them, 'accounts' of their reasons for their actions. And this 'negotiation of accounts' . . . is a mode of explanation quite different from the causal kind: instead of explaining a particular event by showing how, in the circumstances of its occurrence it is an instance of a general law, a person's particular action is explained by discovering what in particular he was trying to do in executing it: Jones' *reason* for crossing the road is that he believed he could buy tobacco on the other side. The *particular* is explained here by the *particular*.

Michael Argyle outlines a range of methodological strategies useful in the analysis of *social situations*. He suggests discovering *goals* by means of interviewing people about which goals they typically pursue in specific situations. To achieve insight into particular goal structures people may also be asked 'to rate the extent to which the main goals for each situation are (1) in conflict, (2) involve routes to one another, (3) are independent, or (4) co-operative.' For a discovery of *repertoires of elements*, the observer may either develop elements 'from his own perceptions of behaviour in the situation' or by grouping small units of behaviour into larger units by means of sequence analysis. Elements may also be discovered by using the 'perceptions and categorizations of participants'. *Rules* may be inferred from systematic observation of be-

haviour from reports of participants. Rules may also be discovered by means of rule-breaking experiments. The discovery
of *sequences* involves the study of probability transitions between the elements of a social situation so that specific chains
of action may be generated. For a discovery of *roles*, rules may
be consulted to describe the roles. Roles may also be inferred
from observation or interviewing. In order to discover the
concepts used in action, Argyle suggests asking people to rate
specific concepts for their salience in particular situations.
Aspects of the *physical environment* may be measured more or
less straightforwardly. And *social skills competence* may be
assessed 'by measures of effectiveness (e.g., goods sold by a
salesperson), observation of role-playing, ratings in real-life
situations, tests of social competence, and various kinds of
self-rating.'

Ragnar Rommetveit addresses the analysis of *meaning* in
action. We may first try to establish the meaning of an action
for the performer by inviting an account from him, as

what the agent does – at least with respect to some aspects – *is known to
him.* His account may be partial, deceptive, and replete with
justifications. . . . The fact remains, though, that he is, in some sense
and at some level, informed about 'real intentions' in a way that
outside observers cannot possibly be. Only he can thus reliably
inform us about awareness of means–ends-separation and potential
states of intrinsic motivation in streams of his life.

We may then try to further specify the meanings of an action
for participants and bystanders by collecting their accounts.
The action meanings provided may differ considerably from
each other as

self-accounts will at all levels tend to differ in characteristic ways
from those offered by outside observers. What from the outside may
appear as a routine in some public game will often, from the position
of the agent himself within his own private world, be imbued with
intrinsic motivation or intention.

Thus, we must not be surprised when somebody who is mowing his lawn may perform other meaningful actions with the same behaviour, according to the accounts obtained. For example, he may also be beautifying his garden, exercising his muscles, avoiding his wife, conforming to the expectations of his neighbours, keeping up property values and angering his neighbour.

Peter Collett concerns himself with the analysis of *action in time*. He raises a number of methodological problems in this area of study. Although the proper study of action must adopt a unit approach in order to become able 'to examine people's actions as they are temporarily constituted and responded to', he thinks that we need to accept that there are no *natural* units of behaviour. From this it follows that the actual units used in the analysis of action processes are not observer-independent:

The segments that the investigator identifies will depend on his status as observer. Obviously, as a discipline develops, its members are likely to reach greater consensus, and with the introduction of workable notation systems there is the possibility of fairly good agreement among investors. But such scientific conventions should not be taken to reflect the actual state of affairs in the world. They are, and can be no more than a convenient means of imposing order on what is observed.

In other words, the analysis of action in time must, in some way, start from structuring the behaviour stream in a *certain way*. Such structuring may be 'etic', involving only the investigator's point of view, or it may be 'emic', relying on the ways in which people subjectively structure the behaviour of others. The 'emic' approach may be used in two ways, both involving certain drawbacks:

Having asked someone to view an action sequence we can either require him to identify the units while he is watching it or have him report on the units afterwards. Each procedure has its limitations; the former because it demands that the subject performs two tasks simultaneously, the latter because it relies on perfect recall. Furthermore, both methods remove the process of subjective construction from the interactive context within which it normally occurs. When we endeavour to make sense of someone else they are usually present, and in most instances doing the same. In these circumstances we seldom monitor others as an end in itself. We do not pursue knowledge for its own sake, but rather as a means to steering our own actions.

Jens Allwood, Marga Kreckel and Rolv Blakar are concerned with specific analyses of *communicative action*. Their methodological strategies may all be characterized as 'etic', as involving only their own standpoints of reconstruction.

Allwood suggests that the various 'felicity conditions' involved in communicative action may be studied by investigating the various verbs we use in order to characterize a communicative action as felicitous in certain ways. Such verbs of communication 'do not usually refer to a communicative action *in toto* but rather they could be said to refer to certain definite aspects of a communicative action from a certain perspective.' Allwood differentiates verbs of communication according to whether they refer to behavioural characteristics of communicative action ('whistle, lisp, mutter, mumble') or parameters of information organization ('refer, predicate, stress, emphasize') or expressive dimensions ('groan, whimper, swear, complain') or evocative parameters ('state, assert, lie, boast') or obligating parameters ('accuse, sentence, testify, appeal') or contextual characteristics ('quote, approve, accept, reject').

Kreckel takes naturally occurring discourse as her raw-data base. She then considers 'tone-units', 'melodic units made up of specific pitch contours' as the elementary organizational forms involved in discourse: 'They break up the stretch of discourse into chunks of messages.' That is, a tone-unit is seen as 'the block or unit of particular meaning the *speaker wishes to convey.*' Thus an utterance such as 'You never told me you'd never marry me' may involve two distinct messages or tone-units: '//You never told me// you'd never marry me//'. Tone-units are differentiated from each other thus:

Within each tone unit there is a point of prominence, representing the speaker's choice of information focus . . . The information focus is realized as phonological prominence or as *focal stress*, indicated by features of loudness, the most extreme pitch within the tone-unit, or length of tonic segment.

The tone-units may then be further investigated in terms of 'inter-unit-structure', or 'cohesion' between messages, and in terms of 'intra-unit-structure', or the distribution of 'new' and 'given' due to 'differences in focal stress' within a message.

As pointed out, Blakar and his collaborators used, basically, an experimental design for the study of clinical aspects of communicative action, but they also treated the discourse generated by the experiments as a raw-data base for further investigation. For example, in the context of their first study, a 'more qualitatively oriented analysis was also carried out':

Three types of analysis were conducted in order to identify further differences and similarities in patterns of communication between the two groups of couples:
1. The tapes were blind-scored by a communication oriented student trained in clinical psychology.
2. A detailed analysis (on utterance level) of the organization of the communication process was carried out.
3. The emotional climate was assessed on a set of five-point scales.

The clinical evaluation was used to assess whether the experimental difference between the two groups would correspond to clinical judgement. The communication process analysis was conducted in order to determine '*why* the Group S couples failed when the communication conflict was induced. The rating-analysis of the emotional climate involved scales of the following type: 'To what extent is the interaction characterized by warmth (openness, confidence, helplessness, intimacy, mutual respect, and so on)?'   .

The overall methodological approach of Blakar and his collaborators involves ongoing critical appraisal and subsequent change of the methods used and, particularly, extensive replication of the general research design under variable social conditions.

David Clarke addresses the possibility of research into a *syntax of action*. One method for the representation of syntactic structure, Clarke suggests, would be to use 'speech act terms as main descriptions' of the action events in an activity sequence 'with a series of sub-parameters which have values particular to that class.' For example:

'THREAT', A, B, x, y, z

could be used to represent A's threat to B that x will befall him unless he carries out requirements y within (time) limits z.

This approach may be backed by 'emic' studies where people's natural categorizations of action structures are taken into account. In all, Clarke suggests the following research strategy:

The first step, then, in the preferred approach to the analysis of behaviour sequences, would be to gather a number of instances of the type to be studied, together with as much background information as possible . . .
The next step is to attempt an analysis of *each case in turn*, sticking at first as closely as possible to the beliefs and concepts supplied by the actors . . .
The procedure so far, though necessary, is far from sufficient. The attributions made of actors and events on the basis of lay pre-theoretical intuitions must be turned into a workable model with some predictive capability. . . . Ideally, some kind of model of the general process needs to be constructed which can express the interrelation of all the elements in the analysis and their effects on behaviour. This could take a concrete realization, such as a computer simulation, or an abstract one, such as a generative grammar of action . . .
Next, the model has to be put through its paces, and tested for its adequacy. The first task is to reproduce from the model the particular sequences of events that went into its construction. Later, it will have to match the real system in the production of word sequences

given novel circumstances as input. All of which is like the requirements made of a generative grammar . . .

Rom Harré, finally, though not concerned with any specific
empirical research problem, but with the issue of *social change*
in quite general terms, raises a number of important
methodological issues. He points out that a relevant part of
our methodological work must be concerned with the conceptual analysis of the phenomena we wish to study: 'The issue of
the nature of social change can hardly be sensibly addressed
without a careful analysis of social forms, that which might
change.' Conceptual analysis reveals, at least as an 'ideal type',
the general componential structure of a phenomenon, in the
case of Harré's theme, the 'evolutionary' structure of social
change, among other aspects. He also implies that social
psychological knowledge, in order to be able to aid in contriving the change of existing social practices, must rely on
methods that adequately represent the componential structure
of practices: 'The knowledge social psychologists profess
ought to make us particularly good at revealing the inner
structure of such practices.'

4   *Conclusion*

Critics may note the frequent programmatic and proto-
scientific character of many of the arguments proposed in this
volume. They may also complain about the general lack of
rigorous empirical research. Yet, it is a particular feature of the
new social psychology as a science in 'emergence' (Ginsburg
1978) that substantive and methodological issues are debated
as if they were encountered for the *first time*, as if they were *just
discovered*. It is a characteristic of this discovery phase that
various lines of argument will perhaps prove to be transient;
others will stand up to the various empirical tests to which
they will be put and prove fruitful. The winners in the race of
ideas cannot be decided at this point, and whether the arguments collected in this book will all eventually find acceptance

or not, I believe, nonetheless, that the future development of social psychology cannot do without them.

References

M. Argyle, 1969, *Social Interaction*, London: Methuen

N. Armistead (Ed.), 1974, *Reconstructing Social Psychology*, Harmondsworth: Penguin

M. Brenner, P. Marsh and M. Brenner (Eds.), 1978, *The Social Contexts of Method*, London: Croom Helm

P. Collett (Ed.), 1977, *Social Rules and Social Behaviour*, Oxford: Blackwell

S. Duncan and D. W. Fiske, 1977, *Face-to-Face Interaction: Research, Methods, and Theory*, Hillsdale, N.J.: Lawrence Erlbaum Associates

A. Gauld and J. Shotter, 1977, *Human Action and Its Psychological Investigation*, London: Routledge & Kegan Paul

G. P. Ginsburg, 1978, 'The Description and Explanation of Situated Action: An Emergent Paradigm in Social Psychological Research', paper presented at the annual meeting of the Society of Experimental Social Psychology, 10 November, Princeton University

G. P. Ginsburg (Ed.), 1979, *Emerging Strategies in Social Psychological Research*, Chichester: Wiley

H. P. Grice, 1975, 'Logic and Conversation', in: P. Cole and J. L. Morgan (Eds.), *Syntax and Semantics*, Vol. 3, *Speech Acts*, New York: Academic Press

R. Harré, 1979, *Social Being, A Theory for Social Psychology*, Oxford: Blackwell

R. Harré and P. F. Secord, 1972, *The Explanation of Social Behaviour*, Oxford: Blackwell

R. D. Mann et al., 1967, *Interpersonal Styles and Group Development*, New York: Wiley

J. Shotter, 1975, *Images of Man in Psychological Research*, London: Methuen

L. H. Strickland, F. E. Aboud and K. J. Gergen, 1976, *Social Psychology in Transition*, New York: Plenum Press

H. Tajfel and C. Fraser, 1978, *Introducing Social Psychology*, Harmondsworth: Penguin

L. Wittgenstein, 1968, *Philosophical Investigations*, Oxford: Blackwell

Action, Joint Action and Intentionality

JOHN SHOTTER   *Nottingham University*

'Tis here, but yet confus'd
Knavery's plain face is never seen till us'd.
Iago: Act 2, Scene 1, Othello

1   *Introduction: The 'Crisis' in Contemporary Experimental Social Psychology*

As usually defined, psychology is thought of as the science of behaviour, and social psychology as that branch of the science which studies either how 'individuals are influenced by the actual, imagined, or implied presence of others' (Allport 1954) or, more recently, the psychological aspects of the process of social interaction itself (Argyle 1969). As a science, its paramount aim is taken to be that of discovering general laws by use of systematic observation, usually within the context of controlled experimentation. But experimental social psychology has for some time now been under attack and supposedly in a state of 'crisis' (Smith 1972; Gergen 1973; McGuire 1973; Strickland, Aboud and Gergen 1976). Many criticisms have been levelled at the 'experimental' side of the research process itself. Difficulties have been found, for instance, both with attempts to formulate 'theories' and also with attempts to test them.

Many such 'theories' have been formulated, for example,

cognitive dissonance theory, social comparison theory, balance theory, and so on. Besides being inadequately defined, and only understood because experimenters using them come from the same or similar socializing communities as their subjects (Bem 1967), none are notions of a very fundamental kind: their appearance in the world is not understood in terms of some deep properties of the social world in the same way as, for instance, some phenomena in the physical world are understood, i.e., as arising out of the fundamental properties of space and time. They appear merely as the names of empirical generalizations, indicating common aspects of our social world current, perhaps only at this point in history (Gergen 1973). Rather than 'theories' they should more properly be called 'heuristics', statements serving merely to order our perceptions and to direct our attention to phenomena which might otherwise go unnoticed. But if that is the function they serve, then they are clearly not amenable to empirical test, for they provide the terms within which our observations are made. In fact, says McGuire (1973), 'we social psychologists have tended to use the manipulational laboratory experiment not to test our hypotheses but to demonstrate their obvious truth.' 'Theories' are abandoned, not because they fail to conform with external reality, but because they fail to explicate properly the intuitions they were meant to illustrate.

To move beyond the 'crisis' in social psychology, an effort must be made, I think, to link the data of social life to some more fundamental notions than those presently available. To this end, I want to attempt to do two things in this paper: First, I shall investigate a number of conceptual categories which seem to be fundamental to any account of a social world, notions such as *action, joint action,* and *intention,* as well as those of *person, self* and *agency,* but especially *time* and *intentionality,* these constituting a whole intrinsically interrelated web or network of concepts. Concerning the structure of intentionality, I want to suggest that mental activity is 'specificatory' in nature, and that, in structuralist (Culler 1976) terms, what we grasp in a person's actions or expressions is a process of specification, a successive expression of differences, specifying aspect after aspect of a synchronically present whole. And that we understand his action, not by referring it to already known general rules, laws, or principles (nor by any mysterious emphatic sharing of his thoughts), but by constructing with him in the course of *joint action* a shared synchronically present whole within which each action or expression plays its part, its meaning being understood in terms of the special entities in that world and only in that world.

This idea is, of course, borrowed from structural linguistics: there it is claimed that the significance of an event or act is to be understood not in terms of its place in a temporal sequence of events, not in a *diachronic* perspective but in a *synchronic* one, in which the event has a place within a system of differences which are *all simultaneously present* (Culler 1976).

Following the outline of such a conceptual web, I want, secondly, to set these fundamental notions to work in making sense of some well-known but puzzling everyday phenomena: a. the fact that people are able normally to understand one another's actions or expressions in the *process* of their performance, without having to wait for such expressions to be 'completed' in some way, and b. the fact that people often construct *social worlds* between themselves in terms of which they are able to explain themselves to one another, whilst at the same time experiencing a *personal world* which is in some respects unique.

2   *Preliminary Remarks on Action, Joint Action, Social Worlds and Personal Worlds*

I can now state my purposes in this paper. While avoiding talk of Kuhn (1962), 'new paradigms', 'paradigm switches', and the like, my purpose in general is to explore some aspects of the view that, instead of taking human nature as something 'fixed', as 'already there', as 'existing independently of anything which we might do or think about', we take *changefulness* as the basic constant of humankind. What if 'human nature' is a continuously changing and developing *artifact,* a 'product'

constructed and reconstructed in the process of people's interactions with one another? I want to avoid talk here of
concern with such a view as being a 'paradigm switch', a 'new
paradigm' to replace the 'old', for it seems to me that the 'old'
view of ourselves, as having, from the classical perspective, a
certain kind of fixed nature, still has a part to play.

Just as we can effect a 'gestalt switch' from one to another
view of an ambiguous figure, so in life it would seem,
'switching' from a view of ourselves as basically changeable or
transformable to a view of ourselves as basically fixed and
unchangeable is a real possibility for us also. Unlike with most
ambiguous figures, however, both modes of existence remain, I want to suggest, *synchronically present,* one as figure in
the context of the other as ground; the changeable or transformable only existing in the context of the fixed and unchangeable, and vice versa. Such an ability, and what it means,
should not go uninvestigated. Thus at various points in this
paper (though it is to one side of my main purpose) I shall
touch upon the complementarity of these two otherwise
incommensurable perspectives, *the causal-explanatory* and the
hermeneutical-understanding perspectives, as we may call them;
though I shall argue that they are not simply or symmetrically
complementary, for the quasi-causal laws of the explanatory
approach can only have their being within a hermeneutical
framework, a shared and agreed system of interpretation
(Gauld and Shotter 1977, pp. 97–98).

While such are my concerns in general, specifically I want to
explore human action as a form-producing process. Rather
than a rule-using, or 'rule-following animal' (as Peters 1958,
p. 5, and other philosophers of a Wittgensteinian persuasion
suggest, for example, Winch 1958), I want to study people as
primarily form-creators (and thus as rule-makers) and only
secondarily as form-, plan-, or rule-users. To take such a
'creative' view of human action is to treat it as a formative
process in its own right, as a continuous sequence of transformation rather than as merely a sequence of discrete events, as a
developing process rather than as merely a (changing)
medium through which other (more constant) factors exert

their determining influence, as in the idea of people as rule-following animals, an interpretation which, once again, expresses the classical preference for the invariable as the essence of things. Viewing human action not as a sequence of well-defined events but as something which develops in time, which involves a passage from something less to more definite, emphasizes the fact that while we can, on occasions, act deliberately, according to rule, plan, or script, and so on, we need not always necessarily do so. Often we act simply upon the basis of our 'thoughts and feelings' we say, in terms of the situation 'as we saw it'.

In such cases we do not find it easy to give a well articulated account of why we acted as we did, even though we know 'we had our reasons'; we simply felt that our action was 'required by' the 'situation' we were in, our 'circumstances' 'demanded' it. For example, each sentence of what I have struggled to write so far has been determined, of course, by my following of many 'rules', but it also expresses a certain aspect of a-situation-as-I-understand-it, and seems to be 'required' by that situation to such an extent that only certain forms of words will correctly express it (although sometimes I judge incorrectly). Thus each sentence both helps to express or to constitute that 'situation' and must be understood in the context of it, as a part is related to a whole; each sentence helps to create the 'world' in which it appears. All truly *personal* actions have this quality, of necessity; they are part of, as I shall call it, a *personal world.* Many social or joint actions have it too: utterances in a dialogue, moves in a game, a quarrel, love-making, an industrial negotiation, for example, in fact any action in an interaction in which an individual must interweave his actions in with the unpredictable actions of others. Such interaction involves a shaping or formative process; the participants have to build up their respective lines of conduct by constant interpretation of each other's ongoing lines of action as indicated in their expressions. In the course of such a process a *social world* can be created and each action understood in its context.

In attempting to understand the idiosyncratic actions of

individuals, whether acting alone or in a group, rather than referring to rules, to anything social, impersonal, or common to everyone, it is often necessary to characterize their situation as they saw it, to grasp the *personal or social world* in which they acted, and to understand the part their action played in such a world. To reconstruct that 'world' in such a way, that puzzling or enigmatic actions are provided with reasonable interpretations, is the hermeneutical task here. Rather than assuming that we all live in an already established common world, and that our actions are distinguished from one another merely by the different rules that we choose to follow, the account above puts human action into quite a different perspective: it is seen as a formative process conducted by the actors themselves (actors make their own acts); it is not seen as produced by a variety of external factors, be they rules, roles, norms, needs, attitudes, and so on, coming to expression through the medium of human conduct, but as constructed by actors by what they take into account; in group life it is not seen as caused by, or as a reaction to, objective structures but as a process of building up joint actions, people and groups exerting their influence upon one another not directly but indirectly through interpretations.

Such an 'in-process' view of human action need not, it is important to note, preclude the existence of structure in the personal and social worlds so fabricated. Rules, norms, roles, statuses, and the like obviously have a kind of existence, and are indeed central features in any account of human social life. But their importance in *this* perspective (in the causal-explanatory perspective things are different) cannot be in their alleged determination of action, nor in their alleged existence as parts of a self-operating societal system. As concepts they are important only as they enter into and determine our thought about action; but that is a different matter, a matter of the interpretations and expressions out of which joint actions are formed. And the manner and extent to which they may enter into that process can vary from situation to situation, depending upon what people take into account and how they assess it. Thus on this view the sociological account of social interaction, for instance, while important (when one is in the causal–explanatory frame of mind), reduces the true state of affairs; in the process–perspective social interaction is between *people* not roles. And in interaction their need is not always simply to express their role, they must interpret and cope with what confronts them, be it a practical problem, a topic of conversation, or both. It is only in highly ritualistic, pre-established forms of social interaction that the direction and content of conduct can be explained by rule/role models; usually the direction and content of the exchange is fashioned out of what people in interaction have to deal with.

3 *Intentionality, Time and Action*

Gauld and I (Gauld and Shotter 1977) suggested that intentionality[1] is a fundamental and irreducible feature, or better, a presupposition of all thought, all conceptual activity, and all action. As such, it would seem, it can only be noticed or grasped (or not); it cannot be further described or defined. Under such circumstances metaphor is the only recourse; and metaphor will abound in the account that follows as my purpose is not to give a philosophical analysis of intentionality, but to attempt to build a 'formative process' model of intentionality to illuminate the nature of the process-view of human action, hence, ultimately, to clarify methodological issues.

TIME

As a preliminary it is necessary to discuss the nature of time, for in a process–perspective it has quite a different quality to it than the uniform left-right flow to which we are used in our conventional representations of it.

1 We used the spelling 'intensionality' to emphasize that 'intentions' are only one among the class of phenomena to which 'intensionality' may be attributed: remembering, perceiving, feeling, and so on, may be intensional too.

When acting, one does not experience a sequence of disconnected objective events, one simply replacing the other, but a succession without, as Bergson puts it somewhere, an *externally defined* 'before' and 'after'. There is a flowing succession of interpenetrating phases, each containing aspects of what has already happened and of what is yet to come. For instance, when I say the word 'cat', I shape my mouth for the vowel before I let the initial consonant go, and even as I am moving from that consonant to the vowel, I am beginning to shape my mouth for the final consonant (Liberman et al. 1957; Liberman 1970). The phases of the word are thus mutually interpenetrating, it is not made up of externally definable elements; they are all reciprocally implicated or intrinsically interrelated, they are, ethnomethodologists would say, irredeemably indexical. There is, for instance, no pure /k/ sound, as the saying of 'keep cool cat' should illustrate; all the initial consonants are coloured by the vowel that follows them. The 'specious' present, the moment of my control of my action would seem to be influenced both by my past and my future. It can be influenced by what I have just done but which has now passed 'outside' my agency to control further, and has thus, strictly speaking, become a part of my immediate environment. Such a product remains 'on hand' but not (as we shall see below) as an object, but as a tool, a structured means, a set of meanings, for use in forming my further conduct. My action can also be influenced by my 'intention', by the 'object' at which I seem to be aiming in my actions, by, Dewey (1896) would say, the current 'redistribution of tensions' or 'transformation of structure' I experience in my world.

About the structure of action, 'l'effort intellectuel', Bergson (1920, p. 188) says,

This operation, which is the very operation of life, consists in the gradual passage from the less realized to the more realized, from the intensive to the extensive, from the reciprocal implication of parts to their juxtaposition.

In other words, in taking the uninvolved, external observer view of behaviour appropriate to the causal-explanatory framework, behaviour is viewed as a sequence of externally defined, objective events which, as such, can exist in isolation from one another. This suggests a *spatialized* view of time, in which time is seen merely as a fourth dimension of space. Such a spatialized view is quite inadequate for capturing the structure of one's experience from a standpoint 'in' action: there one experiences not a sequence of disconnected events, with one state of mind simply replacing another, but an indivisible, heterogeneous continuity, in which successive phases cohere without ceasing to be qualitatively diverse. This is a *meaningful continuity* with an altogether different structure to it from the kind of spatial continuity possessed by points in (or upon) a time.

The passage from a less to a more realized form is already familiar to us in psychology in Chomsky's account of the derivation of a sentence. In that there is no simple *left-to-right* juxtaposition of *structurally independent* parts, but a *top-down* differentiation of wholes into their *structurally dependent* (or reciprocally implied) parts. If we take such structures as defining a temporal ordering, a 'topochronology' we may call it, then, rather than defining a time metrically, by a numbered point on a line, the 'place' occupied by an event in such a structurally dependent whole may be defined *topologically*, in terms of the superordinate event which contains it as a part.

Consider a life:

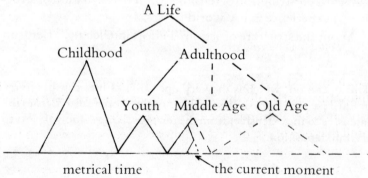

It has a certain temporal structure to it. Topologically, today's event is the latest part of the structure to be derived so far; all other events can be found located or 'placed' between certain other events, and contained within more overarching ones. Above, perhaps inadvisedly, I have confounded a topological with a metrical ordering by projecting the structure onto a line of numbered points, thus illustrating the confusion we fall into when we ask 'Upon what day exactly did I lose my youth?' Strictly, a topology is incommensurable with a metric, time may go slowly or quickly within a topological scheme of things, though it does provide a clear ordering. Just as with a metric, events are located in strict relation to one another; however, within a topological scheme, time is no longer a one-dimensional line: it has a *structure* to it.

Not only does such a view of time allow the past to be 'revocable', in the sense that different structures (as with Chomsky's ambiguous sentences) may be erected over the same flow of past experience, but the completed part of the structure offers to the uncompleted part only limited styles of completion, for example, events appropriate in youth are inappropriate in middle-age; living has, one might say, a 'grammar' to it. There are many other interesting features of such a view of time, not least the light it throws upon so-called subjective and pathological 'distortions' of one's time sense. It would be beside the point to explore these here; it is the way in which the structure of what has been completed-so-far 'specifies' how one may go on that is important in what follows below.

INTENTIONALITY AND INTENTIONS

The notion of intentionality was introduced into modern philosophy essentially by Brentano. In trying to clarify the distinction between mental and physical phenomena, he proposed that one of the main differences between the two was to be found in the fact that unlike physical ones, mental phenomena are characterized by the 'intentional in-existence' (of the intended object); an object, even if it does not have a real existence outside the mind, exists 'in' all mental activity. To put the matter in his own words (Brentano 1973, p. 88):

Every mental phenomenon is characterized by what the Scholastics of the Middle Ages called the intentional (or mental) inexistence of an object, and what we might call, though not wholly unambiguously, reference to a content, direction toward an object (which is not to be understood as meaning a thing), or immanent objectivity. Every mental phenomenon includes something as an object within itself, although they all do not do so in the same way. In presentation something is presented, in judgement something is affirmed or denied, in love loved, in hate hated, in desire desired and so on.

In other words, mental phenomena are related to one another not externally by casual relations, but by the relations of 'containment' or 'implication' in a way that we have already explored. It is not that a mental act 'points to' something as a sign-post points to a town, where sign-post and town exist as external to, and defined independently of one another; a mental act would seem to be 'in' the world towards an aspect of which it is directed, it is an intrinsic part of such a world, intensionally rather than extensionally related to it.

Thus we may take 'intentionality' to be an already given property of a world of form-producing processes, with 'meaning something', 'containing something', and so on, being an intrinsic property of all mental activity. As Gauld and myself (1977, p. 114) say, regarding thought:

Thought must from the very beginning have some tendency to 'point beyond itself' to a 'something' however vague which is other than itself. Without such a pointing, the process of conceptually dividing the world could not get a toehold from which to begin. You cannot divide up the world in thought unless you have an inkling that there is a world. Without that inkling (which contains within itself the possibility of error) one's experiences could not lead one to the belief in a world of objects. Any process of inference from present data presupposes, and could not arrive at, some apprehension of a reality beyond and outside the immediate thought.'

And we add, in case our language is misleading:

> It would perhaps be better to say that in thinking the thinker points beyond his momentary self, his self as engaged in thinking *that* thought. For to talk of thoughts 'pointing beyond' themselves is to make them sound like momentary agents in their own right. Furthermore, the object of a thought is not thought of as set over against that thought; it is thought of as set over against the thinker as he now is.' (p. 115)

All mental phenomena, no matter how primitive, no matter how vague, are intentional; intentional phenomena cannot be derived from phenomena which in essence are non-intentional, action cannot be derived from non-action. Well articulated processes simply have their origins in less well articulated processes of the same kind; not in some other kind of phenomena altogether.

In the passage from the less to the more well-realized something is formed, or perhaps better, forming occurs; momentary 'product forms' are continuously created (and perhaps dissolved) in the flowing movement, as perhaps 'ripples, waves, and vortices are created and dissolved in a flowing stream of water' (Bohm 1973, p. 95). As an analogy for formative processes, a stream of water is, however, inadequate, for a process of growth or irreversible transformation is involved. This idea is captured, Bohm suggests, in the original meaning of the word 'form' in ancient Greek philosophy; as a verb it meant, according to Bohm, an inner *forming activity,* which is the cause of the growth of things, and of the development and differentiation of their various essential forms. As Bohm (1973, p. 95) outlines:

> For example in the case of an oak tree, what is indicated by the term 'formal cause' is the whole inner movement of sap, cell growth, articulation of branches, leaves, etc., which is characteristic of that kind of tree, and different from that taking place in other kinds of trees. In more modern language, it would be better to describe this as the *formative cause,* to emphasize that what is involved is not a mere form imposed from without, but rather *an ordered and structured inner movement that is essential to what things are.'*

As well as a model for the process–aspect of intentionality, there is perhaps also a model for an intention to be drawn from this example, a model for later reference.

In the same way that an intention is said to 'contain' or 'point to' its object, so an acorn may be said to 'contain' or 'point to' an oak tree. But an acorn certainly does not contain an oak tree, or anything like it, even in miniature. It is best seen as the *structured medium or means* through which, in interaction with its surroundings, an oak tree forms, developing itself as the structured means for its own further development or growth. Furthermore, although an acorn specifies the production of an oak tree from it, and not any other kind of tree, it does not specify the tree that grows from it exactly (number of branches, twigs, leaves, and so on), for the tree grows in unpredictable interaction with its surroundings. In the same way, an intention may specify a whole range of acceptable realizations, the actual one realized being formulated in interaction with other relevant contingencies. An intention, then, as I will suggest at greater length in a moment, may be thought of as a specified yet further specifiable means through which one can work towards an end; its already realized aspects limiting and specifying what one may yet do in the attempt to more fully realize it.

Although more metaphors and models could be offered in an effort to illuminate yet further aspects of intentionality, other matters are pressing and space is limited. The aspects touched upon will be sufficient for our subsequent purposes. They are, to summarize: a. the temporal flow of mental activity from less to more realized states and, as a corollary of this, the importance of less realized states of affairs in *specifying* their own further realization; b. the tendency of all mental phenomena 'to point beyond themselves'; and c. the 'intrinsic interrelatedness' of all mental phenomena such that, as Gauld and myself (1977, p. 145) put it:

Without certain beliefs, intentions would disintegrate, without intentions or action-tendencies wants would collapse into idle wishes, without the exercise of a conceptual capacity to think of the future intentions and expectancies could not be sustained.

As in discussing the 'intrinsic interrelatedness' of the phases of the word 'cat' earlier, the matter is best expressed, perhaps, by saying that 'belief', 'intention', 'action', 'self', 'agency', 'person', and so on, are all different *phases* of the same unity. An intentional world thus has quite a different unity to it than a mechanistic world of physically isolable objects held together by external forces; everything in an intentional world is intrinsically interrelated to everything else.[2]

I want to turn now to a discussion of the 'specificatory' nature of mental activity and the yet further 'specifiable' nature of its momentary products, and attempt to construct a more detailed model of what might be involved in the realization of an intention. My aim is to illuminate how, even when expressions may remain irredeemably indexical, that is, less than fully realized, vague and utterly context dependent, their import, especially in the back-and-forth of interaction, may still nonetheless be grasped.

In discussing how a thought can 'point beyond itself', can be 'of' something, Gauld and myself (1977, p. 127) suggest that it could be said to have a 'specificatory function or aspect': it specifies

as it were upon a grid of intersecting co-ordinates, some state of affairs beyond itself. The specifying function does not exhaust

2 A quotation from Whitehead (1975, pp. 114–115) is relevant here. In discussing 'the fallacy of simple location' he says: '. . . my theory involves the entire abandonment of the notion that simple location is the primary way in which things are involved in space-time. In a certain sense, everything is everywhere at all times. For every location involves an aspect of itself in every other location. Thus every spatio-temporal standpoint mirrors the world.' In the light of the special theory of relativity, however, such a view cannot be allowed to stand. We now accept that there are no 'world wide instants', that causal influence takes time to travel. A similar but more complex view results in which every location mirrors not *the* world but *a* limited world with itself at the centre. This I shall suggest is the nature of a *personal world*.

thought – there is, prima facie, a difference between thoughts in which the specified state of affairs is affirmed, and those in which it is merely supposed – but it is a sine qua non of there being any thought at all.'

The 'specificatory' nature of mental activity is a central pre-supposition of *structuralism* (Culler 1976) as well as in the approaches of such psychologists as Neisser (1976), Kelly (1955), Gibson and Gibson (1955), myself (1975), and others. While Gauld and myself (1977) discuss mental activity further to show how 'specificatory function' terminology and 'pro-position' terminology may be related. I shall take it here, without any further elaboration, that mental activity functions to structure a whole into a system of intrinsically inter-related or reciprocally implicated parts, each part being known in terms of its relations to all the others in the system. The point about such a system of perceptually distinguishable but physi-cally inseparable 'parts', is that the momentary 'parts' pro-duced are always open to yet further differentiation and specification, *but only in terms of what they already are*; they are, we may say, 'further specifiable'. This is a point I shall explore further below.

William James (1890, p. 253), in discussing what kind of mental fact a person's 'intention of saying a thing' is, suggests that it often begins with only an extremely vague 'feeling of tendency'; such

. . . 'tendencies' are not only descriptions from without, but they are among the *objects* of the stream, which is thus aware of them from within, and must be described as in very large measure constituted of *feelings* of *tendency*, often so vague that we are unable to name them at all.

In attempting to grasp further the nature of what is involved in the expression of an intention, I want, following Johnson (1971), to consider a 'feeling of tendency' we can name: the 'initial difficulty' from out of which *a question* is formulated. In general, however, I think we must accept that such 'tenden-cies' are not nameable as falling into any particular class before they issue in an expression which formulates them; they are just intentions to say or to do something appropriate in some way to the circumstances. The problem with such 'feelings' is what is the nature of our knowledge of them; in what sense does one know them?

Johnson asks us to consider as an example a history student asking his tutor quite a complex question: 'What are the differences in the present day societies of England and Scotland which can be explained in terms of the historical fact that England was invaded and conquered by the Norman French in 1066, while Scotland had no similar experience of invasion and therefore remained a relatively homogeneous society?' Let us suppose that this is not a rhetorical question, but that the student is genuinely puzzled about the answer. How then does the student succeed in asking his question? What is the nature of the source from which he draws it?

As Johnson remarks, this much is clear: the student cannot be referring to some objective 'question in itself', an aspect of a so-called 'cognitive structure' floating vaguely somewhere in his mind, and be simply recording its properties in language. Such an idea is absurd as it leads immediately to further problems of the type it was meant to solve, for what might be the source of the supposed objective question? Certainly it cannot be something simply caused in the student by the objective environment in which he finds himself (the person of his tutor, his own current brain states, and so on), for how could he then call such a question 'his' question? How could 'he' take responsibility both for its content and for its current formulation if he merely found it occuring within him? How could he know that that was the question 'he' wanted to ask? Further, he would require, as Anscombe (1957, p. 57) puts it, 'a very queer and special sort of seeing eye in the middle of the acting' to 'see' such an object, a special sense organ with which we might observe (or not, if we so preferred) the nature of our own mental activity. But as both Anscombe (1957) and Gauld and myself (1977) argue, paradigms of observation-knowledge are just not applicable to one's knowledge of one's own intentions and actions;[3] knowledge of quite a different kind is involved.

If objective knowledge of the kind gained in observation is not involved, what kind of knowledge is? The question does not just 'come out of the blue' to the student.

Let us return once again to James' vague 'feelings of tendency' and to the source of the student's question in his 'initial difficulty'. How might the student 'use' this difficulty (and the answer is prejudged by the use of the word 'use' rather than 'refer') to arrive at his question? Well, he could perhaps be said to use it as one might use any tool or material as a means or medium in achieving an end: one acts 'through' it, its nature specifying to a degree what one may do with it, its further specification being up to you. Rather than an objective thing, an 'initial difficulty' may be a datum of such a 'specifiable' (Johnson 1971) nature. As such, a person may be said not to know or be aware of it as an objective thing at all, only to know it practically, to the extent that he 'uses' it or 'works through its medium'. And just as the blind man feels, not his stick in the palm of his hand, but the character of the terrain at its tip, so may we be said to experience not our 'feelings of tendency' in themselves, but the 'ends' or 'objects' towards which they may lead. But the analogy above is not quite right, for realizing an intention is not like working with a tool or material *external* to ourselves, simply working 'with' it. It is more the case that a 'feeling of difficulty' is an intrinsic aspect or 'phase' of ourselves, and we live 'within' its so far specified structure working towards its greater specification within the limits its previous specification allows.

3 This not to say that observation-knowledge of one's actions may not be involved in their retrospective *evaluation*. As Nisbett and Wilson (1977) and especially Bem (1967, 1972), as well as many others working in and around the attribution theory tradition here discovered, not only are people not aware of *why* they act as they do, the reasons they give for their actions are often inaccurate. When asked to account for their action, people refer not only to *a priori*, implicit causal theories that abound in their culture, but also, seemingly, to their own observations of their own behaviour, as helpful sources of information upon which to base their

To summarize: the model for the realization of an intention offered has two aspects or components to it. One component is the initial 'feelings of tendency' from which the expression of one's action seems to issue. Such feelings are known, it suggests, not objectively, but only vaguely in terms of their possible further specification in practice, or more strictly, in terms of their *already specified further specifiability*. Although often only momentary product-forms, with no more than a fleeting existence, such 'feelings' may (as in a dialogue, say) provide the basis for further action, being transformed as one's circumstances change. The other component of the model is a formative process, an inner forming activity that is essential to what a person's intention is, that is, its already specified but yet further specifiable nature. Just as the whole inner movement of an oak tree in its growth (in its structured passage through time from less to more modes of being) is characteristic of the kind of tree it is, with its source in an acorn, so the action of a person is characterized by the intention, the phase of his being, in which the action has its source.

The metaphors and models in this section illustrate some of the properties of the 'worlds' within which human action has its being. Such worlds are unitary worlds of intrinsically interrelated entities awaiting yet further differentiation; worlds full of vague yet further specifiable products of human action; worlds in motion which, in the very character of their motion, indicate the style of what is yet to come. In such

---

account. For example: 'I *told* the girl I loved her, so I suppose I must have done, at the time.' Such results reveal the peculiar nature of our accounting practices. However, there is nothing in this work to suggest that when one says for example, 'I want coffee' or 'I am unhappy' that one is *a.* using implicit causal theories, *b.* observing oneself, or *c.* mistaken. Without the basic trustworthiness of such 'non-observational self-ascriptions' (Abelson 1977), the untrustworthiness of our *a posteriori* accounts could not be established.

What Nisbett and Wilson miss, however, is that the situations in which people are unable to account for the influences affecting their behavioural outcomes are *social* situations, ones in which individuals are not themselves wholly responsible for what happens; the outcomes result from *joint action.*

worlds action can in and of itself have a structure and order to it without such an order needing to be determined by externally defined rules.

4   *Action and Interaction: Social and Personal Worlds*

I want to turn now to the discussion of action and interaction, and the creation of social and personal worlds. I want to show a. that the 'workings' of such worlds are just 'invisible' to us, but no less full of charm and strangeness, as the world of modern physics, and b. that, in investigating actions in them, a hermeneutical (understanding) approach should first be applied to construct the 'world' (as a unity whole) within the context of which an action (as a proper part of the whole) can be seen to have its *sense*. Only then is a search worthwhile for the method, rule, or device by which members of that world achieve such a sense. If the sense was made routinely, then the device sought will already be a part of members' competence in that world. If the sense was not made routinely, then the device discovered may be offered as a possible addition to that competence, as is the case with noviciate members not yet well versed in the ways of such a social world.

The peculiar charm and strangeness of 'social worlds' resides in the paradox that while people quite clearly do construct their own ways of life for themselves, their own 'worlds', they none the less experience them as 'given', as 'realities' existing externally to and independently of them, and as containing things which, even before they actually find them or become conscious of them, are thought of as existing 'somewhere' in that world: the thesis explored below then is that people, although unaware of doing so, construct social worlds of meaning between themselves in the course of social interaction, and in so doing, determine the form of their own consciousness, their own modes of being in the world, their own categories of thought, perception and action.

ACTION

Currently, psychology and social psychology are taken to be sciences of behaviour, but as the concept of action is central to my whole endeavour here, let me begin by pointing out the traditional distinction people draw between action and behaviour, between acts and events, between things people *do* and things which merely happen to them, within them, or around them, outside of their agency to control. While boats, bombs and barnacles behave, we *recognize* people as being able to act; and it is the special quality of human action, especially its *intentional* nature, its ability to 'point to' something beyond itself, that we shall find crucial in its ability to indicate a 'world'.

The distinction between action and behaviour is crucial in everyday life, where we are continually concerned with whether people *themselves* intended what they did, or whether it happened by accident, or with what a person meant by his action. It is only because people themselves know, in at least some important cases, whether they intended their activity or not, and whether they achieved what they meant to achieve (or whether they made a mistake), that such questions about their actions make any sense; beings unable to distinguish between what *they* intended and what just happened irrespective of their agency would find such questions quite senseless. Besides being crucial in everyday life, the distinction is most certainly crucial in science (Shotter 1975). If people are unable to distinguish between what just happens, by itself, and what happens only as a result of their intended action, there would be no basis for empirical inquiries in science at all, no way of doing controlled experiments.

We thus approach human action in a quite different way to the way we approach other behaviour; a quite different set of interpretative assumptions (or rules) are involved. Gauld and myself (1977, pp. 42 – 45) set out some of them. Central is the assumption that actions are initiated and/or guided or controlled *by agents*, by people themselves. Rather than describing events and their regularities impersonally, without reference to their authorship, people are treated as the authors of their own actions.

There seem to be a number of good reasons for this: first, as Winch (1958, p. 32) points out, 'the notion of following a rule is logically inseparable from the notion of making a mistake.' In other words, unlike the motions of planets in their orbits, actions have criteria of success or failure; people need to evaluate or 'monitor' (Harré and Secord 1972) their actions in relation to these in the course of their performance. Often, of course, they fail to meet the appropriate criteria, then they may be censured; on some occasions they succeed, then we may congratulate them. We do not congratulate the moon for having managed to stay in its orbit last night, but we do congratulate young Johnny for managing not to fall off his new skateboard this afternoon.

The mistakes and errors to which human action is prone do not issue from it being governed by 'looser' laws than motions in the natural world, for what rules there are in social life, as Chomsky has shown in the case of language, are extremely precise, and prescribe very fine distinctions on occasion. Mistakes and errors occur because skill, effort, and care is required in *applying* and implementing them. As Ryle (1963, p. 29) remarks:

The well-regulated clock keeps good time and the well-drilled circus seal performs its tricks flawlessly, yet we do not call them 'intelligent'. We reserve this title for the persons responsible for their performances. To be intelligent is not merely to satisfy criteria, but to apply them . . .

But even more than skill at applying criteria is involved if people are to be treated as the authors of their actions, for they may still, so to speak, 'be going through the motions'. As Gauld and myself (1977, p. 44) point out:

accepting a criterion as *the* criterion... by which the success or otherwise of an action is to be measured involves not just applying it to one's directed movements, but as it were *committing oneself* to fulfilling it, guiding one's self-expression in accordance with its requirements.

One's *self* is involved in one's acting such that success or failure of one's action is *one's* success or failure. And the mark of such commitment is not the meeting of certain criteria in the making of one's movements but the skilful relating of one's motions to one's own intentions, to one's inner 'feelings of tendency'. In such a case, people's actual patterns of movement are irrelevant, it is the way that they 'go on' (to use a Wittgensteinian phrase) from one phase of their activity to the next that counts.

Human action would seem to be unique not because, from an external observer's point of view, no other behaviour is quite like it, but because it is only about human behaviour that we are able to make *and sustain* certain assumptions. Observing a projectile now (as beneficiaries of Cartesian metaphysics and modern science) we ascribe the pattern of its trajectory to the operation of impersonal general laws, but in observing people's motions we still ascribe their trajectories *to them*; we still think of them as controlling their own movements in relation to their own thoughts and feelings. And such ascriptions in this case 'work', for we do, so to speak, see 'through' their actions to their thoughts and feelings. This is not to say that we actually see their objective thoughts and their objective feelings; as such, not only are these completely hidden from us, but if our earlier account of 'intentions' is correct, they are as almost unknown to other people as they are to us. On our earlier account, what we see in a person's action is *his use* of the thought or feeling in which it had its source. People's actions are thus understood when their 'intentions', as something to be used, are as plain to us as they are to them; then we can 'go on' as they go on.

Such an understanding is achieved, not by referring to general laws or rules, nor by sharing thoughts or feelings, but by *constructing,* on the basis of at least the above assumptions, the whole context (or 'world') within which the action or

expression played its part (or had its sense). Such constructions or interpretations may, of course, be wrong. But there is
no reason for supposing that they should not be subjected to
just as much critical scrutiny and testing as theories in the
natural sciences; and in this sense, a hermeneutical science is
just as feasible as an explanatory-causal science. Consensual
understanding is achieved when, in *negotiation* with those
whose actions one is attempting to understand (and therein lies
its difference with a natural science), a *joint* 'way of going on'
from the action or actions in question is constructed *and agreed*
(Habermas 1972). Understanding in the hermeneutical view
is not achieved by, as mentioned earlier, re-experiencing
people's thoughts or feelings, nor when one knows how to
'pass', or to re-enact the actions in question by 'going through
the motions'. In neither case can the *sense* and *significance* of
people's actions be discovered in that way.

While logically possible, such a negotiated consensual
understanding is, of course, difficult to achieve in practice;
negotiation has to stop sometime, and some people or groups
of people will always feel that interpretations have been
imposed upon them by others. This is no less of a problem
when natural scientific methods are used in the study of
human affairs (Habermas 1972). These most important considerations must be discussed elsewhere, however; here we
must turn now to problems in the 'explanation' of social
behaviour.

An approach to the study of human action has been proposed in which workers have noted the distinction between
action and behaviour, and have claimed that while behaviour
may be explained by reference to general laws, human actions
cannot be so explained; they must be 'explained' by discovering *the reasons* people have for doing them, the rational considerations in terms of which they, as rational social agents, in the
perspective of their social world, structured their actions in the
course of their execution. Thus, instead of people being
treated as mechanisms caused to behave like mindless billiard
balls by they-know-not-what forces acting upon them exter-

nally, people are to be treated as entities able to explain themselves by giving, or at least by negotiating with those who are investigating them, 'accounts' of their reasons for their actions. And this 'negotiation of accounts', it has been pointed out, is a mode of explanation quite different from the causal kind: instead of explaining a particular event by showing how, in the circumstances of its occurrence it is an instance of a general law, a person's particular action is explained by discovering what in particular he was trying to do in executing it: Jones' *reason* for crossing the road is that he believed he could buy tobacco on the other side. The *particular* is being explained here by the *particular*. Rather than an instance of a general law, his action is being treated as the precise adjustment of a unique self to his own special circumstances as he saw them; an adjustment in which he could, of course, have failed.

A sphere of *autonomous*, skilful action has been marked out here; in this sphere men are not caused to act by events outside themselves, but are the originators of their own actions. In such a sphere, as Hollis (1977) remarks, 'rational action is its own explanation', that is, Jones is *there* as an agent in his action, and 'he' is executing it in terms of certain grounds and other rational considerations. His actions are explained when, roughly speaking, those grounds and considerations are as plain to us as to him. The considerations in terms of which he acts explain his action. The understanding achieved here may be *used as an explanation,* that is, a generalization, when it is offered in the context of the assumption that in such circumstances as Jones' *all* other rational agents would have done the same.

So far so good: we have succeeded in opposing, at least in theory, man-the-mechanism with man-the-autonomous-rational-social-agent, and in showing that there is a mode of rational explanation which can legitimately be applied to his conduct. The most well known approach in social psychology in this sphere is Harré's and Secord's (1972) *ethogenics*, and in this chapter I want to continue to share with them the problem of how to treat people for-the-purposes-of-science, as rational, social agents, able to act as the source of their own actions. But there is something very wrong, I think, with their approach to this problem in which a. they take *deliberate* activity, activity in which people seemingly refer to a 'theory', an 'idea', a 'grammar', or some other 'cognitive structure' somewhere *in-their-heads* in structuring their activity, as a model for *all* that people do, and b. see people's activity as determined in some way by factors external to it, by pre-established 'grammars of the social order' (Harré and Secord 1972, p. 123). 'In order to understand what people do, one must see their activities in terms of deliberate followings of rules...' (p. 15)

But as Hollis (1977) shows, actors who are creatures of rules are still passive in the sense that the actions they perform are not 'their' actions. To learn which rules people are following in their actions is not to learn a. their intentions in following them, nor b. why they put themselves under the guidance of those rules. Reference to rules may answer the 'how' question, but the 'what' and the 'why' question remain. If there is nothing more to discover in *ethogeny* than, as Harré and Secord (1972, p. 9) put it, 'the "generative mechanisms" that give rise to behaviour', then once again, as in the behaviourist paradigm, the idea of people themselves, as individual personalities, being the authors of their own actions disappears.

Besides the threat to self and genuine individuality in Harré and Secord's approach, there is also a threat to genuine creativity and development. They suggest that a social individual is an entity 'which consciously self-monitors its performance and is capable of anticipatory commentary...', as if it is always possible to know what one is doing while one is doing it, as if there is always a script, plan, or rule to which to refer in structuring one's actions. However, there are many everyday activities, it seems to me, in which we remain deeply ignorant as to what exactly it is that we are doing, not because the 'scripts' supposedly in us somewhere are too vague or too deeply buried to bring out into the light of day, but because the formative influences shaping our conduct are not wholly there *in-our-individual-heads* to be brought out: in our everyday affairs we must act not only in an unpredictable environment, but our actions are influenced by the unpredictable actions of others. Hence other forms of action require analysis other than just autonomous action: besides acting autonomously, people also interact as well as acting jointly (and heteronomously, that is, subject to the rule of externally imposed laws). And in interacting or acting jointly they do things collectively, they lack the 'power' (Harré 1970) to do things singly. It is in this sphere then, not in that of deliberate followings of rules, that we may expect to find 'developmental' phenomena (Gauld and Shotter 1977), the growth of the general factors that make routinely meaningful action possible.

This then will be my concern in the remainder of this section: the analysis of the *joint action* (to use Blummer's 1965/66 term) involved in developing the grounds for routinely meaningful action. I shall be concerned with such activities as discussions, industrial negotiations, football matches, tutorials, greetings, insults, promises, listening to academic papers, and so on, using joint action as a model to some extent as help in understanding more unstructured interactions like general conversation, and just 'playing around'. Such activities as these cannot wholly be performed simply by following the rules or referring to pre-established plans; they are, none the less, actions with a particular *style* to them: people seem *committed* by one phase of their activity to behaving in one way rather than another in the next. Whilst friendly conversations differ from philosophical debates which differ from psychotherapy which differs from formal interviews, and so on, people know in which activity they are engaged and conduct themselves accordingly. Elsewhere (Shotter 1973a, b, 1974) I have explored the growth of people's 'personal powers' in social interaction; here I want to explore people's 'social powers'. They have the power, I think, to create and sustain a 'social world' between them in such activities, a seemingly 'external' and 'objective' world in terms of which, when required as autonomous agents to do so, *they can give their reasons for their actions,* and have them understood and accepted by those, and only those, who understand with them the same 'world of meaning'. And this, as we shall see, is a quite different way of accounting for one's actions, of giving them a rational explanation, than in terms of rule-, plan-, or script-following. It involves grasping the 'intentional structure' of the 'world' from which the action draws its sense, grasping it not objectively but practically, knowing how to use the context it provides to go on as the people in it go on.

A personal world, I suggest, has the same intentional structure to it as a social world and thus possesses most of the other properties of social worlds discussed below. But what people lack when acting all alone is access to the processes in which a *common* sense can be constructed; joint action is essential to the construction of a common context within 'what I see' can be contrasted with 'what everybody sees'. It is not so much that in joint action 'agreements' are made, but that, as Winch (1958, p. 50) puts it, 'action with a sense . . . goes together with certain other actions in the sense that it commits the agent to behaving in one way rather than another in the future'; and that commitment is a *moral* commitment. Strangers meeting one another's glances in the park seem to establish a shared commitment of a kind quite different from that if their glances had never met, but no 'agreements' have been made here; they have merely 'recognized' one another as creatures with *possibly* agreeing assumptions about the interpretation of the world. A more precise 'agreement' remains to be constructed.

THE NATURE AND STRUCTURE OF SOCIAL AND PERSONAL WORLDS

In discussing the nature and structure of the 'social worlds' constructed in the course of joint action, I want to make two interrelated points: the first is simply that in the world of practical human affairs, men must often interlace their actions in with those of others, hence, what they as individuals desire and what actually happens *are often two quite different things.*

Vico (1744; see also Pompa 1975; Berlin 1976) was the first to note the importance of this phenomenon. As the results of joint action cannot be traced back to the intentions or desires of particular individuals (as we normally assume the products of actions can), they can take on a seemingly 'objective' and 'external' quality. They may seem to have the quality of impersonal, just-happening events and thus it seems necessary to seek their external causes just as one would for other impersonal, just-happening events. Rather than being attributed to an author, their occurrence is attributed to an external force or agency 'outside' of the people involved; 'social norms', 'role demands', or some such other influence acting upon people and structuring their action is invoked. A paradigm example here is the movement of the wine glass on the *Ouija* board. Clearly it does not move unless people's fingers are on it. But so strong is the conviction that its movements cannot be traced back to any intentions of the people involved, while its movements none the less display intelligence, that they are attributed to an external spirit, acting through the medium of the people present – the workings of such social processes as these remain quite invisible to the people involved in them. Laing's (1971) 'knots' are examples of the ways in which people unknowingly trap themselves within the 'micro-social worlds' they construct between them, 'worlds' too small or too restricted for people's self-expression.

The second point is that unintended though the results of joint action may be, such action remains, nonetheless, *intentional*, in the sense of 'pointing beyond itself' already discussed at length above. Such action 'points to' a realm (or realms) of other possible actions, to a 'world of meaning or reference' which seems to make its appearance even as the action occurs, and can thus function as *the context in which the sense of the action is understood* and a reply to it formulated. The reply may transform, or specify the already specified context yet further, and so on, until a common or joint product of the exchange is formed which is the responsibility of neither of the parties to its construction.

These two features of the 'worlds' so produced, their impersonality and their intentional structure, are well described by Merleau-Ponty (1962, p. 416) when he says:

Ahead of what I can see and perceive, there is, it is true, nothing actually visible, but my world is carried forward by lines of intentionality which trace out in advance at least *the style* of what is to come ... Husserl uses the terms protentions and retentions for the intentionalities which anchor me to an environment. They do not run from a central *I*, but from my perceptual field itself, so to speak, which draws along in its wake its own horizon of retentions, and bites into the future with its own protentions.'

I as an individual personality remain distinct from 'the world' in which I find myself; that world confronts me with, among other things, problems which I must solve if I am to go on in it. My perception seems to express a *given* situation within which I, by my personal acts may create others. My perceptual experience feels as if, Merleau-Ponty (1962, p. 215) suggests, 'it comes not from my own being, the one for which I am responsible and for which I make decisions, but another self which has already sided with the world, which is already open to certain of its aspects and synchronized with them.' It is created, we might say, by the 'natural powers' (Merleau-Ponty 1962, p. 215; Shotter 1973, 1974), the protentions and retentions, the assumptions I use and through which I work in coping with my circumstances. Even 'personal worlds' may thus be impersonal in the sense that, what we may wish and desire is one thing, while the nature and structure of the 'world' within which we find ourselves, is another. But they are not common worlds in which what one confronts is also confronted in the same way by everyone else.

THE REFLEXIVE, MORALLY COERCIVE, AND INCORRIGIBLE NATURE OF 'SOCIAL WORLDS'

The nature of socially constructed realities is such as to render all Popper's (1963) strictures about falsifiability quite beside the point, for such worlds are both *morally coercive* and *reflexive*. That is, a. they provide a world in terms of which a person who inhabits it *must* determine his action; for example, rational Skinnerians *must* see the human world in terms of stimuli and responses, and *must* structure their explanations in terms of schedules of reinforcement and so on, if they want to remain living, that is, in a Skinnerian world. Its other members, actual or potential, exert a morally coercive force upon them, in that sense. And b. in so determining people's actions, there is no way in which their actions can lead to results *beyond* that reality; it is reflexive in the sense that, no matter what happens, it is understood and dealt with in terms that the reality provides. Piaget (1971) calls this the self–regulating property of structures.

Let me illustrate with an example: when the Azande of Africa are faced with important decisions, Evans–Pritchard (1937) tells us, decisions about whom to marry, or where to build their house, and so on, they consult a spirit oracle. They do it by first gathering a substance from the bark of a certain type of tree and then, after having prepared it in a seance-like ceremony, they feed it to a small chicken. The Azande have decided beforehand whether the death of the chicken will denote a 'yes' or a 'no' answer, and the oracle, working through the medium of the chicken's living or dying, gives them an unequivocal answer to their question.

We, with our western 'scientific' knowledge, 'know' that the tree bark used by the Azande contains a poison that kills some chickens but not all. Knowing the oracle's bark is 'really' poison, *we* wonder what would happen when, for instance, someone else consulted the oracle about the same question and got a contradictory answer? What if the oracle is contradicted by later events, the house site floods, the wife becomes a whore? How is it possible for the Azande to continue to believe in oracles in the face of so many evident contradictions in their faith? (The same way, in fact, that we all, including Skinnerians, maintains our beliefs.)

What '*we*' would call contradictions are not contradictions for the Azande; they are only contradictions *for us*, as we view the events from within the reality of western science. While we look at oracular practices to determine whether oracles exist or not, the Azande *know* that oracles exist; that is the beginning premise of their particular mode of rationality. Everything that happens they experience as supporting that initial assumption in some way. And they explain away apparent failures by what Evans-Pritchard (1937, p. 330) calls 'secondary elaborations of belief'. When he tried to confront them with apparent failures of the oracle, they only laughed or met his arguments,

sometimes by point-blank assertions, sometimes by one of the evasive secondary elaborations of belief ... sometimes by polite pity, but always by an entanglement of linguistic obstacles, for one cannot well express in its language objections not formulated by a culture.'

They said that a taboo must have been breached, or that sorcerers, witches, ghosts, or gods must have intervened; these 'mystical' notions reaffirming, in fact, the very reality of a world in which oracles are a basic feature. The Azande explain the failure of the oracles by retaining as an initial premise, the unquestioned absolute reality of oracles; their reality is *morally coercive* in the sense that it provides the terms in which they as social agents *must* structure their actions. 'Witchcraft, oracles, and magic form an intellectually coherent system', says Evans-Pritchard (1937, p. 476),

Each explains and proves the others. Death is proof of witchcraft. It is avenged by magic. The achievement of vengeance-magic is proved by the poison-oracle. The accuracy of the poison-oracle is determined by the king's oracle, which is above suspicion.

These are the terms in which the Azande experience their world. They are reflexive when, by using 'secondary elaborations of belief', apparent refutations are turned into verifications of the oracle's existence. Their beliefs are thus *incorrigible* in the sense that there is no way in which they can ever be discovered to be false.

We 'scientists' feel thankful that we are not as the Azande, trapped within a web of obviously false beliefs from which we cannot escape. But this same irrefutability, Lakatos (1970) has shown, is also a property of all the great scientific research programmes. How is it then that if both the Azande and, say, our Newtonian 'realities' are or were irrefutable in principle, have we managed to transcend our Newtonian beliefs while the Azande, seemingly, have no hope of transcending theirs? The answer can be found, I believe, although I have no space to discuss it at length here, in the phenomenological distinction Schutz (1953) and Garfinkel (1967) draw between the rational properties of scientific and commonsense activities, between taking a *theoretic* and a *practical* interest in the world. Taking the former attitude, we assume the 'interpretative rule' when confronting phenomena that we know nothing of them and that they are not what they seem; thus we must construct theories about them. Taking the latter attitude, we take our commonsense knowledge and our social competencies for granted and things *are* accepted as being what they seem to be. We possess a 'scientific attitude' that the Azande lack; even though they may as individuals disagree as to the proper interpretation of puzzling phenomena, they do not as we do disagree upon the whole nature of the appropriate interpretative framework, their understanding is always 'within' it.

UNDERSTANDING IN AND OF SOCIAL WORLDS

Our understanding of a phenomenon is always from a position 'within' an interpretative framework, even if that framework constructs an impersonal world regulated by causal laws. Our explanation of natural phenomena requires us to interpret them *as if* they were regulated by laws. We have already discussed our understanding of human phenomena, and the different interpretative assumptions with which we approach them. Understanding them is not, I have claimed, a matter of seeking *the* grammars of *the* social order (as if these already existed in social worlds before *any* people, so to speak, came along to inhabit them). It is a matter, at every stage, both practical and theoretical, of constructing common and agreed worlds. Being able to live by, and use, grammars presupposes everywhere the existence of the general conditions in terms of which grammars may be developed. Denying that one meets these conditions is tantamount to denying one access to a social world; it is to refuse to recognize one's status as a person in fact.

Consider what happens when someone shouts, 'Hey, you!' at you: what is that person doing, what is he saying, even when he shouts it at you in the most general of contexts? We might answer by following Austin (1962), seeking the 'speech act' that the utterance performs: it is hardly a greeting or salutation of any kind, but neither is it necessarily an insult, although it does seem to be an incivility of some kind. As it is more than just an exclamation, let us call it, for want of some-thing better, a directed-attention-demander, an unwieldy but seemingly accurate description. But is it accurate? If that was the function to be served, surely 'Hey' or 'Hello there' would have done just as well. But neither expression seems to say the same thing at all. While the person is perhaps demand-ing attention with his speech act, he is saying much more: at least in his use of the vernacular he is recognizing one's status as a person, as a being able to use language and indicate intentions in his expressions. 'Hey' could equally well have been addressed to a dog; as such it leaves one nonplussed as to how to go on to reply to it; it involves no attempt to make any sense. Should one act frightened as a dog might when sur-prised by a loud noise, or what? 'Hey, you!' creates in its very utterance a world in which you are not personally recognized but are already assigned a role, that of paying attention, of giving recognition to the other that you await his next move; as such your role is a subservient one. 'Hello there' may surprise you, may get your attention, and so on, but it constructs a quite different kind of social world, a world of civility and tolerance in which you are invited to play the part of an equal, to reply in kind as a personal other: 'Oh hello there, I'm so-and-so.'

Let us move now from a general context to more specific ones, for we have still not encountered the speaker as an individual; the sense of his utterance, and thus our reply to it, will depend upon where and who we both are. If you are the managing director of a large company, just unlocking the door of your Rolls in your firm's underground carpark, and the parking attendant shouts 'Hey you!' at you, you may be prepared to give him the benefit of the doubt and ignore it, or you may feel sufficiently incensed to discover who he is and make an appointment to see him the next day. If you are not the owner of the Rolls you are just unlocking, your 'reply' may be to run. If you are the managing director and you have just turned down a request by the parking attendant to marry your daughter, you may consider running again (especially if he is bigger than you), and so on. As an utterance, 'Hey, you!' specifies in general a social world with a certain style to it, even when heard by quite young children. Although it is further specifiable in various ways, it cannot easily be transformed into one of a different kind, in which the subservience imputed to the 'you' is changed into equality or dominance, say.

Two things are illustrated in the examples above. The first is that 'Hey, you!' draws its sense mostly from the very general interpretative assumptions we apply in making sense of the actions of agents and very little from anything like a rule. Straight away it specifies a style of exchange which may (or may not), with further specification in a particular context, become *established* as a clear and distinct form of social exchange, that is, become *as if* governed by rules. The second point, which follows from the first, is that as the exchange is not initially a 'rule-governed' exchange, to attempt to understand it as one (on analogy with TG-grammar or dramaturgy) is to distort the 'developmental' aspect of its nature. The particular sense of the utterance, the particular author's particular intention in uttering it, is understood practically by perceiving it as occurring in a world with a particular intentional structure to it (see Merleau-Ponty's account quoted earlier). As interaction proceeds that structure is transformed accordingly, and one's perceptions of it change. Theoretically, the sense in the author's action may be understood, to repeat the by now familiar hermeneutical formula, by constructing an account, in negotiation with those whose action one is attempting to understand, of a common and agreed world of meaning, an account of a way of going on from the action in question. Such negotiated and agreed accounts of ways-of-going-on actually are rules.

Essential to the establishment of rules, of regularities, repeatabilities, stabilities is humankind's moral sensibility and people's capacity to understand how to be responsible for their own actions. If we can retain that capacity, to use a remark by Hanna Arendt (1959, p. 254), then,

even if there is no truth, men can be truthful, and even if there is no reliable certainty, men can be reliable.

And that, when we put the changefulness of humankind at the centre of things as we have in this paper, is perhaps the best for which we can ever hope; but surely that should be quite enough.

References

R. Abelson, 1977, *Persons: A Study in Philosophical Psychology,* Basingstoke: Macmillan

G. W. Allport, 1954, 'The Historical Background of Modern Social Psychology', in: G. Lindzey (Ed.), *Handbook of Social Psychology*, Vol. 1, Cambridge, Mass: Addison-Wesley

G. E. M. Anscombe, 1957, *Intention,* Oxford: Blackwell

H. Arendt, 1959, *The Human Condition,* New York: Doubleday Anchor Books

M. Argyle, 1969, *Social Interaction,* London: Methuen

J. Austin, 1962, *How to Do Things with Words,* Oxford: Clarendon

H. Bergson, 1920, *Mind-Energy,* London: Macmillan

I. Berlin, 1976, *Vico and Herder: Two Studies in the History of Ideas,* London: Hogarth

D. J. Bem, 1967, 'Self-Perception: An Alternative Interpretation of Cognitive Dissonance Phenomena', *Psychological Review,* Vol. 74, pp. 183 – 200

D. J. Bem, 1972, 'Self-Perception Theory', in: L. Berkowitz (Ed.), *Advances in Experimental Social Psychology,* Vol. 6, New York: Academic Press

H. Blummer, 1965/66, 'Sociological Implications of the Thought of George Herbert Mead', *American Journal of Sociology,* Vol. 71, pp. 535–44

D. Bohm, 1973, 'Human Nature as the Product of Our Mental Models', in: J. Bentall (Ed.), *The Limits of Human Nature,* London: Allen Lane

F. Brentano, 1973, *Psychology from an Empirical Standpoint,* London: Routledge and Kegan Paul

J. Culler, 1976, *Saussure,* London: Fontana

J. Dewey, 1896, 'The Concept of the Reflex Arc in Psychology', *Psychological Review,* Vol. 3, pp. 13–32

E. E. Evans-Pritchard, 1937, *Witchcraft, Oracles and Magic Among the Azande,* London: Oxford University Press

H. Garfinkel, 1967, *Studies in Ethnomethodology.* Englewood Cliffs, N.J: Prentice-Hall

A. Gauld and J. Shotter, 1977, *Human Action and its Psychological Investigation,* London: Routledge and Kegan Paul

K. Gergen, 1973, 'Social Psychology as History', *Journal of Personality and Social Psychology,* Vol. 26, pp. 309–320

J. J. Gibson and E. J. Gibson, 1955, 'Perceptual Learning: Differentation or Enrichment?' *Psychological Review,* Vol. 62, pp. 32–41

J. Habermas, 1972, *Knowledge and Human Interests,* London: Heinemann

R. Harré, 1970, 'Powers', *British Journal of the Philosophy of Science,* Vol. 21, pp. 81–101

R. Harré and P. F. Secord, 1972, *The Explanation of Social Behaviour,* Oxford: Blackwell

M. Hollis, 1977, *Models of Man,* Cambridge: Cambridge University Press

W. James, 1890, *Principles of Psychology,* Vol. 1, London: Macmillan

D. M. Johnson, 1971, 'A Formulation Model of Perceptual Knowledge', *American Philosophical Quarterly*, Vol. 8, pp. 54–62

G. Kelly, 1955, *The Psychology of Personal Constructs,* New York: Norton

T. S. Kuhn, 1962, *The Structure of Scientific Revolutions,* Chicago: Chicago University Press

I. Lakatos, 1970, 'Falsification and the Methodology of Scientific Research Programmes', in: I. Lakatos and A. Musgrave (Eds.), *Criticism and the Growth of Knowledge,* Cambridge: Cambridge University Press

A. M. Liberman, 1970, 'The Grammars of Speech and Language', *Cognitive Psychology,* Vol. 1, pp. 301–325

A. M. Liberman, F. S. Cooper, D. P. Shankweiler and M. Studdert-Kennedy, 1967, 'Perception of the Speech Code', *Psychological Review,* Vol. 74, pp. 431–61

W. J. McGuire, 1973, 'The Yin and the Yan of Progress in Social Psychology', *Journal of Personality and Social Psychology,* Vol. 26, pp. 446–456

M. Merleau-Ponty, 1962, *Phenomenology of Perception,* London: Routledge and Kegan Paul

U. Neisser, 1976, *Cognition and Reality,* San Francisco: Freeman

R. E. Nisbett and T. D. Wilson, 1977, 'Telling More than We Can Know: Verbal Reports an Mental Processes', *Psychological Review,* Vol. 84, pp. 231–59

R. S. Peters, 1958, *The Concept of Motivation,* London: Routledge and Kegan Paul

J. Piaget, 1971, *Structuralism,* London: Routledge and Kegan Paul

L. Pompa, 1975, Vico: *A Study of the 'New Science',* Cambridge: Cambridge University Press

K. R. Popper, 1963, *Conjectures and Refutations,* London: Routledge and Kegan Paul

G. Ryle, 1963, *The Concept of Mind,* Harmondsworth: Peregine Books

A. Schutz, 1953, 'Common-Sense and Scientific Interpretation of Human Action', *Philosophy and Phenomenological Research,* Vol. 14, pp. 1–38

J. R. Searle, 1969, *Speech Acts: An Essay in the Philosophy of Language,* Cambridge University Press

J. Shotter, 1973a, 'Prolegomena to an Understanding of Play', *Journal for the Theory of Social Behaviour,* Vol. 3

J. Shotter, 1973b, 'Acquired Powers: the Transformation of Natural into Personal Powers', *Journal for the Theory of Social Behaviour,* Vol. 3, pp. 141–156

J. Shotter, 1974, 'The Development of Personal Powers', in: M. P. M. Richards (Ed.), *The Integration of a Child into a Social World,* Cambridge: Cambridge University Press

J. Shotter, 1975, *Images of Man in Psychological Research,* London: Methuen

J. Shotter, 1978, 'The Cultural Context of Communication Studies: Theoretical and Methodological Issues', in: A. Lock (Ed.), *Action, Gesture and Symbol,* London: Academic Press

M. B. Smith, 1972, 'Is Experimental Social Psychology Progressing?', *Journal of Experimental and Social Psychology,* Vol. 8, pp. 86–96

L. H. Strickland, F. E. Aboud and K. J. Gergen, 1976, (Eds.), *Social Psychology in Transition,* New York: Plenum Press

A. N. Whitehead, 1975, *Science and the Modern World,* London: Fontana

P. Winch, 1958, *The Idea of a Social Science and its Relations to Philosophy,* London; Routledge and Kegan Paul

The Analysis of Social Situations

MICHAEL ARGYLE   *Oxford University*

---

1   *Introduction*

A number of recent studies by Milgram, Zimbardo and others have demonstrated the extraordinary extent to which behaviour is affected by situations. If we want to explain social behaviour we must explain how situations influence it.

Several ways of analysing situations have been proposed in the past, but it will be argued that none of these are able to account for the effects of situations on behaviour. A new model is proposed here, in which situations are analysed as systems of communication, using an analogy with games. This suggests a number of different features of situations, such as goal structure, repertoire of elements, etc., and research is reported on each of these features. The practical implications of this line of thinking include new ways of social skills training for people who cannot cope with particular situations, modification of problem situations, for example by changing the rules or the environmental setting, ways of resolving inter-group conflict, and new ways of matching individuals to jobs.

The experiment by Milgram (1974) showed that normal members of the public would give what they thought were near-fatal electric shocks to another person, in 65 per cent of cases, if ordered to do so by the experimenter. In the experiment by Zimbardo et al. (1973) normal university students, who were asked to play the role of prison guards, did so in such a tyrannical way that other students, ordered to be convicts, became emotionally distressed, and the experiment had to be terminated. Studies of religious sects show that people who are quite normal on week-days can speak with tongues, handle snakes, and have near-psychotic experiences on Sundays (Argyle and Beit-Hallahmi 1975).

Research on person-situation interaction has studied the percentages of variance due to persons, situations, and $P \times S$ interaction; the last two are usually found to be at least as great as the first. Other studies have found functional relationships of the form $B = f(P, S)$, for example, showing how anxiety is a function of trait anxiety and the stressfulness of situations (Endler and Magnusson 1976). This kind of work makes it necessary to find dimensions or categories of situations, such as stressfulness, cooperative-competitive, and the like. A currently popular way of finding such dimensions of situations is by means of multi-dimensional scaling, in which subjects indicate how similar a number of situations are to each other, so that the underlying dimensions which they are using can be extracted statistically. Myron Wish (1975) used this method for finding the dimensionality of eight different kinds of social events and eight role-relations. He obtained the following dimensions:

friendly – hostile
cooperative – competitive
intense – superficial
equal – unequal
informal – formal
task-oriented – not task-oriented

These dimensions were not all independent; the first two are correlated, for example. These dimensions are most valuable, and have appeared in other studies. However, they do not tell the whole story. Consider the combination *task-oriented, unequal, friendly, intense* and *cooperative*: this includes such situations as going to the dentist, being psychoanalaysed, saying confession, having a tennis lesson, having a philosophy tutorial, discussing work problems with the boss, and discussing domestic problems with father. (It is difficult to assess them for formality.) If someone has difficulties with one of these situations, as clients for social skills training often do, then they need to know more than the fact that the situation is task-oriented, unequal, friendly, etc. If we want to understand one of these situations to the point where we can predict or explain the sequence of events in it, we need to know more. What is it about situations which it would be useful to know, and which would provide sufficient information for these purposes?

I propose to use games as models for other social situations. In each case the participants agree to follow certain rules; they pursue certain goals, and only certain moves are recognised as relevant acts. In his analysis of games, Avedon (1971) proposed the following features:

1. purpose (i.e., how to win)
2. procedure for action (i.e., moves)
3. rules
4. number of participants
5. roles of participants
6. results, or pay-off
7. abilities and skills required
8. interactive patterns, e.g., competition between teams
9. physical environment
10. equipment required.

The list of features of situations which I have been using, and which has developed independently, is as follows:

1. goal structure
2. repertoire of elements
3. rules
4. sequences of behaviour
5. concepts
6. environmental setting
7. roles
8. skills and difficulties (Argyle, 1976)

These could be divided up differently; for example, roles could be a subdivision of rules, and sequences are closely linked with repertoire. I believe that these features are inter-dependent and form a system, so that only certain combinations of goals, rules, etc., are possible. I shall give a number of examples of one feature generating other features. In using the game analogy, I am using 'game' in a rather general sense, and want to underplay the element of competition, which is often absent from social situations. It can, therefore, include the kinds of situation which Harré and Secord (1972) call 'rituals' and 'entertainments'.

A rather different view of situations is held by symbolic interactionists, who maintain that interactors are continuously renegotiating the shared definition of the situation. I agree that participants do alter the nature of situations along dimensions like friendly-hostile, or tense-relaxed, within a given situational framework, e.g., a tennis lesson or a visit to the dentist. They may also be able to modify the rules; for example, a series of seminars, at family meals, may develop a local modification of these. I also agree that participants sometimes change the nature of the situation entirely as when a philosophy tutorial turns into psychotherapy, or a tennis lesson into a love affair. However, when this happens, there is a transition to another socially defined situational structure, rather like a change from tennis to squash; in each case there is a discontinuity. It is also true that new situations gradually evolve in the culture, as in the case of brainstorming, T-groups and encounter groups. The same is true of the gradual development of games, like rugby football.

2   Goal Structure

Why do people enter social situations, indeed why do they engage in social behaviour at all? A functional account would suppose that they are motivated to do so, i.e., they expect that certain needs will be satisfied, certain goals obtained. We must add that people have learnt that certain needs will be satisfied in certain situations. Further, situations have developed as cultural institutions because they do satisfy these needs. Thus meals are situations for satisfying the hunger drive, classrooms for satisfying the desire to learn (and to teach). We should perhaps distinguish between needs and drives on the one hand, and goals on the other. A may be hungry (a state of need), and desire to eat at a particular restaurant (a goal, which leads to need reduction). This is not an absolute distinction since goals, which are routes to need satisfaction, acquire secondary drive properties themselves. In addition to needs, like hunger and thirst, there are also drives, like sex, achievement and affiliation, which are not based on any bodily deficit, though they are accompanied by physiological arousal. Another problem is that situations *arouse* needs and drives, as well as satisfying them. Someone who is not very hungry may have his appetite aroused by the smell and sight of food in the restaurant; he anticipates both the arousal of the drive and its satisfaction. Sometimes, it is primarily the arousal which is sought, rather than its reduction, as at fairs, and noisy parties.

The needs, drives and goals which are satisfied by a situation also form a *structure*, that is, if a person is pursuing more than one goal, or if there is more than one person there. We shall analyse situations in terms of the relations between two or more *goals*.

1.0 ONE PERSON, TWO GOALS

1.1 *One goal leads to another.* Using the terminology of forces and barriers devised by Lewin (1935), such a structure can be represented as follows:

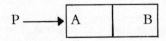

Here P desires goals A and B, where A leads to B. For example, P wants to eat at a certain restaurant A and also wants to eat a dish B which this restaurant happens to serve.

1.2 *Two goals in conflict.* As Lewin (1935) has shown, there are three kinds of conflict:

Double approach conflict

$$\overset{+}{B}\longrightarrow \textcircled{P} \longleftarrow \overset{+}{A}$$

For example, a person wants to go to two different restaurants.

Double avoidance conflict

$$\overset{-}{B}\longrightarrow \textcircled{P} \longleftarrow \overset{-}{A}$$

For example, a pupil does not want to do either Latin or Greek. As Lewin's analysis shows, a double avoidance conflict is only a problem if there is a boundary, so that P has to go to either A or B.

Approach–avoidance conflict

$$P \underset{\longleftarrow}{\overset{\longrightarrow}{\rule{3cm}{0pt}}} \overset{+-}{A}$$

For example, a child wants to stroke a horse's nose, and is also afraid to do so. This is of particular importance in psychology; it is found that the avoidance component falls off faster with distance, thus creating an equilibrium position; this can be generalised to approach drives like affiliation in relation to intimacy (Argyle and Dean 1965).

2.0 TWO PERSONS, ONE GOAL EACH

2.1 *Cooperation.* Two people might pursue the same goal, as in affiliative and sexual behaviour, and cooperative work. Or they may pursue different goals, as in the case of people preparing and eating a meal. These two cases could be represented in Lewinian terms as:

$$\begin{matrix} P \searrow \\ Q \nearrow \end{matrix} \text{ joint action} \longrightarrow A$$

$$\begin{matrix} P \searrow \\ Q \nearrow \end{matrix} \text{ joint action} \begin{matrix} \nearrow A \\ \searrow B \end{matrix}$$

In games theory terminology, this is a non–zero–sum game, like:

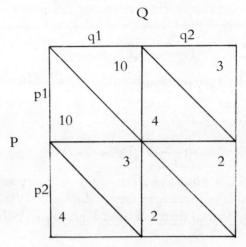

This is a straightforward case where cooperative action $p_1 q_1$ is most rewarding for both parties.

Cooperation may involve elements of conflict. In situations devoted to affiliative or sexual activity for example, one person may want to go faster or further than the other. There are more complex cases, like the Prisoner's Dilemma Game, where each party is tempted by the possibility of larger gains to shift from cooperative action (Jones and Gerard 1967).

2.2 *Competition and conflict.* Here, if A attains his goals, B does not. Examples are competing for food, to win races, or to get jobs. This can be represented in game theory terms as a zero-sum game. Here, whatever one wins, the other loses. In experimental games the meaning of competition is not always clear: are subjects trying to maximise their individual gains, or their lead over the other player (Chadwick Jones 1976)? In any case, real-life competition need not be a zero-sum game, since one may gain without the other losing anything, or losing very much, as when two people hope to win a raffle.

Cases of direct conflict are a little different, for example, when A wants to persuade B to do something which B does not want to do. They are not necessarily competing over food or jobs, but again if one gains the other loses.

All these cases can be represented as:

P◄——————┼——————►Q

2.3 *Altruistic concern for other.* Here, the goal attainment by one is a source of satisfaction to the other, rather like the route-to-goal situation in 1.1; for example, a mother is made happy by her child enjoying his supper.

2.4 *Independent goals.* P and Q may be pursuing quite unrelated goals, as when a hostess is displaying her skill at cooking, and a guest is displaying his skill at conversation.

3.0 TWO PERSONS, TWO GOALS EACH

There are many possible combinations here, of which I shall mention two.

3.1 *Assertiveness.* P wants to persuade Q to do something which Q does not want to do; for example, a husband wants to persuade his wife to go to a certain place for their summer holiday. Each has a second goal – to sustain good relations with the other. If P wins, he also loses some of Q's goodwill and damages the relationship, and if Q wins likewise. This can be represented as:

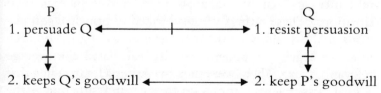

P   Q
1. persuade Q ◄————————┼————————► 1. resist persuasion

2. keeps Q's goodwill ◄————————► 2. keep P's goodwill

On this somewhat speculative analysis there is one inter-personal conflict, two similar intra-personal conflicts and one cooperative linkage of goals.

3.2 *Supervision.* The supervisor, S, wants members of his work-group, W, to work hard, but they may want to take it fairly easy. The supervisor also wants to keep on good terms with his men; if he does, research shows that they will probably work harder (Argyle 1972), so this is a route to his other goal. The men want to keep his good opinion, but they will not do so if they do not do much work, so they have an internal conflict.

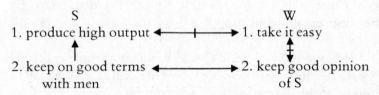

Here there is one inter-personal conflict, one intra-personal conflict, one route-to-goal link, and one cooperative link.

AN INVESTIGATION OF GOAL STRUCTURE

This study was carried out with nurses and occupational therapy students. The first stage consisted of open-ended interviews to find the goals which the girls thought were relevant to a number of common situations. The interviews produced long lists of goals; others were added from lists of needs by Murray (1938) and others, and the total list was reduced to a shorter list of 21 main goals.

In the first two studies samples of 60 and 37 girls rated the relevance of each of the goals to each role in each of 8 situations. These ratings were subjected to principal components analysis, showing the main groupings of goals for each role. For each component we also calculated the average relevance score. There were thus two criteria for deciding that a goal was relevant for a given role and situation – the emergence of a principal component, and the average relevance score. In most cases there were three such main goals. For example, in the case of a nurse and patient encounter the following goals were most relevant:

nurse	patient
mutual acceptance	mutual acceptance
take care of other	obtaining information
look after self	own well-being

In a second study we studied 'goal structures' – degree of conflict or instrumentality between the goals found in the first study. Thirty-six further subjects rated the degree of conflict v. compatability of pairs of goals on 5-point scales, and also the direction of instrumentality or interference.

Two examples of the goal structures found are shown below. These figures show one-way and two-way instrumental relationships, one-way interference, and two-way interference or conflict, independence, and average levels of conflict within and between persons. In the nurse-patient encounter there is a small amount of conflict (4.16 on a 1–5 scale) between well-being of nurse and patient. In the complaint situation there is a lot of conflict, especially over dominance; if a complainer concentrated on persuasion rather than dominance he might be more successful (see Argyle, Furnham and Graham in press).

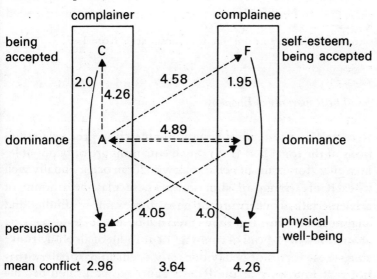

Fig 1: Complaint

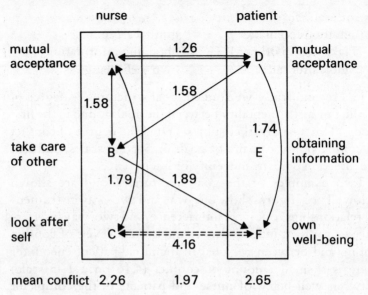

Fig 2: Nurse-patient

Note for Figures

> ——————————————▶ instrumental relationship
> ◀——————————————▶ two-way instrumental relationship
> — — — — — — ▶ interference
> ◀====== two-way inference

Numbers refer to amount of conflict on a scale from 1–5.

3 The Repertoire of Elements

Research on personality-situation interaction produces equations of the form B = (P,S). Such equations are only possible, however, for forms of behaviour which can occur equally well in each of a range of situations. These may be amount of anxiety, talk, conformity or gaze, for example (Endler and Magnusson 1976). But they could not be level of bidding (i.e., at auction sale), speed of running, or amount of alcohol drunk, since these forms of behaviour only occur in particular situations. It follows that the P × S approach is limited to universally applicable categories of behaviour, and cannot incorporate forms of behaviour unique to situations or groups of situations.

Early research on behaviour in groups led to sets of categories such as those of Bales (1950) which were believed to be applicable to all kinds of group behaviour. In fact, later research on different social settings has produced quite different sets of categories for behaviour in the classroom (e.g., Flanders 1960), doctor-patient interaction (Byrne and Long 1976), children at play (Blurton-Jones 1972), and so on. The categories of behaviour which appear to be useful for studying behaviour in different situations are very different.

The hypothesis I want to develop is that each basic kind of social situation has a characteristic repertoire of elements. To some extent these elements follow from, and could be deduced from, the goals of the situation; the elements are the moves which are needed to attain the goals. Thus problem-solving requires moves like 'makes suggestion', 'asks question', 'disagrees', and so on. To some extent the repertoire is the product of cultural development, in the course of which different ways of reaching the goals are worked out. This is reflected also in the emergence of different rule systems. Thus buying and selling can be done by auction sale, with its special rules, and a rather limited number of moves by the buyers, who can only bid or not bid.

The meaning of an element of behaviour is partly given by the situational setting. For example, if A glances at B, this may be seen as (a) a threat, leading to a fight, among rival groups of football hooligans, (b) a threat, leading to flight, if the experimenter stares at motorists at a stop-light, or other readers in libraries, (c) a request for help, if the experimenter has collapsed on the underground, (d) the beginning of courtship (Argyle and Cook 1976). In a fundamental sense the meaning of a social act depends on the situation, rather than on the subjective intentions of the actor. If a person raises a cup of coffee to his lips, this is an act of coffee drinking, regardless of what he may be thinking about (Rubenstein 1977).

A further part of the hypothesis is that the semiotic structure of the repertoire is characteristic of the situation. What I mean by semiotic structure is the way certain acts are perceived and responded to as equivalent or similar, while others, perhaps equally similar in physical terms, are sharply contrasted. The hypothesis is obviously true in the case of games, where small differences in the way a ball is hit or thrown, or the point at which it lands, make a great difference.

In order to study repertoires some decision must be reached about the size of units to be used. Some investigators have taken the complete utterance and accompanying or equivalent non-verbal elements as the unit. However most investigators have chosen to take speech acts within utterances, for example, information followed by a question (Bales 1950). Some have taken the phonemic clause, a smaller unit (Boomer 1978). Some have taken a hierarchy of units of different sizes (e.g. Sinclair and Coulthard 1975).

There are three ways of discovering the repertoire of elements.

CONSTRUCTION BY THE INVESTIGATOR

In the so-called 'etic' approach, the investigator develops categories from his own perceptions of behaviour in the situation. The categories will therefore reflect his own interests to some extent. Thus there are numerous category schemes for interaction in the classroom; some include 'asks higher-order question', some do not, and so on (Simon and Boyer 1974). The categories are also limited to what observers are able to record reliably, which usually keeps the number of categories small. However, Byrne and Long (1976) obtained 59 categories of doctor behaviour – they didn't have any for the patient.

EXTRACTION BY SEQUENCE ANALYSIS

If a sequence analysis is made, using fairly small units of behaviour, it is possible to arrive at larger units in two ways. If element A has exactly the same antecedents and consequents as

B, then A and B can be grouped together as equivalent; otherwise they must be distinguished. For example, Kendon (1975) found that for a couple kissing on a park bench, the girl had two main kinds of smile in terms of their consequences: one led to her being kissed, the other led to withdrawal. Van Hooff (1973) produced a grouping of equivalent elements of chimpanzee social behaviour based on similarities of consequents and antecedents.

PERCEPTION BY PARTICIPANTS

In the so-called 'emic' approach, the perceptions and categorisations of participants are the criterion. There may be some variation between them, but unless there is a considerable degree of sharing of concepts communication would be impossible. This method has been little used in the development of category schemes, but an example is given below.

We showed above that repertoires to some extent follow from goal structure, together with the cultural development of rule systems. Repertoires can also be manipulated independently. Shapiro (1976) carried out an experiment in which the experimental variable was a change of repertoire. He found that if questions were not permitted, special difficulties for interactors were created, in particular in handing over the floor to another speaker.

AN INVESTIGATION OF THE REPERTOIRE OF FOUR SITUATIONS

Graham, Argyle, Clarke and Maxwell (in press) studied the repertoire, as perceived by participants, in the following situations: an evening at home, visiting the doctor, a sporting occasion with someone of the same sex, and a first date. Interviews were held with a sample of members of the Oxford Psychology Department subject panel, who were female, married and under the age of 35. Elements of three kinds were elicited: activities, types of utterance, and feelings. A total of

194 elements was obtained for the four situations. In a second stage, a further sample of ten subjects from the same subculture were asked to check the items which they considered normal and typical for each situation. There was no obvious cut-off point, and we accepted all items which 40 per cent of the sample agreed to, giving 91, 65, 76 and 91 respectively, for the four situations. The greatest differences between situations were for activities, e.g., at the doctor's; a substantial proportion of the conversation and feeling elements were common to all four situations, though there were also items unique to situations, e.g., 'ask if disease is serious', and 'hope treatment will work'.

A third stage of the study produced larger groupings of these items in terms of possible substitution. This followed a grammatical model, in which classes of words can be discovered by finding possible substitutes in sentences, e.g., in 'the boy ate a bun', *boy* can be replaced by *girl* or *dog*, but not by *bun*, *ate*, or *slowly*. A third sample of ten subjects were asked individually to group the elements for each situation in terms of possible substitution. The results were analysed by hierarchical cluster analysis, and dendrograms obtained. A cut-off point of 65 per cent agreement was selected; this reduced the numbers of items or clusters to 49, 53, 46 and 48. An example of a cluster was 'sit and watch other people'/'read magazines'. Perhaps the main result is that items do not fall into equivalence classes nearly as readily as words do, and to this extent the linguistic model is inapplicable.

A STUDY OF THE SEMIOTIC STRUCTURE OF ELEMENTS IN TWO SITUATIONS

Duncan (1969) contrasted experimental and structural approaches to social psychology. The following study combined both methods. Argyle, Graham and Kreckel (unpublished) studied the ways in which elements of behaviour were grouped and contrasted in two situations. The situations were a young man and a young woman, on a date, and at work in an office. Twenty-six elements of behaviour were used, which could occur equally in either situation. Twenty subjects rated each element on ten rating scales, regarding each element as if it had been directed to them by the person of the other sex. The data were analysed by hierarchical cluster analysis. As predicted, there was a very clear separation of task and personal issues in the work situation, but not in the date. For example, questions about work and about private life fell into very distant clusters for work, but were seen as very similar for the date. While the main division for the work situation was between task and personal/social, in the date the main clusters were of positive and negative behaviour.

4   Rules

Continuing our analogy between social situations and games, I want to propose that all social situations are rule-governed. There could not be a game between a team following the rules of, say hockey, and a team following the rules of rugby football, or between someone playing chess and someone playing tennis. Some of the rules can be described in terms of repertoire, they are rules about which moves are allowed and which are not. Closely related are 'constitutive rules' which define what counts as a 'goal', a 'no-ball', etc. Rules are primarily regulations about how the game is to be played, which must be agreed to and followed by all players (Collett 1977). If a rule is broken, the game is usually stopped, and further rules prescribe what sanctions shall be imposed – a free kick, etc. Even the most fiercely competitive and aggressive games can only take place if both sides abide by the rules, of boxing or wrestling, for example. Rules are developed gradually, as cultural products, as ways of handling certain situations; they can be changed, but changes are slow. The rules have to be learnt, by children, as part of their socialization, by new members of organisations, and by people from other cultures.

How are the rules of social situations discovered?

OBSERVATION OF BEHAVIOUR

In principle the rules of most games could probably be discovered by observation, in particular observing when sanctions
are imposed and when play is stopped. In the case of complex
games, like cricket, this would be very difficult because of the
use of a number of concepts like 'declare', 'not out', etc.,
which would be difficult to observe. Such concepts are discussed in a later section. In social situations rule-breaking may
lead to visible disruption of behaviour – as when someone tries
to make a speech during a church service or a chamber concert.
Or there might be signs of disapproval, verbal or non-verbal.
Very often, however, there is little disruption and no sanctions
are used, for example if someone made a rude noise on a polite
occasion, so observation is not the easiest way in which to
discover rules.

REPORTS OF PARTICIPANTS

They may not be able to state the rules very clearly, but they
have little difficulty in judging whether they have been
broken. This is similar to the rules of grammar – few can state
them, but most people can follow them correctly, and can tell
when a mistake has been made. A study using this method is
described below, using reports of disapproval and disruption.

STUDY OF REACTIONS TO RULE-BREAKING

The experimental breaking of rules was first used by Garfinkel
(1963), in an experiment on noughts and crosses, where the
experimenter placed his mark on one of the lines. We have
used this method in a more controlled experimental way to
study the rules of interruption – an example of a sequence rule;
subjects were asked to judge experimentally varied instances
of interruption. It was found that the latter is most acceptable

at the end of a sentence rather than at the end of a phrase, though this was better than the middle of a phrase, and that it was irrelevant how long the person interrupted had been speaking (Argyle 1975). In another experiment I asked subjects to rate instances of rule-breaking on a number of scales, the main factor found was degree of disruptiveness. At one pole were rules *intrinsic* to situations, where breaking them brought things to a complete stop – e.g., a candidate at interview insists on asking all the questions. Such intrinsic rules are quite different from norms or conventions, like which clothes should be worn.

THE DISCOVERY OF GENERATIVE RULES

The rules of grammar are known as 'generative rules', since they are capable (if they are correct) of generating all legitimate sentences in the language. Such rules are discovered by rather different methods – postulation of rule systems, generating sentences from them, and making progressive corrections to the rules. This is more like testing a high-level scientific hypothesis; the deductions from such generative rules include a lot of 'surface' rules of the kind we have been discussing.

Our procedure has been to take formal situations, in this case games, as models for less formal situations, as recommended by Harré and Secord (1972). But are less formal situations governed by rules at all? Clearly some situations are more rule-bound than others. Price and Bouffard (1974) asked subjects to rate the appropriateness of 15 kinds of behaviour in 15 situations. It was found that the situations varied greatly in 'constraint', i.e., the number of things not permitted: at one extreme were church services and job interviews, at the other were being in one's own room, or in a park. As the study reported below shows however, even the most informal situations are governed by some rules.

It may be argued that the rules of situations are not fixed, but changeable; Piaget (1932) showed that even children are capable of altering the rules of games. In the case of most games however the rules have developed very slowly in the course of history, as in the emergence of rugger from soccer, and tennis from real tennis. The same is true of formal social situations, like committees, lectures, interviews, and seeing the doctor. Less formal situations, with fewer intrinsic rules, are probably more subject to local variations and the emergence of local conventions, for example, about family meals, and coffee at work. In both formal and informal situations there can be gradual changes, but these changes take place slowly, in the case of formal situations very slowly.

It must be emphasized that there is play within the rules. Just as the play of football depends on individual and joint skills and strategies, within the framework of the rules, the same is true of behaviour in social situations.

Rules are developed so that the goals of situations can be attained. Some of these are common to many different situations, such as:

1. Maintaining communication – rules about turn-taking, and use of common language.
2. Preventing withdrawal – rules about equity, division of rewards (see below).
3. Preventing aggression – rules about restraint of violence by rules of ritual aggression, e.g., among football hooligans (Marsh, Rosser and Harré 1978).
4. Coordinating behaviour – driving on the same side of the road, having morning coffee at the same time (Bach 1975).
5. Achieving cooperation – keeping quiet at concerts (Bach 1975).

Turning to the goal structure of specific situations, it is evident that more than one set of rules will do the job. For example, buying and selling can be done by barter, bargaining, auction sale, raffle, or in fixed-price shops; the latter can be further divided into supermarkets and personal selling methods. The goal of taking open-air exercise with a ball in a group of people can be met in a larger number of ways. Here the rules represent not so much a limited set of logical alternatives as in the case of selling, but more a set of elaborate cultural constructions; the same could be said of some social situations like dinner parties, weddings and religious ceremonies.

An experimental demonstration of goal structure leading to rule development is Thibaut and Faucheux's experiment (1965): when two players were given unequal power in a game-playing experiment, the *more* powerful initiated the establishment of rules for some degree of equity, to ensure that the other player didn't withdraw from the situation. Mann (1969) carried out a field study showing the emergence of rules as a function of goals. The queues for Australian football games last for over 24 hours; rules have developed about how much time out is allowed (2–3 hours at a time), staking claims by property (wooden boxes), and turn-taking in groups. Queue jumpers are rarely attacked, but simply booed. They are kept out by the closeness of the queue. This is an example of the emergence and negotiation of local rules modifying more general cultural rules or deciding how they should be applied.

A STUDY OF THE RULES IN DIFFERENT SITUATIONS

Two studies were carried out by Argyle, Graham, Campbell and White (unpublished). In each, a list of possible rules was obtained by pilot interviews, 124 rules in one case, 20 in the other. Samples of subjects were asked to rate the applicability of each rule to each of 25 and 8 situations, respectively. It was found that there was a considerable degree of consensus about the rules for each situation, and that some rules were fairly specific, others very general. The most general rules were 'be polite', 'be friendly', 'don't embarrass other people', and 'don't make other people feel small'.

5 *Sequences*

Just as situations have characteristic repertoires of elements, so also do they have characteristic sequences of these elements.

The sequence of acts form the route to the goals of the interactions. In the case of games the sequence usually takes the form of alternate moves, each responsive to the last, in an attempt to defeat the other player. An auction sale has a similar structure of alternating, competitive moves. So do sessions of boasting, or story-telling. Most social situations, however, are more cooperative and less competitive. In selling, for example, there are such cooperative sequences, between customer C and sales person S, as:

C: asks to see goods
S: produces, demonstrates goods

C: asks for price, or other information
S: gives information

C: asks to buy, pays
S: wraps up and hands over goods

Sometimes longer sequences are needed to carry out the inter-personal task. For example, a doctor-patient consultation, involving doctor D and patient P, would contain the following stages:

D: greets patient
   asks what problem is
P: describes symptoms
D: asks follow-up questions
D: examines patient
D: makes diagnosis, explains to P
P: asks questions to clarify
D: suggests treatment

It would be impossible for these phases to be carried out in a different order.

We can partly analyse social behaviour into two-step sequences. Some of these are universal to all situations: questions lead to answers, and instructions or requests lead to action (or refusal). Some two-step sequences are based on special situational rules, like bidding at auction sales. Others are not so much rules as natural psychological tendencies, such as response-matching, the effects of reinforcement, and the effects of friendly and hostile behaviour.

Three-step sequences are more complex:

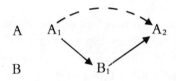

In addition to the two-step linkages A_1B_1 and B_1A_2, there is also a connection A_1A_2.

The $A_1 - A_2$ link reflects the persistence of A's planned social behaviour, for example he asks permission to smoke and then does so.

The same occurs in four-step sequences, when A_2 is a response to feedback, and is a piece of corrective action. Examples of such corrective action can be seen in the social survey interview involving an interviewer I and a respondent R (Brenner 1980).

I_1:   asks question
R_1:   gives inadequate answer, or does not understand
       question
I_2:   clarifies and repeats question
R_2:   gives adequate answer

---

or

I_1:   asks question
R_1:   refuses to answer
I_2:   explains purpose and importance of survey; repeats
        question
R_2:   gives adequate answer

In each case, I_2 is a modified version of I_1, as a result of R's move R_1, with the intention of eliciting a proper answer (R_2). There is continuity between I_1 and I_2, related to I's goals, based on R's feedback (R_1).

It is useful to distinguish cases where one person has most of the initiative, like interviewing and teaching, and cases of real negotiation or discussion where both can initiate equally well (Jones and Gerard 1967). The simple three-step and four-step models fit the first case quite well, but the second is more complicated. If there is persistent goal-seeking by both interactors, there may be interlocking, back-to-back three-step sequences, as in the following example, from a selection interview:

I_1 How well did you do at physics at school?
R_1 Not very well, I was better at chemistry.
I_2 What were your A level results?
R_2 I got a C in physics, but an A in chemistry.
I_3 That's very good.

There are two four-step sequences here: $I_1 R_1 I_2 R_2$ and $R_1 I_2 R_2 I_3$. There is persistence and continuity between R_1 and R_2, as well as I_1 and I_2. Although I has the initiative, R can also pursue his goals.

Larger sequences of interaction can be generated by use of repeated cycles, closely reflecting the nature of the situation. For example teaching uses cycles like:

Teacher: lectures, explains with examples
           asks question
Pupil: replies

An encounter between two people getting to know one another might repeat the following cycle:

A: asks question
B: replies; asks A the same question

   Interaction sequences can be divided into episodes or phrases. There may be shifts of topic, or other aspects of interaction. Committee meetings, meals and formal occasions have clearer episodes than less formal ones. Episodes of different sizes can be located by asking observers to indicate the break-points while watching video-tapes. Episodes may consist of repeated cycles, as in classroom interaction, or run through once, as in greetings. An episode involves temporary agreement to collaborate in a familar sequence, and is started by episode-negotiating signals, which may be verbal or non-verbal. We gave an example above, of the main episodes in doctor-patient consultation; here the order of the episodes follows from the nature of the task. In a selection interview, the main episodes are: welcome – interviewer asks questions – candidate is invited to ask questions – ending. Here, the order of the second and third episodes is a matter of convention, and could be reversed.

   The basic method for analysing sequences is to study transition probabilities, i.e., the possibility that one act will lead to another, representing a so-called Markov chain:

Next Act

		A	B	C
	A	5	90	5
Last Act	B	10	10	80
	C	35	35	30

Here it can be seen that A leads to B, and B to C. Larger chains can be discovered by 'chain analysis'. If AB is the most common sequence, AB is called D, and the analysis repeated, with D as an element, and this is repeated indefinitely (Dawkins 1976).

A STUDY OF SEQUENCES IN FOUR SITUATIONS

In the study of four situations (going to the doctor, etc.) described above, a study was made of the ordering of the groups of elements judged to be substitutable, together with remaining ungrouped elements. A sample of ten subjects were given cards with the individual or clustered elements written on them, and asked to arrange them in a typical sequence for each situation. The information was entered into a transitional probability matrix, and analysed by chain analysis. Each of our four situations yielded a number of chains; the doctor situation produced the most, the evening at home the least. An example is:

1. make appointment
2. drive to destination
3. park the car
4. arrive
5. see receptionist.

6   *Roles*

Most situations contain a number of different roles, i.e., there are positions for which there are different pattern of behaviour and different rules. The game analogy shows that in some games, like cricket, there are a number of different roles, but it does not show how these roles have come about. Roles are usually discussed in relation to social organizations, which have roles like doctor, nurse, patient etc. Here we are concerned with roles in social situations, though these may be part of organizational roles. We can define roles in terms of the model behaviour of, e.g., doctors on ward rounds, or in terms of the expectations, and demands of others, i.e., the rules. I shall adopt the first definition here.

I suggest that situational roles come about for three main reasons.

DIFFERENT GOALS

When two people are drawn to a situation to pursue different goals, their roles will be different. Usually these goals will be, at least partly, complementary and cooperative, and the joint behaviour satisfies different goals. Examples are buying and selling, teaching and learning, being a doctor and a patient.

DIVISION OF LABOUR

When there is a joint task to be done, there is often division of labour. In a restaurant, waitresses, cooks, barman and the person at the till divide up the work. Different industrial workers and their equipment are linked in 'socio-technical systems'. As organizations become larger, the more complex is the division of labour, and the more complex the possible situational role-structure.

SOCIAL CONTROL AND LEADERSHIP

One individual may have the power to reward or punish others in the situation. Teachers and interviewers, for example, have such power. 'Equal-unequal' was one of Wish's dimensions of situations. How do such differences of power come about? A group of four can function quite well without a leader; larger groups progressively need an informal leader, a formal leader, and then two or more levels of leadership. There is a rather crucial point at which the position of leader (or chairman) is established, and someone is formally appointed to this position. Organizations usually have a hierarchical structure, and positions differ in the power they command, the relations with other positions, with interlocking complementary roles, and in the style of leadership that is given and received. The extent of this hierarchical structure, such as the number of levels, is a product of sheer size, and also of the nature of the technology – under mass production, for example, there is a larger span of control and a 'flatter' structure (Blauner 1964).

INFORMAL ROLES

These are rather different; owing to the existence of different personalities in a situation, different people may react to it in different ways. However, the nature of the situation creates a limited and characteristic set of opportunities of this kind. In many groups there is a 'socio-emotional' leader – who looks after the social as opposed to the task aspects of the situation. In juries and some work groups there is often a 'leader of the opposition'. (Argyle 1969). Mann et al. (1967) found some interesting roles which often appeared in the Harvard variety of T-group – including 'distressed females' and 'sexual scapegoat' – a male who had doubts about his masculinity and invited the group to study him.

I said above that situational roles may reflect organizational roles. They may also come into conflict. Whyte (1948) found that there was often trouble in restaurants between waitresses and cooks, since the waitresses had to give orders to cooks – who are of higher status than waitresses. Situations are also affected by society-wide roles of age, sex and social class. This too can create conflicts with situational roles, for example, when a teacher is younger than his pupils.

The role structure of a situation may be discovered in several ways.

1 *Books of rules.* For formal situations, like committees, and for games, the book of rules also describes the roles.

2 *Observation.* This is the anthropological method, and can be used for example to describe the different roles in a ceremony.

3 *Interviews.* This will yield information about the less visible aspects of roles, and information about expectations, i.e., the rules governing positions.

4 *Study of the socially mobile.* Anyone who has changed jobs, sex, class, or nationality can produce a wealth of information about differences of roles.

7 Concepts

In order to deal with complex stimuli or problems or to perform skills, it is necessary to possess the relevant concepts. In order to play cricket it is necessary to be familiar with such concepts as 'out', 'declare', 'no-ball', 'l.b.w.', and so on. In addition, the higher levels of skill may depend on the acquisition of additional concepts. In chess, for example, it soon becomes necessary to know about 'check by discovery', 'fork', and so on. These new concepts may refer to more complex aspects of the state of the game, or to larger units of performance. In most skills, the more skilled performer is able to run off larger strings of performance automatically, and these will be conceptualized. In Scottish Country Dancing it is essential to master sequences like 'reels of three', 'highland schottische' and 'grand chain'. The more advanced performer knows also about 'rondel', 'half Mairi's wedding' and 'General Stuart setting step'.

In order to deal with people, individuals use personal constructs (Kelly 1955). Individuals vary in the complexity of their constructs, using a larger or smaller number of independent dimensions. They use salient dimensions reflecting their main preoccupation – with race, class, intelligence, sexual attractiveness, and so on. The links between their constructs constitute 'implicit personality theories', about how constructs are related to one another, e.g., race and intelligence.

We should expect that people would be more socially competent in situations (a) if they are cognitively complex, i.e., use a number of independent construct dimensions, and (b) if their constructs are relevant to the situations in question. There is a certain amount of indirect evidence that more complex persons are more socially skilled: older children are more complex (and more skilled); more complex people are more accurate at person perception, mainly because they are less prone to halo effect, and can recognise that someone is, for example, both intelligent and dishonest. Jaspars (unpublished) found that more complex teachers could deal better with classroom problems like cheating and lateness if spontaneous reactions were studied. If they were given time to reflect the non-complex teachers could solve these problems too.

Within different social groups particular dimensions become important, because they are the distinguishing features of the group, or the dimensions along which the group believes itself to be superior to other groups (Tajfel 1970). Schizophrenics, who are socially very inadequate, are found to have a specific cognitive deficit – lack of stable constructs for categorising other people (Bannister and Salmon 1966).

Concepts are needed to deal with social interaction. Study of the giving and reciprocation of gifts in Japan shows that three concepts are involved, corresponding to three principles governing gift-giving. These are:

1 *Gimu* – a life long indebtedness and loyalty to parents and ancestors, which is never paid off.
2 *Giri* – the exact repayment of debts and obligations, which has a definite time limit.
3 *Ninjo* – natural desires and feelings (Morsbach 1977).

This example shows that concepts may have a complex intellectual background, and extensive links with other ideas. Committee meetings require the mastery of a number of concepts like 'straw vote', 'casting vote', 'nem con', 'unanimous', 'abstain', and so on. The concepts for everyday social interaction have not so far been much studied, though it is known that there are interesting cultural differences.

TWO STUDIES OF THE CONCEPTS USED IN DIFFERENT SITUATIONS

Forgas, Argyle and Ginsburg (unpublished) studied a group of 14 research psychologists. Each person completed a set of 36 ratings scales to describe the behaviour of each person, including the rater, in four situations – morning coffee, going to the pub, seminars, and parties at the home of the senior member of the group. The ratings were analysed by multi-dimensional scaling, to find the underlying dimensions being used. In the social situations there were two dimensions – extraversion and evaluation (as an enjoyable companion). In the seminar situation, however, there were three quite different dimensions – dominance, supportiveness and creativity.

Argyle, Forgas, Ginsburg and Campbell (unpublished) carried out a study with a group of housewives and a group of students, who were asked to rate the relevance of 36 bipolar constructs in 4 situations and for 7 target groups. Factor analyses showed that the constructs produced rather different factors in each situation. However there was a friendly-extraversion factor in each situation, which was rated as high relevant. Work-related constructs, like industrious, competent and dependable, were much less relevant in work situations than in social ones. Different constructs were found relevant for different target groups. For example, the relevant scales for children were judged to be *well-behaved* and *noisy*, while for professional people the most relevant scales were *competence* and *high-status*. It appeared that the most relevant scales were those that reflected the nature of the interaction with different target groups.

8   *Physical Environment*

Barker and Wright (1954) defined their 'behaviour settings' as combinations of 'studying patterns of behaviour', i.e., our rules, roles and repertoire, and environmental setting. We too want to emphasize the physical setting as an important feature of situations. The environment causes behaviour, as is shown by studies of the effects of overcrowding, for example. The environment is also created for purposes of interaction, i.e., in the pursuit of goals, by architects, planners and by anyone who furnishes, decorates or merely arranges a room. However, someone who, for example, arranges the furniture in a room, does so in the expectation that this will affect social interaction in some way; therefore we can concentrate on environment as a cause of behaviour.

Several aspects of physical environment have been shown to influence behaviour:

1 *Proximity* produces greater intimacy, discomfort when past a certain distance, and progressive aversion of gaze.

2 *Crowding* produces high arousal, discomfort, aggressive behaviour in males, laughter (tension release), withdrawal from social contact, and emotional disturbance, if prolonged.

3 *Orientation.* Side-by-side creates a more cooperative and friendly relationship; facing opposite creates an atmosphere of competition and conflict, unless two people are eating a meal.

4 *Barriers* to vision or locomotion create privacy, reduce intimacy, there is less talk and reduced arousal.

5 *Furniture arrangement* produces various combinations of the factors above, together with creation of private spaces. Desks can be placed to dominate the room, chairs placed to suggest friendly chat, sofas of different designs suggest varying degrees of intimacy.

6 *Colour and decoration.* Colours affect emotional state – red and yellow for warmth and cheerfulness, dark blue and brown for gloom. The nature of the furnishings can suggest interrogation, romance, office work, or important decision-taking. People seen in a pretty room are liked more than the same people seen in an ugly room. Chairs placed by a fire suggest reading or chatting.

7 *Heat and noise.* If it is too hot or noisy, people are aroused and put in a bad mood; they will like the people they meet less, help less, and give larger electric shocks in experiments.

8 *Equipment.* In many situations special equipment is needed,

which extends the range of social behaviour possible. These might include blackboard and chalk, pointer, and overhead projector, or bottles of drink and glasses, or various toys and games. A number of cooperative toys are now available, which like see-saws and table tennis take two to play with, thus reducing one major form of conflict between pairs of children (Wrightsman 1977; Moos 1976; Canter 1975).

9   Skills and Difficulties

Every social situation presents certain difficulties, and these need certain social skills in order to deal with them. The same is true of games. Polo, high diving, pole-vaulting, each present obvious difficulties, and require special skills. They also create some degree of anxiety, which must be controlled. There are a number of general skills which are each used in several games – riding horses, swimming, hitting balls, etc. The same is probably true of social skills (Argyle 1969).

Social competence can be assessed by measures of effectiveness (e.g., goods sold by a salesperson), observation of role-playing, ratings in real-life situations, tests of social competence, and various kinds of self-rating. Self-reports show primarily how comfortable versus how anxious a person feels in a situation, which is not quite the same as his effectiveness (Argyle, in press).

There have been a number of studies of the situations which people find difficult or uncomfortable. The factors or clusters which are obtained vary with the range of situations studied, and the statistical procedures used. The areas of difficulty are as follows:

1. assertiveness situations: e.g., having to stand up for your rights.
2. performing in public.
3. conflict, dealing with hostile people.
4. intimate situations, especially with the opposite sex.
5. meeting strangers.
6. dealing with people in authority.

7. fear of disapproval, criticism, making mistakes, looking foolish; this does not correspond to particular situations in our sense (e.g., Stratton and Moore 1977; Richardson and Tasto 1976).)

Our previous analysis can help us to account for these difficulties, and also suggest the skills which would solve the problem. We suggested a possible goal-structure for assertiveness, with various intra- and inter-personal conflicts. The solution might be to increase the interpersonal rewards provided, or to persuade the other that the suggested action is either in his interest or in line with principles which he accepts. Difficulties with strangers (i.e., making friends) and with the opposite sex are very common among candidates for social skills training. The trouble is that they have failed to learn certain basic social skills, such as rewardingness, non-verbal communication (e.g., for liking), and sustaining conversation (Trower, Bryant and Argyle 1978).

There are theoretical grounds for expecting other forms of social difficulty, which did not appear in the studies cited above, perhaps because they were not included in the lists of situations studied:

1. *Unfamiliar situations*, for example, where the rules, goals or concepts are unknown. Visiting a foreign country, joining a new organization, first going to an encounter group or a psychoanalyst are examples.

2. *Complex situations*, where a number of different people have to be attended to at once, several different goals pursued, and so on.

10 *Applications*

1.0 SOCIAL SKILLS TRAINING

Social skills training (SST) by means of role-playing and allied methods is widely used for socially inadequate neurotic patients, for training teachers, salesmen, interviewers, and other professional social skills performers, as well as for members of the public who want to improve their skills. I believe that these forms of training can be made more effective by making use of our understanding of social interaction processes, including the analysis of situations.

A considerable number of the neurotic patients to whom we have given SST have reported difficulty with quite specific situations – often more specific than the factors listed earlier. In some of these cases we discovered that the patient had failed to understand correctly certain features of the situation in question. People who were afraid to go to parties didn't know what parties were for (goal structure), or what you were supposed to do at them (repertoire and rules). Candidates at interviews commonly mistake the goals and think interviews are for vocational guidance, or get the rules wrong, and think they are going to ask the questions. For such people we have given instructions about the features of the situations in question. Sometimes this has been done didactically, drawing partly on published findings, and partly on the experience of the trainers. Another approach has been to work with a group of individuals, all of whom have difficulties with, for example, dating. The experience of those present in the group is used – and it is necessary to have some people who are confident that they can handle the situation; in the course of an hour it is possible to arrive at an agreed list of the main goals, rules and repertoire, the main difficulties and how they can be tackled.

It may in addition be necessary to give behavioural SST, so that trainees can master some of the skills needed in the situation. Where the optimal skills are not known from the literature, analysis of the features of a situation can sometimes suggest ways of dealing with the problems involved, as we showed above in the case of assertiveness.

2.0 DEBUGGING PROBLEM SITUATIONS

Behaviour is more affected by situations and by P $\times$ S interaction than it is by personality factors alone, yet emotionally disturbed and delinquent behaviour is dealt with almost entirely by trying to change persons. We now know how situations might be changed instead, and here are some examples.

2.1 *Change the elements.* Brainstorming groups, for stimulating creativity, were produced by ruling out part of the usual repertoire of group discussion – criticism and disagreement. T-groups are groups in which the only topic of conversation permitted is what is happening in the group; this means that the normal repertoire is extended to allow direct personal comments. Encounter groups too involve an extension of the usual repertoire – to include bodily contact between strangers.

2.2 *Change of roles (1).* We mentioned above Whyte's study of restaurants. He solved the difficulty of waitresses giving orders to the higher status cooks by the introduction of a 'spindle': waitresses wrote their orders and pinned them to the spindle; the cooks looked over the orders, and cooked them in whatever order was convenient.

2.3 *Changes of roles (2).* Uneducated psychiatric patients think that all that is required of them is to take a pill and wait to get better. This is not the view of psychiatrists. To resolve this problem some hospitals now provide pre-therapy training for the role of psychiatric patient.

2.4 *Changing the environment.* Sommer (1969) improved things in an old people's home by moving the furniture. Previously the chairs were in rows round the walls of large day-rooms, and the inmates sat in a stupor staring into space. Sommer grouped the chairs round coffee tables, which greatly increased the level of social interaction.

2.5 *Changing communication structures.* Several of the studies by the Tavistock Institute for Human Relations involved re-designing socio-technical, or work-flow systems. For example, Longwall coalmining was re-organized by including on each shift men who did the three main jobs of cutting, filling and stonework, whereas before they were on different shifts and were often uncooperative (Trist et al. 1963).

These are one or two examples of changing situations. When a situation has been analysed in terms of the features introduced in this chapter, many possible ways of modifying it can be suggested.

3.0 PERSONALITY ASSESSMENT

The implications of interactionism, and of our ideas about situations, for personality assessment, have not yet been worked out. There is space here only for an initial exploration of the problem.

3.1 *Selection*. The first point to emphasize is that performance at the interview itself should usually be disregarded, since the interview is so different from the situations to be faced on the job. Secondly, a very clear idea is needed about the range of situations of which the job will consist. Evidence should then be sought by the performance of candidates in situations as similar as possible to these job situations. The job description should provide detailed information about the range of tasks to be done, and provide evidence about the skills and the motivations which are relevant to them. If the tasks are new to the candidates (e.g., for astronauts), measures of the relevant skills can be obtained by special tests: motivation can be assessed by study of choice of leisure activities, or by investigation of preferred activities as by the Strong and Kuder inventories (see Argyle 1972).

3.2 *Vocational guidance*. Here, the emphasis is on finding a job that will satisfy the client, and one which will make use of his abilities. More attention should be paid here to his choice of leisure activities. In considering a wide range of possible occupations, as is usually done, greater attention should be paid to the range of situations and demands within each. This means that more research is needed into jobs from this point of view. Some may turn out to consist of rather diverse situations and the corresponding skills.

3.3 *Appraisal.* In the British Civil Service and in many large firms, there is an annual attempt to appraise the effectiveness of staff, and to discuss it with them at an appraisal interview. If someone is not doing well this is assumed to be his fault, to be dealt with by encouragement, reduced salary, demotion, or the sack. From an interactionist point of view this may be a mistake: perhaps the job is simply too difficult, and should be redesigned; perhaps the person does not match this job and should be moved to a different one. The approach developed in this chapter suggests some principles for re-design of jobs, and also principles for moving people to different ones. Something is known about the most effective skills in this kind of interview (Argyle 1978), but these should be used with full awareness of how persons and situations interact.

4.0 HELPING WITH INTER-GROUP CONFLICT

Very often conflict between groups is based on real conflicts of interests. Often however this is a minor factor, and the real trouble is differences in style of behaviour. There may be situations in one culture which are totally new, and do not exist in the other. Newcomers to Oxford need to learn what to do at dessert, collections, vivas, bump suppers, meetings of Congregation, and other situations. More commonly the same basic situation takes a somewhat different form in two cultures. Here are some examples of cultural differences in the features of behaviour and situations which have been described in this chapter.

4.1 *Goal structure.* In Indonesia, humility is valued more than assertiveness, in India wealth and power are not valued, in much of the Far East the preservation of 'face' is a very important goal (Trandis et al. 1972).

4.2 *Repertoire.* Non-verbal signals are used differently in different cultures – touch may be added to the repertoire (Arabs), negative facial expressions not used (Japan), proximity used differently, for example. There may be a large number of personal pronouns. In Botswana there is no word for thank-you; instead both hands are stretched out to receive (McCallin personal communication).

4.3 *Rules.* There are elaborate rules for gifts in Japan, alcohol is forbidden in Moslem countries, bribes are normal in Africa and India, selling may be done by bargaining. In Gonja only social superiors ask questions, since this implies power.

4.4 *Concepts.* We mentioned the concepts governing Japanese gift-giving. Australian aboriginals have smoky fires in their houses because of the spiritual value of fires, and it is difficult to visit them since you are not supposed to invade their territory, and should be invited to cross the boundary of it. There may be special words for styles of behaviour, such as the Mexican 'machismo', Spanish 'honour' and Yiddish 'chutzpuh'.

4.5 *Roles.* The role of women is totally different in Arab culture, as is the role of the aged in cultures who revere them. Styles of leadership are often more authoritarian, while caste and class barriers may work very differently.

4.6 *Environment.* In Japan, and other parts of the world, furniture is totally different; different climates result in quite different kinds of clothes.

4.7 *Skills and difficulties.* Different rule systems and repertoires create special difficulties, and require special skills. For example if selling is done by bargaining the necessary skills must be learnt; similarly there are skills for bribery, greetings, the approved forms of courtship, and so on.

Training to perform competently in another culture can be done by learning the new rules, as in the Culture Assimilator (Fiedler et al. 1971), or by coaching in the other culture's style of non-verbal communication (Collet 1971). Whatever method of training is used, it is necessary to find out first which are the most crucial areas of difference, that can give rise to difficulties. These may be far from obvious. Aboriginal ideas about fires, territory and other matters, the Botswana thank-you, Japanese gift-giving, Japanese facial expressions, Arab bodily contact, African bribery, have led to a great deal of trouble for those who did not understand these features of local behaviour.

References

M. Argyle, 1969, *Social Interaction*, London: Methuen

M. Argyle, 1972, *The Social Psychology of Work*, London: Allen Lane

M. Argyle, 1976, 'Personality and Social Behaviour,' in: R. Harré (Ed.), *Personality*, Oxford: Blackwell

M. Argyle, 1978, *The Psychology of Interpersonal Behaviour, 3rd Edition*, Harmondsworth: Penguin Books

M. Argyle, in press, 'Interaction Skills and Social Competence,' in: M. P. Feldmann and J. Orford (Eds.), *The Social Psychology of Psychological Problems*, London: Wiley

M. Argyle and B. Beit-Hallahmi, 1974, *The Social Psychology of Religion*, London: Routledge & Kegan Paul

M. Argyle and M. Cook, 1976, *Gaze and Mutual Gaze*, London: Cambridge University Press

M. Argyle and J. Dean, 1965, 'Eye-Contact, Distance and Affiliation,' *Sociometry*, Vol. 28, pp. 289–304

M. Argyle, A. Furnham and J. A. Graham, in press, *Social Situations*, Cambridge: Cambridge University Press

E. M. Avedon, 1971, 'The Structural Elements of Games,' in: E. M. Avedon and B. Sutton-Smith (Eds.), *The Study of Games*, New York: Wiley

K. Bach, 1975, 'Analytical Social Philosophy, Basic Concepts,' *Journal for the Theory of Social Behaviour*, Vol. 5, pp. 189–214

R. F. Bales, 1950, *Interaction Process Analysis*, Cambridge, Mass.: Addison-Wesley

D. Bannister and P. Salmon, 1966, 'Schizophrenic Thought Disorder: Specific or Diffuse?,' *British Journal of Medical Psychology*, Vol. 39, pp. 215–219

R. G. Barker and H. F. Wright, 1954, *Midwest and Its Children: The Psychological Ecology of an American Town*, Evanston, Ill.: Row-Peterson

R. Blauner, 1964, *Alienation and Freedom*, Chicago: University of Chicago Press

N. Blurton-Jones (Ed.), 1972, *Ethological Studies of Child Behaviour*, London: Cambridge University Press

D. S. Boomer, 1978, 'The Phonemic Clause: Speech Unit in Human Communication,' in: A. W. Siegman and S. Feldstein (Eds.), *Nonverbal Behaviour and Communication*, Hillsdale, N.J.: Erlbaum

M. Brenner, 1980, 'Skills in the Research Interview', in: M Argyle (Ed.), *Manual of Social Skills*, London: Methuen

P. S. Byrne and B. E. L. Long, 1976, *Doctors Talking to Patients*, London: HMSO

D. Canter et al., 1975, *Environmental Interaction: Psychological Approaches to Our Physical Surroundings*, Guildford: Surrey University Press

J. K. Chadwick-Jones, 1976, *Social Exchange Theory*, London: Academic Press

P. Collett, 1971, 'On Training Englishman in the Non-Verbal Behaviour of Arabs: An Experiment in Intercultural Communication,' *International Journal of Psychology*, Vol. 6, pp. 209–215

P. Collett (Ed.), 1977, *Social Rules and Social Behaviour*, Oxford: Blackwell

R. Dawkins, 1976, 'Hierarchical Organisation: A Candidate Principle for Ethology,' in: P. P. G. Bateson and R. A. Hinde (Eds.), *Growing Points in Ethology*, London: Cambridge University Press

S. Duncan, 1969, 'Non-Verbal Communication,' *Psychological Bulletin*, Vol. 72, pp. 118–137

N. S. Endler and D. Magnusson (Eds.), 1976, *Interactional Psychology and Personality*, Washington: Hemisphere

F. E. Fiedler, R. Mitchell and H. Triandis, 1971, 'The Culture Assimilator: An Approach to Cross-Cultural Training,' *Journal of Applied Psychology*, Vol. 55, pp. 95–102

N. A. Flanders, 1970, *Analyzing Teaching Behavior*, Reading, Mass.: Addison-Wesley

H. Garfinkel, 1963, 'Trust and Stable Actions,' in: O. J. Harvey (Ed.), *Motivation and Social Interaction*, New York: Ronald

J. A. Graham, M. Argyle, D. D. Clarke and S. Maxwell, in press, *The Sequential Structure of Social Episodes*, Semiotica

R. Harré and P. F. Secord, 1972, *The Explanation of Social Behaviour*, Oxford: Blackwell

E. E. Jones and H. B. Gerard, 1967, *Foundations of Social Psychology*, New York: Wiley

G. A. Kelly, 1955, *The Psychology of Personal Constructs*, New York: Norton

A. Kendon, 1975, *Some Functions of the Face in a Kissing Round*, Semiotica, Vol. 15, pp. 299–334

K. Lewin, 1935, *A Dynamic Theory of Personality*, New York: McGraw-Hill

L. Mann, 1970, 'The Social Psychology of Waiting Lines,' *American Scientist*, Vol. 58, pp. 390–398

R. D. Mann et al., 1967, *Interpersonal Styles and Group Development*, New York: Wiley

P. Marsh, E. Rosser and R. Harré, 1978, *The Rules of Disorder*, London: Routledge & Kegan Paul

S. Milgram, 1974, *Obedience to Authority*, New York: Harper and Row

R. H. Moos, 1976, *The Human Context*, New York: Wiley

H. Morsbach, 1977, 'The Psychological Importance of Ritualised Gift Exchange in Modern Japan,' *Annals of the New York Academy of Science*, Vol. 293, pp. 98–113

H. A. Murray, 1938, *Exploration in Personality*, New York: Oxford University Press

J. Piaget, 1932, *The Moral Judgement of the Child*, London: Routledge & Kegan Paul

R. H. Price and D. L. Bouffard, 1974, 'Behavioural Appropriateness and Situational Constraint as Dimensions of Social Behaviour,' *Journal of Personality and Social Psychology*, Vol. 30, pp. 579–586

F. C. Richardson and D. L. Tasto, 1976, 'Development and Factor Analysis of a Social Anxiety Inventory,' *Behaviour Therapy*, Vol. 7, pp. 453–462

D. Rubenstein, 1977, 'The Concept of Action in the Social Sciences,' *Journal for the Theory of Social Behaviour*, Vol. 7, pp. 209–236

D. Shapiro, 1976, 'Resources Required in the Construction and Reconstruction of Conversation,' mimeo

A. Simon and E. G. Boyer (Eds.), 1974, 'Mirrors for Behaviour,' 3rd Edition, *Classroom Interaction Newsletter*, Wyncote, Penn.: Communication Materials Center

J. Sinclair and R. M. Coulthard, 1975, *Towards an Analysis of Discourse: The English Used by Teachers and Pupils*, London: Oxford University Press

R. Sommer, 1969, *Personal Space*, Englewood Cliffs, N.J.: Prentice-Hall

T. T. Stratton and C. L. Moore, 1977, 'Application of the Robust Factor Concept to the Fear Survey Schedule,' *Journal of Behavior Therapy and Experimental Psychiatry*, Vol. 8, pp. 229–235

H. Tajfel, 1970, 'Experiments in Intergroup Discrimination,' *Scientific American*, Vol. 223, pp. 96–102

J. Thibaut and C. Faucheux, 1965, 'The Development of Contractual Norms in a Bargaining Situation under Two Types of Stress,' *Journal of Experimental Social Psychology*, Vol. 1, pp. 89–102

H. Triandis et al., 1972, *The Analysis of Subjective Culture*, New York: Wiley

E. L. Trist et al., 1963, *Organizational Choice,* London: Tavistock

P. Trower, B. Bryant and M. Argyle, 1978, *Social Skills and Mental Health*, London: Methuen

J. A. Van Hooff, 1973, 'A Structural Analysis of the Social Behaviour of a Semi-Captive Group of Chimpanzees,' in: M. von Cranach and I. Vine (Eds.), *Social Communication and Movement*, London: Academic Press

W. F. Whyte, 1948, *Human Relations in the Restaurant Industry*, New York: McGraw-Hill

M. Wish, 1975, 'Role and Personal Expectations about Interpersonal Communication,' US-Japan seminar, University of California, San Diego, mimeo

L. S. Wrightsman, 1977, *Social Psychology*, Monterey, Cal.: Brooks-Cole

P. G. Zimbardo, 1973, A Pirandella Prison, *New York Times Sunday Magazine*, 8 April, pp. 38–60

On 'Meanings' of Acts and What is Meant and Made Known by What is Said in a Pluralistic Social World

RAGNAR ROMMETVEIT *Oslo University*

1 *Introduction*

Mainstream sociological, psychological, sociolinguistic and psycholinguistic research is, in my opinion, pervaded by false, though very seductive, monistic assumptions about our language and the world. Much of what I have recently written on language, thought and communication (see, for example, Rommetveit 1978 and 1979) may, in fact, be conceived of as crusades against such explicitly held and/or tacitly endorsed assumptions and, hence, by those who do not share my view, as a Quixotic fight against fictitious evils. Nevertheless, in the first part of this paper, I will continue my crusade against 'literal' meanings of utterances and 'public' meanings of acts.

My main purpose, though, is to explore some important implications of a consistently pluralistic set of assumptions. How shall we assess 'meanings' of acts and determine what is meant, understood and made known by what is said if we take it for granted that people differ not only with respect to *what they know and believe about the world*, but to some extent even with respect to *what they mean by what they are saying*? What are, given such conditions, the mechanisms of negotiation and reciprocal control in the construction of human intersubjectivity? How can states of shared social reality be attained in encounters between different private worlds?

These are some of the, admittedly, very complex issues I want to pursue in this paper. What happens when monistic assumptions about natural language and our social world are replaced by a consistently pluralistic outlook is thus a subtle transformation of some basic problems of human communication. Mutual understanding can then no longer be accounted for in terms of either unequivocally shared knowledge of the world or linguistically mediated literal meaning. It becomes to a considerable extent a matter of, for example, actual and reciprocally assumed control of what is meant by what is said and of, in some sense, a self-fulfilling *faith* in a shared world. Also, the study of human communication becomes an enquiry into a hitherto largely unexplored range of possible, sustained and/or only temporarily established states of partially shared social realities.

2   On 'Public Meanings' of Acts and 'Literal Meanings' of Utterances

Within social science today we can witness a growing concern with issues that were considered taboo in respectable academic environments for quite some time. The term 'meanings' has thus entered the scene of scientific discourse again, not only within linguistics, but also within psychology and sociology. This may well be a symptom of a very healthy and warranted emancipation from the tyranny of a rather puritan and poorly understood social scientific variant of 'positivist' philosophy. It is high time that we, as Ginsburg (1979) proposes, consider *meanings of actions for the participants* worthy of scientific explication.

My sympathy with Wittgenstein (1968) in his struggle to explicate meaning, however, leads me to watch the present re-entry of the problem of meaning with considerable scepticism. My worries are of the following kind: Is the current search for meaning, in particular *when combined with postulates about 'literal' or 'public meaning'*, in part a search for some novel Archimedian point to replace abandoned information processing paradigms, illusional behaviourist axioms, or brittle reductionist notions? And, if so, will not those, who today seek safety in 'literal' or 'public meaning' and the presumed universal wisdom embedded in ordinary language, soon and necessarily become disillusioned once more and seek salvation elsewhere?

Let us now briefly examine one such case of a rather dramatic re-entry of 'meaning', namely my friend and colleague Jan Smedslund's re-definition of the data of scientific psychology as *the public meanings of a person's act*. The term 'act' is used by Smedslund in this context in a wide sense, including any segment of any activity of a person. He proposes the following ideal procedures for determining meaning (Smedslund 1969, p. 6):

1. The *total meaning* of the act X to person P in situation S at time t is determined by the set of statements which to P in S at t are implied, contradicted, or those whose likelihood of being true is changed, given that X occurs.
2. Ths *strict meaning* of X to P in S at t is determined by the set of statements which to P in S at t are implied or contradicted, given that X occurs.
3. The *direct meaning* of X to P in S at t is determined by the set of statements which to P in S at t are equivalent with the statement that X occurs.
4. The *total public meaning* of X in community Y in S at t is the part of the total meanings of X to all individual members of Y in S at t which is shared, i.e., the intersection of all the individual sets.
5. The *strict public meaning* of X in Y in S at t is the part of the strict meanings of X to all individual members of Y in S at t which is shared.
6. The *direct public meaning* of X in Y in S at t is the part of the direct meanings of X to all individual members of Y in S at t which is shared.

What is achieved by making the public meanings of a person's act the data of scientific psychology is thus a reversal of the orthodox behaviourist account of mental phenomena in terms of covert and presumed 'objective' behaviour: The invariant and basic feature of human behaviour, in the re-defined psychology, is assumed to reside in its public meaning, and the latter is to be determined by *sets of statements*.

Public meanings of a person's acts are thus, as far as they exist, necessarily objective, since, according to Smedslund's definition, they are shared by independent observers. He continues (p. 6):

It is further assumed that not only does a person recognize and understand such meanings, but that whenever he himself acts in a given community, the public meanings of his acts are, at some level, intentional. This means that whenever a person acts in a given community, he has, at some level, a communicative intent which is defined primarily by the public meaning of his act. The qualification 'at some level' refers to the fact that the communicative intent need not be conscious to the actor. He may lack the incentive or the habitual orientation toward reflection, he may be inclined to avoid reflection (defensiveness), or he may lack the necessary intellectual power. The qualification 'at some level' also refers to the existence of conscious or unconscious deceit, where the expressed meaning does not correspond with the subjective facts.

Smedslund's notion of meanings of *acts* is thus very similar to Schank's notion of *conceptual action*. Schank argues (1975, p. 42): 'The real meaning of each ACT is the set of inferences that are possibly true when that ACT is present.' And the 'psychological reality' of public meanings is further corroborated by philosophical and sociological explication of the social nature of acts. As Harré (1978, p. 49) puts it: 'Since a social act is *constituted* by its place in a humanly constructed social reality, it is what folk take it to be'. The 'strict public meaning' of some social act is hence, if we follow Smedslund and Harré, necessarily unequivocal and, in some sense, 'objective'. The postulation of a communicative intent in every act, moreover, paves the way for an application of *a general theory of acts of speech* to *human action in general*.

A basic assumption in *Searle's theory of speech acts* is his 'principle of expressibility', that is, the principle that *whatever can be meant can also be said*. Searle (1974, p. 20) thus takes it to be an analytic truth about language that '. . . for any speaker S whenever S means (intends to convey, wishes to communicate in an utterance, etc.) X then it is possible that there is some E such that E is an exact expression of, or formulation of, X'. This has the consequence that cases where the speaker does not say exactly what he means, the principle cases of which are *nonliteralness*, *vagueness*, *ambiguity* and *incompleteness*, are not at the theoretical core of linguistic communication. It is assumed accordingly that for any possible speech act there is a possible linguistic element which (given the context of the utterance) is sufficient to determine that *its literal utterance* is a performance of precisely that speech act (see Searle 1974, p. 21).

The notion of meaning, tabooed for a long time, is thus, in Smedslund's re-definition of psychology and Searle's theory of speech acts, given a welcome equal to that of the prodigal son in the Bible. *What is meant* is not only made the core question of human communication and action; it is also assumed that it is *in principle* possible, without any residuals, to explicate what is meant in terms of contextually appropriate literal expressions and/or, in some sense, publicly transparent acts.

I have elsewhere (Rommetveit 1978 and 1979) argued that Searle's theory of speech acts is a Trojan horse by which seductive monistic assumptions about a perfect human 'Interpretationsgemeinschaft' (community of interpretation) are invading sociolinguistic discourse analysis, and that they do so in the guise of postulated unequivocal literal meanings of expressions. I have shown, moreover, how the Platonic and/or implicitly normative nature of such presumedly unequivocal meanings are revealed when we try to capture them in actual human discourse. The same, I shall argue, is bound to happen to Smedslund's public meanings when we start searching for them in real human interaction. And this has to be so because human communication and interaction take place in a pluralistic, only partially shared, and only fragmentarily known social world.

Literal meaning of utterances and public meanings of acts can thus, given the boundaries of Searle's and Smedslund's theories of meaning, serve as Archimedian points in discourse analysis and scientific psychology only under certain idealized conditions. Searle's theory, for instance, is *not* assumed to be valid within a semiotic domain characterized by vagueness, ambiguity, and incompleteness. And Smedslund's assumption that a person's communicative intent is primarily determined by the public meaning of his act does *not* hold if, for example, the person lacks 'the incentive or the habitual orientation toward reflection' or 'the necessary intellectual power'. We may hence ask: Precisely *how* reflective, knowledgeable, and intellectually capable does a person need to be? And more generally: Is not Searle's, and possibly also Smedslund's, list of *exceptions and reservations* essentially an enumeration of *basic existential conditions of human interaction and discourse*?

Let us now, despite this general suspicion, engage in a search for public meanings of specific and relatively simple everyday acts in accordance with Smedslund's definition of such meanings. Let us consider first Menzel's mystery case '*What was Mr. Smith doing behind the lawn-mower?*' Mr. Smith, who lives in a house in the suburbs, is, on a certain Saturday morning, seen pushing a machine around on the grass. The machine is a lawn-mower, and Menzel (1978, p. 147) comments upon the meanings the behaviour may have as follows:

... while it is (almost unquestionably) true that Mr. Smith is mowing his lawn, there are a number of other things which he is also doing by the same behaviour:
he is beautifying his garden;
he is exercising his muscles;
he is avoiding his wife;
he is conforming to the expectations of his neighbours;
he is keeping up property values in Scarsdale;
and he is angering his new neighbour, Mr. Ifabrumliz, who prefers

to sleep late, and feels that Smith's mowing is a criticism of his, Ifabrumliz's, unkept lawn.

Menzel shows by this, and a number of other examples, that most streams of behaviour can be conceptualized as *acts* in more than one way. It may at times be possible to indicate a certain 'minimum meaning' (such as *mowing the lawn* in the above example). That meaning, however, does not necessarily have the greatest explanatory value, or, in any sense, supply the 'true' motive power. Menzel's conclusion, after several case studies of meanings of specific acts, is thus that (1978, p. 148) '. . . it is fallacious to insist on determining "the" meaning of an act, as though there necessarily were one which is somehow the most fundamental or real one'. I may add, after a considerable number of case studies of presumed 'literal' meanings of utterances (Rommetveit 1974): A search for 'the' (public) meaning of an act seems to be as futile as a search for 'the' (literal) meaning of a verbal expression. Let me now try to show in some detail why the mystery of Mr. Smith's doings that Saturday morning cannot be solved by Smedslund's ideal procedures for determining public meanings of acts.

Notice, first of all, that the total public meaning of the act has to be assessed as *the intersection* of all individual sets of statements which to all members of Mr. Smith's community are implied, contradicted, or whose likelihood of being true are changed, given that his mysterious behaviour occurs. Those few people who know Mr. Smith and his wife very well may thus be of the opinion that he is 'really' avoiding his wife. Such statements are *not* implied to the majority of community members who know him less well, however, and consequently are *not* part of the public meaning of his act. But what if those who know Mr. Smith best insist that he is *merely* avoiding his wife, or exercising his muscles? What if they provide evidence that Mr. Smith is wholeheartedly *against* snobbish gardens and the upkeeping of property values in Scarsdale, yet so eager to get away from his wife and to have some physical exercise that he, quite unaware of what others may think about him, has grabbed the lawn-mower and started mowing the lawn? And what if a considerable minority in Scarsdale holds the opinion that *lawns are more beautiful if people let the grass grow until the clover has blossomed*, whereas a majority prefer *neatly kept lawns*?

These issues indicate the kind of problems we encounter when we seriously try to assess the public meaning of an act as defined by Smedslund: We discover that the intersection of all individual meanings, *unless the community happens to be perfectly homogeneous*, shrinks to a trivial minimum (in this case: to *mowing the lawn* as distinguished from all other possible acts). This will, obviously, also be the solution of the mysteries of the public meanings of other particular acts such as, for example, *what Mr. Smith is doing at the assembly line* in the factory where he is employed. The engagements and perspectives of his fellow workers, his employer, the trade union leader in the factory and other divergently politically engaged members of the community are bound to be such that the intersection of the statements implied, contradicted, etc., *to all of them* by his act will, if we disregard the trivial minimum, be the zero set.

But let us also, in order to explicate Smedslund's assumption that the agent at some level has a communicative intent which is primarily determined by the public meaning of his act, examine *the fate of the deviant in an otherwise perfectly homogeneous community*. Let us now assume for instance, that Scarsdale is a suburb in which everybody, *except Mr. Smith*, is fond of neatly kept lawns, and that everybody, except him, also conceives of lawn-moving as a means of beautifying the garden and keeping up property values. Mr. Smith, however, is of an entirely different opinion and mows his lawn when and only when he notices that the clover blossoms have faded and/or when he feels an urgent need to exercise his muscles. What is, in such a case, *the public meaning of*, and *the communicative intent inherent in*, his act on that Saturday morning? Is his behaviour devoid of public meaning (since the intersection of what is implied to *him* and to *others* is zero), yet erroneously interpreted by neighbours and incidental passers-by as an instance of conventional beautifying of gardens and keeping up property values? Or is Mr. Smith in this case, whether his attitude towards the majority ideology is one of reflective rejection or agnostic innocence, bound to conform to that majority ideology *in his communicative intent*?

Some such questions may, as clearly indicated by Smedslund, be settled by further investigation of particular background and context features. The meanings of Mr. Smith's activity that morning to those who have observed his wife-avoiding manoeuvres and deviant style of gardening for years may thus probably, though not necessarily, overlap to a considerable extent. The 'public meaning' of his act may hence clearly transcend the trivial minimum if, for example, we *redefine the community in which the act takes place so as to include only an inner circle of friends and neighbours.*

Notice, however, that the resultant intersection of individual meanings in that case may well turn out to be, for example, *'idiosyncratic' wife avoidance* rather than *'public' upkeeping of property values.* Yet, some very crucial questions remain unanswered even if there is nearly perfect agreement within such an inner circle. If, for example, we still insist that Mr. Smith has a communicative intent, we may ask: To whom is the message inherent in his lawn-mowing addressed? To his wife? To his neighbours and friends? And what if all members of his inner circle of significant others (including Mrs. Smith) maintain that what he is 'really' doing is, for example, getting away from his wife, whereas Mr. Smith himself tells us with an open and honest face that *he is actually in a happy state of intrinsic motivation and is doing nothing at all but using his muscles?*

Let us include as one definite possibility that this is precisely what he will tell us if interrupted while busily pushing the lawn-mower around. How, then, does such a spontaneous and frank comment upon his own behaviour relate to its public meaning? Should it be interpreted merely as *one deviant vote* in a 'public' decision-making process, or has it some unique status in our assessment of the meaning of his act?

Harré (1978, p. 50) maintains: 'The speech which accompanies action has the general role of making action . . . intelligible and warrantable . . . Such speech is *accounting*.' And we may add: What we have achieved by adding our last possibility is merely to include an instance in which Mr. Smith's own account of what he is doing differs sharply and in characteristic ways from those offered by others. He claims he is mowing the lawn because he loves physical exercise and enjoys the activity as such, even though it makes sense to his neighbours and friends primarily as, for example, a wife-avoiding manoeuvre. Let us, hence, try to rephrase the entire mystery of what Mr. Smith was doing behind the lawn-mower that Saturday morning in terms of *attribution theory* and *accounting*.

We may thus, as Eckblad (1977, pp. 83–108) has argued in her brilliant analysis of schemes, plans and intrinsic motivation, in principle conceive of Mr. Smith's whole life as a single composite lens structure in which his uttermost values or goals serve to give meaning to (define, interpret) all of his behaviour. A few possible solutions to the mystery can then be indicated, as in Figure 1, in terms of embeddedness of acts in superordinate means–ends–structures (ascending arrows). And we may make sense of what is going on by accounts such as:

A. Mr. Smith is using his muscles cutting the grass and thus, by making the lawn neat-looking, beautifying the garden. While in that way pleasing his neighbours and keeping up property values in the area, he is at the same time improving his health and, all in all, leading the good life of a conventional Scarsdale citizen (*unbroken* lines in Figure 1).

B. Mr. Smith is using his muscles cutting the grass and thus, by preparing the ground for another crop of long grass and clover blossoms, beautifying the garden *according to his own peculiar standards* and indeed decreasing property values in Scarsdale. But he is at the same time improving his health and, as far as his own deviant conception is concerned, leading a good and independent life (*broken* lines in Figure 1).

C. Mr. Smith is using his muscles cutting the grass merely in order to get away from his wife and anger his neighbour Mr. Ifrabrumliz by the noise he is making, thus evading his obligations as a husband and leading a bad life (*dotted* lines in Figure 1).

What Mr. Smith is doing behind the lawn-mower is in each of these three cases imbued with meaning from successively more inclusive and inherently meaningful patterns: The implications of his act are revealed in plausible chains of attribution of intentions and/or reasons and/or responsibilities and pursued to the uttermost schemes in the all-inclusive means-ends-

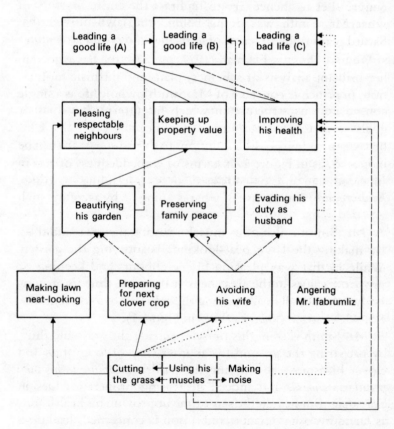

Figure 1: *A modified version of Menzel's mystery: 'What was Mr. Smith doing behind the lawn-mower?'*

structure of his entire personal life. The three accounts are thus different, yet very similar with respect to *level of reflectiveness* and *vertical scope*. And they are strikingly different from a possible account on the part of the agent himself such as, for example, that he is temporarily relieved of all worries concerning the future and the meaning of life and doing nothing but using his muscles.

The pure physical activity component of pushing a lawn-mower, however, may indeed vary greatly as far as subjective experience is concerned: It may under certain conditions be a chore and a necessary evil, yet, under other conditions, a truly pleasant and intrinsically satisfying activity. The 'orientation toward reflection' is in the latter case, moreover, nearly zero, and the state of mind in fact characterized by no awareness of *means-ends-separation* nor of *intention* at all (Eckblad 1977, p. 108). And this is, according to Bateson (1973, p. 134), also *the habitual orientation towards acts in a Balinese society* in which children '. . . learn to see life . . . as composed of rote sequences inherently satisfying in themselves'. Derivation of meanings of acts by reference to superordinate and/or future goals, on the other hand, is a distinctive feature of Protestant ethics (Weber 1958).

Scarsdale is, unfortunately, neither unequivocally Protestant nor Balinese. Some people there are perhaps most of the time painfully aware of doing something in order to achieve some future end, whereas others are at least part of the time unreflectively engaged in an immediate here-and-now. There are thus people who actually hate physical effort, yet mow the lawn in order to increase property values and please the Lord, and who accordingly suffer in anticipation of deferred gratification. Others experience moments of Balinese intrinsic motivation behind their lawn-mowers. The social scientist engaged in assessment of 'public meanings' of acts or in account analysis is accordingly left in a state of bewilderment: What are, under such variant conditions, '*the habitual orientation toward reflection*' (Smędslund 1969, p. 6) *and the appropriate vertical scope in accounting?*

The vertical scope in Figure 1 illustrates what Davidson (1971) has aptly labelled 'the accordion effect' in the attribution of meanings to acts. What Mr. Smith is doing behind the lawn-mower may be squeezed down to a trivial minimum (or even some inherently satisfying component of that minimum). But it may also be stretched out in terms of successively more inclusive means-ends-structures and causal or quasi-causal textures in such a way that its ultimate significance fades away into that 'bottom of being' which according to William James (1962, p. 157) '. . . is left logically opaque to us'. Davidson maintains (1971, p. 22): 'The accordion, which remains the same through the squeezing and stretching, is the action; the changes are in aspects described . . .' And we may add: What *other people* 'take it to be' (Harré 1978, p. 49) accordingly contingent upon the position from which the act is viewed.

Even the 'trivial minimum' meaning of what Mr. Smith is doing may thus remain enigmatic to a peasant from an entirely isolated valley without any knowledge of suburban life: What is going on does not make sense to him because he takes it for granted that grass is something to be harvested and fed to the sheep. And lawn-mowing is indeed a multifaceted entity *even if its trivial minimum meaning is taken for granted*. As Schütz (1951, p. 167) maintains:

If I, with respect to an element S of the world taken for granted, assert: 'S is p', I do so because for my purpose at hand at this particular moment I am interested only in the p-being of S and I am disregarding as not relevant to such purpose that S is also q and r.

The assertion 'S is p' in conjunction with the fact that aspects q and r are disregarded implies in the terminology of Mannheim (1952) and Hundeide (1978) precisely that the event S (the act) is experienced from a particular *position* and, in the terminology of Bateson, Goffman and Minsky, as enclosed within a certain *frame*. Its 'meaning' is accordingly generated from some particular set of *premises for interpretation* (Bateson 1973,

p. 160), a certain *background understanding* (Goffman 1974, p. 22), a given *collection of questions to be asked* (Minsky 1975, p. 246).

A particular position, moreover, implies a definite perspective and hence necessarily a restricted range of possible alternatives against which only specific aspects of the event acquire significance and salience. Wittgenstein (1968, p. 212) maintains: '. . . what I perceive in the dawning of an aspect is not a property of the object, but an internal relation between it and other objects'. These 'other objects', though, are in the attribution of meanings to specific acts provided by the observer himself in terms of *tacitly presupposed alternatives*. What strikes the good Scarsdale citizen who happens to pass by the Smith residence that morning is that Mr. Smith at such an early hour actually is mowing his lawn rather than, for example, *staying in bed with a hangover after a Friday night of excessive drinking at the pub* (see account A). The whereabouts of Mr. Smith's wife and the noise of the lawn-mower are of no concern to him at all. These are salient and significant aspects, however, when the very same act is viewed from the position of *a person prying into Mr. Smith's* marital affairs and personal feuds with Mr. Ifabrumliz (see account C).

The horizontal range of 'meanings' at each vertical level in Figure 1 may thus be read as potential aspects of what is going on, that is, as a set of *meaning potentials* (Rommetveit 1974, p. 108). The immediate 'meaning' of the act to any particular *observer* may hence be assessed in principle as a particular pattern of such aspects, a pattern contingent upon the position, background information, presuppositions, interests and momentary curiosity of that particular observer. Mr. Smith may thus 'actually', that is, *if God's truth about his intention were revealed and his (Mr. Smith's) notoriously low level of reflectiveness forgiven him*, be doing nothing but using his muscles. The predicament of life in a pluralistic social world is such, however, that *even if such were the case, he cannot prevent uninformed by-passers or malicious pryers from reading good citizenship or wife-avoidance into his act.*

God's truth about 'real' intentions will unfortunately (or fortunately) remain unknown to us social scientists. But the best we can do, perhaps, is to examine very carefully the *position of the agent himself* with respect to a vertically and horizontally expanded range of possibilities of the kind suggested in Figure 1. It then becomes obvious that poor Mr. Smith cannot be held responsible for that entire range: Only some of the possibilities are things which, on any particular occasion, he *did intentionally*, others are things that '*befell him*' on that occasion, and still others are probably *misinterpretations* of what he 'actually' did. Intention thus implies agency, but the converse does *not* hold (see Davidson 1971, pp. 3–7). The noise and the resultant neat-looking lawn are clearly aspects which, *if we accept account B as an honest and reliable self-account*, 'befell' Mr. Smith. A passer-by who sees a conventional Scarsdale citizen behind the lawn-mower and a pryer who hears its irritating noise are in that case *wrong*, that is, their positions are such that the meaning of what Mr. Smith is doing *within his private world of taken-for-granted states of affairs and possibilities* that Saturday morning remains hidden to both of them.

We have, thus, probably to assume, as Davidson (1971, p. 12) suggests, that *what the agent does* – at least with respect to some aspects – *is known to him*. His account may be partial, deceptive, and replete with justifications. Thus, Mr. Smith may possibly publicly deny that he is mowing the lawn in order to get away from his wife, whereas prolonged observations of the timing of his gardening activity as related to the location of Mrs. Smith provide evidence that he is lying. The fact remains, though, that he is, in some sense and at some level, informed about 'real intentions' in a way that outside observers cannot possibly be. Only he can thus reliably inform us about awareness of means-ends-separation and potential states of intrinsic motivation in streams of his life. Social scientific accounts of meanings of acts *qua moves in presumedly complex and conventional cultural games* may hence at times take the form of scholastic superstructures imposed upon rare islands of Balinese unreflective innocence in modern Western life.

The *honest self-account* has thus a unique status at every level of the vertical scope of attribution of meanings to acts. And possible discrepancies between a self-account and accounts offered by different 'significant others' at successively higher levels of Figure 1 are revealed in questions such as:

Is Mr. Smith merely using his muscles?

Is he using his muscles solely because he intends to cut the grass, only because he wants to make noise, or for both purposes?

Is Mr. Smith, by avoiding his wife, evading his marital obligations, or is his avoidance actually, given his unfortunate family situation, a wisely planned strategy aimed at preventing futile fights and preserving some family peace?

Does beautification of the garden mean immediate beautification (neat lawn today) or does it entail an expanded time perspective (long grass and clover blossoms a month from now)?

Some of these questions arise out of conditions of *genuine ambiguity* and *multiple meanings* similar to those explored by Wittgenstein (1968, pp. 104–105) in his discussion of the duck-rabbit figure. The passer-by may thus congenially remark, as he is catching Mr. Smith's eyes behind the lawnmower: 'You are out beautifying your garden at such an early hour?' Mr. Smith nods his head, and the good citizen continues his walk with *a corroborated false monistic notion* of genuinely ambiguous garden aesthetics. Getting away from one's wife on a particular occasion, moreover, may from the positions of most outside observers, to the conventional good citizen as well as to the malicious pryer, mean evasion of marital duties. But it may also be a very wise and resigned Mr. Smith's rational solution to a problem he knows infinitely much more about than either the good citizen or the malicious pryer.

Ambiguity at one level can in such cases hardly be solved by reference to public consensus at some higher level. On the contrary: As we expand the scope of accounts vertically, from the lowest possible level towards some superordinate 'meaning of life', we discover that our *public* trivial minimum branches off into different, yet in some sense, successively more meaningful, *private* entities. And self-accounts will at all levels tend to differ in characteristic ways from those offered by outside observers. What from the outside may appear as a routine in some public game will often, from the position of the agent himself within his own private world, be imbued with intrinsic motivation or intention. We may thus at times be willing to make sense of *the acts of other people* by considering them as robot-like beings, yet protest violently against such accounts of *our own personal acts*.

The possible solutions to the mystery depicted in Figure 1 are thus legion: Mr. Smith may be in a happy and innocent state of intrinsically satisfying bodily activity; he may be suffering the pain and entertaining the hope of the good Protestant torturing his flesh in anticipation of remote rewards; he may be avoiding his wife for either one of at least two mutually exclusive reasons; and so on. What remains invariant across the entire range of such possible 'meanings', however, is the trivial minimum that *Mr. Smith is mowing the lawn*. The very expression 'mowing the lawn' is accordingly as *useful* and as *opaque* as a proper name (see Rommetveit 1974, pp. 49–51). It implies *nothing* about higher-order 'meanings' such as those suggested in Figure 1, yet entails them all as *potentials*. And that is precisely the reason why it serves the very important public function of *identifying reference* in a lawn-mowing in an otherwise pluralistic community.

Let me, finally, comment briefly upon acts that differ markedly from lawn-mowing with respect to *interaction and potential communication components* and indicate how different potential aspects of such acts may acquire significance at different stages of life. Consider, for instance, the trivial minimum of *holding hands and singing lullabies at the bedside of a small child*. What is implied by such an act to the middle-aged father engaged in the act, to the child, to observers in different positions? Is the father merely doing his parental duty? Is he comforting the child? Is he spoiling it? Which potential aspects become salient when the act is viewed from the position of the child's teenage brother? Which aspects acquire significance within grandfather's private world of memories and retrospective wisdom?

What is going on in the bedroom in such a case 'means' obviously different things to *the child* and to *the father*. But what? The teenage brother may maintain that his small sister is being over-protected and spoiled, whereas the holding of hands *when viewed from the old man's position* perhaps is transformed into an enigmatic existential bridge between two generations of human life: a middle-aged man consoling an anxious child while actually, though unknowingly, himself seeks comfort and courage in the young hand. Is the 'meaning' of the act *sub specie aeternitatis* thus perhaps embedded in the refrain of the lullaby, though in such a way that it cannot be fully revealed *to the agents* until a late stage of life? Let us listen:

> . . . so sullelee – lullelee – loo
> our boat is drifting ashore
> where one and one don't make two
> but something mysteriously more . . .

3   *On Different Private Words, Patterns of Communication Control, and Dyadic States of Temporary Social Reality*

Kierkegaard maintained that *life is lived forward and understood backward*, and our search for the public meanings of acts seems indeed to be a futile venture. There is apparently no natural end, either in the form of literal meanings of expressions or ultimate knowledge of the world, to the explication of linguistically mediated meaning. The scope of my private world at any given moment is such that there is, according to Schütz (1951, p. 168) '. . . a selection of things and aspects of things relevant to me . . . whereas other things and other aspects are for the time being of no concern to me or even out of view'. Which aspects are focused upon by each of the two participants in any particular case of dyadic interaction are thus in part determined by the individual actor's engagement and perspective. How different *explicitly* introduced referential domains of discourse affect linguistic encoding and decoding, moreover, has been cogently demonstrated in psycholinguistic experiments by Olson (1970) and Deutsch (1976): Which of a set of possible verbal expressions will be used to refer to any particular object is clearly determined by *the range of objects from which the referent must be set apart*. And there is no reason to believe that such referential domains are of less significance when they are tacitly taken for granted, for instance in a case in which two people are talking about some state of affairs (such as Mr. Smith mowing the lawn) from different private perspectives and hence *with different taken-for-granted referential domains of alternatives in mind*.

An essential component of communicative competence in a pluralistic social world, however, is our capacity to adopt the perspectives of *different* 'others' (Rommetveit 1974, p. 59). Initiating a dialogue is, in Merleau-Ponty's words (1962, p. 182), '. . . to transform a certain kind of silence into speech'. Once the other person accepts the invitation to engage in that dialogue, his life situation is temporarily transformed: What is meant *and* understood is from that moment on determined by a joint commitment to a *temporarily shared* social reality, established and continually modified by acts of communication. States of partial or perfect intersubjectivity are thus products of negotiation, elaboration of contracts, and communication control, and they come into being in a subtle interplay of presuppositions and semantic potentialities (see Rommetveit 1974, pp. 79–112).

What any particular observer 'sees' going on in Mr. Smith's garden that Saturday morning is thus an entirely private affair. But it can be *talked about* and hence, at least under certain conditions and in some sense, become *a temporarily shared social reality*. Different aspects of the composite event will then be jointly attended to by both conversation partners depending upon whether it is talked about from the positions of the 'incidental passer-by', the 'deviant', or the 'malicious pryer' (see accounts A, B and C above). What is meant by what is said about it at any particular stage of the conversation, moreover, becomes then a matter of *whose private world is accepted as the foundation of the state of dyadic social reality attained at that very moment.* Let us now explore in some detail how temporary states of partial or even perfect dyadic social reality may be established in encounters between different private worlds.

A framework for such a detailed analysis is indicated in a 'dialogical truth table' (Table 1), and the basic unit to which we assign truth values is *an individual state of belief* with respect to some publicly identifiable state of affairs S of the general form

S is R_i

The state of affairs may thus be the 'trivial minimum' *Mr. Smith's mowing of the lawn.* The essence of the incidental passer-by's private outlook may in that case perhaps be captured in an assertion such as

S is R_j: Mr. Smith's mowing of the lawn is *a manifestation of good, conventional Scarsdale citizenship.*

A characteristic feature of the deviant's interpretation of what is going on, however, appears to be

S is R_k: Mr. Smith's mowing of the lawn is *a preparation for a novel crop of long grass and clover blossoms.*

And a significant aspect of the event when it is viewed from within the private world of the pryer is apparently

S is R_l: Mr. Smith's mowing of the lawn is a *wife-avoiding manoeuvre.*

Assertions such as S is R_j, S is R_k, and S is R_l may, as we shall see later on, enter conversations about Mr. Smith's mowing of the lawn in the form of tacit presuppositions. And *any particular such assertion* of the form S is R_i may in one particular person p_1's private world w_1 either be held *true* (t), be rejected as *false* (f), or remain *undetermined* (u) with respect to truth value. (The

Table 1: *From a binary TRUE/FALSE in an unequivocal monistic world to 19,200 states of dyadic social reality*

	Beliefs								Control	
	I Actual		II Assumed			III Actual			IV Assumed	
	p_1 in w_1	p_2 in w_2	p_2:(p_1 in w_1)	p_1:(p_2 in w_2)		p_1/p_2			p_1:(p_1/p_2)	p_2:(p_1/p_2)
(1)	t	t	(1) t	t	(1)	p_1	p_2	(1)	p_1 p_2	p_1 p_2
(2)	t	f_1	(2) t	f_1	(2)	$p_1 =$	p_2	(2)	p_1 p_2	$p_1 = p_2$
(3)	t	f_2	(3) t	f_2	(3)	p_1	p_2	(3)	p_1 p_2	p_1 p_2
(4)	t	u	(4) t	u				(4)	p_1 p_2	i
(5)	f_1	t	(5) f_1	t				(5)	$p_1 = p_2$	p_1 p_2
(6)	f_1	f_1	(6) f_1	f_1				(6)	$p_1 = p_2$	$p_1 = p_2$
(7)	f_1	f_2	(7) f_1	f_2				(7)	$p_1 = p_2$	p_1 p_2
(8)	f_1	u	(8) f_1	u				(8)	$p_1 = p_2$	i
(9)	f_2	t	(9) f_2	t				(9)	p_1 p_2	p_1 p_2
(10)	f_2	f_1	(10) f_2	f_1				(10)	p_1 p_2	$p_1 = p_2$
(11)	f_2	f_2	(11) f_2	f_2				(11)	p_1 p_2	p_1 p_2
(12)	f_2	u	(12) f_2	u				(12)	p_1 p_2	i
(13)	u	t	(13) u	t				(13)	i	p_1 p_2
(14)	u	f_1	(14) u	f_1				(14)	i	$p_1 = p_2$
(15)	u	f_2	(15) u	f_2				(15)	i	p_1 p_2
(16)	u	u	(16) u	u				(16)	i	i
			(17) t	i						
			(18) f_1	i						
			(19) f_2	i						
			(20) u	i						
			(21) i	t						
			(22) i	f_1						
			(23) i	f_2						
			(24) i	u						
			(25) i	i						

latter case may be described as a state of agnosticism or ignorance, 'don't know'). We are thus so far simply following Kleene and Kripke in their application of a strong three-valued logic. Their term '*undefined*' corresponds to the term '*undetermined*' in the present scheme and is not to be interpreted as an extra truth value (see Kripke 1975, p. 700).

The value 'false', however, must in our dialogical truth table be split into two separate variants f_1 and f_2. The reason for doing so will be revealed later, and the dichotomy may be briefly explained as follows: A person p_1 may in one case deny that S is R_i because he believes S to be *some specified entity other than* R_i. The deviant, for instance, denies that Smith's mowing of the lawn is a manifestation of conventional Scarsdale citizenship because he believes it to be a preparation for a novel crop of long grass and clover blossoms. Let us label such a rejection *falsity* 1 (f_1). P_1's private world may in another case, apart from his rejection of the assertion that S is R_i, be characterized by a state of ignorance with respect to S. A person may for instance deny that Mr. Smith's mowing of the lawn is a manifestation of good citizenship, yet remain entirely open and undetermined with respect to *what else* it may possibly be. This latter condition of rejection will be labelled *falsity* 2 (f_2). Both f_1 and f_2 may at this stage simply be read as *false*, however, since each of them will behave precisely like their mother value in our computation of the three truth values t, f and u of composite dyadic constellations.

Let us now, as a first step towards an explication of very complex states of a partially shared social reality, add another person (p_2 in w_2) and survey the resultant sixteen different dyadic constellations of individual states of belief (see the two left-hand columns under I in Table 1). We may ask: Under which of these conditions can the interpretation R_i of S be said to constitute part of p_1's and p_2's shared social world?

This will be the case, we shall claim, if, and only if, the conjunction of (p_1 in w_1) and (p_2 in w_2) is true. We may accordingly examine every dyadic constellation as a conjunction of the two individual states. The truth values for S is R_i in (p_1 in w_1) and S is R_i in (p_2 in w_2) in Table 1 are thus:

True for case (1)

False for cases (2), (3), (5), (6), (7), (8), (9), (10), (11), (12), (14) and (15).

Undetermined for cases (4), (13) and (16).

Each dyadic combination of actual states of belief, however, represents merely a *potential* dyadic social reality and is bound to remain so until p_1 and p_2 are brought into contact with each other. The fact, for example, that two incidental passers-by believe the same or different things about what is going on behind the lawn-mower is of hardly any significance at all *if they do not know about each other's existence.* It is only when p_2 constitutes part of p_1's social world and vice versa that some state of actual social reality can emerge.

This implies, more specifically, *that p_2 may entertain more or less veridical assumptions about p_1's outlook on the world and vice versa* [p_2: (p_1 in w_1) and p_1: (p_2 in w_2), see columns 3 and 4 in Table 1]. Let us suppose that these assumptions both happen to be valid, that is, that p_2 assumes p_1 to believe precisely what p_1 actually believes *and* that p_1's assumption about p_2's state of belief is equally correct. This means for constellation I (4) of actual beliefs, for example, that p_2 assumes p_1 to believe that S is R_i (l in column 3) whereas p_1 assumes p_2 to be undetermined with respect to that issue (u in column 4). In the four left-hand columns of Table 1 are thus listed, row by row, sixteen different cases of perfect correspondence between dyadic constellations of *actual* and *reciprocally assumed* beliefs.

An actual state of a perfectly shared social reality may now be defined as a conjunction of (p_1 in w_1), (p_2 in w_2), p_2: (p_1 in w_1) and p_1: (p_2 in w_2) that is true:

Some interpretation R_i of S constitutes part of p_1's and p_2's perfectly shared social reality if, and only if, both of them believe that S is R_i and each of them assumes the other to hold that belief.

The only conjunction of actual and reciprocally assumed

states of belief that is true is constellation I (1), II (1) in Table 1. This is a dyadic social reality of perfectly shared and reciprocally assumed *faith*, and only one out of sixteen cases of perfect correspondence between actual and reciprocally assumed states. But what, then, about perfectly shared and reciprocally assumed *agnosticism* (or ignorance)?

The most likely conditions for such a state are obviously constellations I (6), II (6); I (11), II (11); and I (16), II (16). Constellation I (6), II (6) is the case in which both p_1 and p_2 believe, and assume the other to believe, that S is something else than R_i. *What* else S is held to be, however, is not specified. It is possible, therefore, that their shared and mutually acknowledged rejection of the assertion that S is R_i actually entails conflicting outlooks: P may deny that Mr. Smith's mowing of the lawn is a manifestation of good citizenship because he believes that Mr. Smith entertains very deviant notions concerning gardening, whereas p_2 is convinced that the mowing of the lawn is merely a wife-avoiding manoeuvre. But they may also share *the same* alternative belief (for example, that Mr. Smith is preparing the ground for another crop of long grass and clover blossoms).

Constellation I (16), II (16), on the other hand, is a case of fully shared and reciprocally acknowledged orientation of *complete agnosticism* towards S. We are accordingly in this case allowed to engage in assessment of intersecting parts of two different worlds by a procedure of elimination and claim that w_1 and w_2 intersect in an area of perfectly shared and reciprocally assumed ignorance. This implies, more specifically, that for *constellation I (16), II (16) we can eliminate conflicting presuppositions with respect to S as a possible source of misunderstanding in a dialogue between p_1 and p_2.*

Constellation I (11), II (11), finally, is a case of fully shared and reciprocally acknowledged orientation of *partial agnosticism* toward S. Both p_1 and p_2 believe and assume that the other believes that S is *not* R_i. Apart from that, however, they are both ignorant with respect to S and assume the other to be so too. We can therefore in this case also safely exclude the possibility that p_1 and p_2 misunderstand each other because they presuppose different things about S. And it should by now be clear why the single value *false* in the monistic, though only partially known, world of strong three-valued logic must be dichotomized in our dialogical table: Our two variants f_1 and f_2 are indeed a *sine qua non* in a systematic analysis of shared social realities in terms of *agnosticism* as well as faith. Variant f_1 implies nothing about shared ignorance at all, whereas variant f_2 in case I (11), II (11) yields an intersection of the two individual worlds w_1 and w_2 in terms of a perfectly shared and reciprocally acknowledged *partial agnosticism*.

Perfect correspondence is the case in only sixteen out of altogether 16×25 possible dyadic constellations of states of actual and reciprocally assumed belief in Table 1, however. Let us now comment briefly upon some of the remaining 384 combinations.

The first thing we then have to do is to introduce a fifth state of assumed belief. This fifth value, i, may be defined as a state of *absence of assumptions* concerning the other person's state of belief with respect to S. An i in column p_2: (p_1 in w_1) means that p_2 is *ignorant* (or undetermined) with respect to which of the four primary states t, f_1, f_2 or us exists in w_1. We might hence be tempted to define it as the disjunction of those four primary states, that is, as *either* t *or* f_1, *or* f_2 *or* u. This would lead us into serious difficulties, however, since such a disjunction is bound to be *true*. We would accordingly have to accept constellations I (1), II (17); I (1), II (21) and I (1), II (25) as actual states of perfectly shared social reality.

The value i must hence be defined as representing a second-order state with no counterpart in primary states of individual belief at all. An individual can be *undetermined* with respect to some state of affairs S in the sense that he does not know what S *is* or *is not*, but he cannot be fully ignorant of his own lack of determination. He may be said to be entirely ignorant (i) of *another person's state of belief* with respect to S, though, in the sense that he neither knows, nor assumes to know, anything about it. The value u in column p_2; (p_1 in w_1) thus means that p_2 *assumes p_1 to be undetermined with respect to S*, whereas i means that p_2 *is undetermined with respect to which one of the four previously defined primary states t, f_1, f_2 or u exists in w_1*. Let us now explore in detail what happens when people with variant states of *actual* and *reciprocally assumed* belief with respect to an assertion of the form *S is R_i* engage in conversation about the composite state of affairs S.

The basic mechanism of establishing intersubjectivity across different private worlds is *reciprocal role taking*: p_1 attempts to make known to p_2 something about the state of affairs as it appears to him in his own private world w_1 by addressing p_2 on what he assumes to be p_2's premises, p_1: (p_2 in w_2). p_2, on the other hand, tries to make sense of what p_1 is saying by adopting what he assumes to be p_1's private outlook, p_2: (p_1 in w_1), while listening to p_1. There is thus in acts of human communication *an inbuilt circularity*.

However, the circularity inherent in acts of communication does *not* imply that the two participants assume joint or equal responsibility for what is being meant by what is said. The speaker monitors what he says in accordance with what he assumes to be the listener's position, yet in order to make *his own private world* comprehensible to the other. What he says may still turn out to be an incomplete and very poor expression of what he means. But he cannot possibly misunderstand *what he himself intends to make known*. Only he, *not* the listener, can decide *what is being meant* and *whether it is being misunderstood*. Thus, control of the temporarily shared social reality at any given stage of a dialogue is, under conditions of perfect equality or symmetry between partners, in principle, unequivocally determined by *direction of communication*.

This means, more specifically, that reciprocal role taking under condition III (2) IV (6), $p_1 = p_2$; p_1: ($p_1 = p_2$): and p_2: ($p_1 = p_2$) in Table 1 is combined with an unequivocal and reciprocally endorsed *primary contract* or *rule of control*: Each of the two participants has *qua speaker* the privilege of imposing his own private world upon the other and *qua listener* the commitment to try to grasp what the other person, from within *his* private world, is talking about. The speaker, or more generally: *the participant who introduced whatever is being talked about at that moment, is assumed to know what is being meant by what is said.* A relation of *actual* equality or symmetry (condition III (2), $p_1 = p_2$ in Table 1) by no means implies, therefore, *diffusion of* and/or *some vaguely defined status of equality with respect to* control, but merely *absence of actual constraints upon interchangeability of dialogue roles.* Conditions of asymmetry, $p_1 \, p_2$ and $p_1 \, p_2$, must accordingly be defined as *conditions of constraints.* And such conditions are in fact established in every social psychological experiment on dyadic interaction in which the two participants are assigned fixed and different dialogue roles in their joint experimental task (see, for example, Ross, Amabile and Steinmetz 1978; Blakar and Pedersen 1978).

What is implied by *actual control* (column III in Table 1) may thus be explicated and 'operationalized' in terms of particular experimental conditions (see Rommetveit 1979). But such control is also revealed in *institutionally provided constraints* upon communication in particular real-life settings. Every formal educational system, for example, may be said to possess a definite and unequivocal pattern of asymmetry: Topics of discourse are pre-determined by curriculae, and the teacher, by virtue of his superior knowledge and his role as an educator, is the one who is supposed to have the final word concerning *what is meant by what is said.* The progressive teacher may, hence, define his own trade as the art of creating an internal symmetric pattern of reciprocally assumed control within an actual, institutionally given, frame of asymmetry (constellation III (1) IV (6) in Table 1).

States of dyadic social reality may thus be systematically explored qua *products of particular dyadic combinations of actual and reciprocally assumed beliefs under variant conditions of actual and reciprocally assumed communication control.* And let us at this stage return to our dyad and examine the role of *presuppositions* under relatively simple conditions of discourse. Consider, for instance, the following situation:

Two friends, p_1 and p_2, are driving together in a car; p_1 is the driver, p_2 his passenger and guest, and the drive is in fact a guided tour in the neighbourhood of p_1's home. As they are driving along, they pass a big, shabby, derelict-looking building. It is obvious to any observer that the building has been left to decay, but its appearance is otherwise such that it leaves the observer with no clue whatsoever about its previous identity: It may be a forlorn apartment house, an empty office building, a closed-down factory, or something else. As they are passing that building, however, p_1 says to p_2:

There wasn't enough profit from the production.

Let us assume that p_2 is truly ignorant with respect to the identity of the building until this very moment. He may later on, though, inform his wife that there is a closed-down *factory* in the neighbourhood of their friend p_1's home. And he will do so with complete confidence that he is telling the truth. *His state of agnosticism was thus transformed into a state of belief the moment he understood what p_1 told him as they were passing that building.*

This information must in part be explained in terms of shared propositional knowledge of the world as proposed by Labov in his theory of discourse (Labov 1972): What is meant by p_1 as they are passing the building can hardly be understood by p_2 at all unless both of them take it for granted that production takes place in factories rather than, for example, apartment buildings. But *such would also be the case if p_2 were, for example, a fellow passenger in a tourist bus passing that same building.* But in such a case would p_2 later on confidently tell his wife about the factory? If not, why? Under which particular conditions will p_1's presupposition that the building is a factory automatically become p_2's belief?

The case of the two friends, I shall argue, is a simple case of what, in previous casuistic analyses, I have labelled *prolepsis* (Rommetveit 1974, p. 87). p_1's presupposition that the building is a factory is of the form

$$S \text{ is } R_i$$

and the state of dyadic social reality at the moment when he starts talking about insufficient profit is constellation I (4) II (21) III (1) IV (6). A truly proleptic feature of the situation is that p_1 talks *on the assumption that* or *as if* p_2 already knows what he himself knows about the building [t in column p_1: (p_2 in w_2)]. Another essential feature of the situation is the constellation of *p_2's ignorance concerning p_1's state of belief* and the actual constraints upon their conversation due to the fact that *p_1 lives in that area whereas p_2 is a stranger* [i in column p_2: (p_1 in w_1) and $p_1 p_2$ in column III]. The state of dyadic reality *at the moment p_2 understands what p_1 is saying*, I (4) II (21) III (1) IV (1), is under these conditions immediately transformed into the perfectly shared social reality I (1) II (1) III (1) IV (6): p_1's unwarranted assumption that p_2 knows that the building is a factory has *become* true.

The case of the two tourists is, as already indicated, identical as far as *shared abstract propositional knowledge of the world* is concerned. The state of dyadic social reality prior to p_1's utterance, however, is in this latter case I (4) II (13) III (2) IV (6); I (4) II (16) III (2) IV (6); or I (4) II (20) III (2) IV (6). Notice that the constellation of actual constraints upon the situation *and* p_2's assumption concerning p_1's state of belief is now an entirely different one: *p_1 and p_2 are both unfamiliar with that particular neighbourhood* ($p_1 = p_2$ in column III) *and p_2 will in all likelihood take it for granted that p_1 is as ignorant about the identity of the building as he is himself.* He will, hence, even if p_1 speaks on the false assumption that p_2 has also identified it as a factory, necessarily *become aware of*, and probably also *question*, that presupposition.

Let us at this stage return to our initial mystery and see how Table 1 may possibly help us to assess what is *meant*, *understood* and *made known* when our incidental passer-by p_1 engages in conversation about what he saw in Mr. Smith's garden under variant dyadic constellations of states of belief and communication control. A characteristic feature of his private Saturday morning world, we remember, is the general presupposition S is R_j: Mowing the lawn is a manifestation of good, conventional Scarsdale citizenship.

And his story is possibly as follows:

A Saturday morning walk through Scarsdale is really a treat. It's so nice here, a real paradise compared to some other places. I remember driving through the East River district one early Saturday morning last year. What a misery: Ugly houses, unkept gardens, half-naked kids running around while their parents were probably sobering up after last night's booze . . . But people here in Scarsdale deserve their good fortune. We are hard-working people who care about our properties and like to keep the neighbourhood nice and clean. I walked by Mr. Smith's residence, and *Mr. Smith was indeed already busy mowing his lawn.*

Let us assume, moreover, that our passer-by p_1 is a shielded (and, in some sense, innocently egocentric) member of the local establishment who takes it for granted that the person he is addressing, p_2, shares his perspective on what Mr. Smith was doing. A significant component of *what is meant* by what he says is in that case, irrespective of *who* happens to be his conversation partner, captured by inserting the value t for S is R_j in columns I, p_1 in w_1, and II, p_1: (p_2 in w_2) of Table 1.

What is *made known*, however, is clearly contingent upon what the other person, p_2, privately believes and assumes him, p_1, to believe with respect to that issue, and it may also in part be determined by actual and reciprocally assumed control of communication in the encounter between p_1 and p_2. Let us therefore examine what the incidental passer-by p_1 may make known by his Saturday morning report *to different conversation partners*. What happens when he tells his story to his wife, to his seven years' old son, to Mr. Smith's prying neighbour (see account C above), and to another incidental passer-by with a different perspective on what Mr. Smith was doing (see account B above)?

CASE 1, p_2 IS p_1's WIFE

Our incidental passer-by p_1 and his wife p_2 have lived together in Scarsdale for many years as members of the local establishment there. The presupposition *S is R_j* thus constitutes part of their perfectly shared social reality. And he, p_1, is the one who *knows* what happened in Mr. Smith's garden since she, p_2, did not accompany him on his morning walk. The constellation of dyadic social reality and communication control as *the wife is listening to her husband's story* is thus I (1) II (1) III (1) IV (1) in Table 1. And, probably, so thoroughly shared are their presuppositions concerning details of life in Scarsdale that p_1's entire introductory talk about their idyllic suburb might be skipped. What is made known *to his wife* is, even if that were the case, that *Mr. Smith appears to be an exceptionally good and respectable Scarsdale citizen.* The wife's immediate response to subsequent gossip suggesting that the Smiths are leading a Bohemian life will, hence, very likely be one of protest: How can that be? Is not Mr. Smith a particularly conscientious and nice fellow? Didn't her own very trustworthy husband observe him busily mowing his lawn early one Saturday morning?

CASE 2, p_2 IS p_1's SEVEN YEARS' OLD SON

The young boy is not yet fully familiar with his parents' outlook on Scarsdale life, and his state of belief with respect to the significance of lawn-mowing is still one of innocent ignorance (*i* in column II, p_2: (p_1 in w_1) and *u* in column I, p_2 in w_2, of Table 1). His situation when listening to his father's Saturday morning report is thus similar to that of *the stranger on* a *guided tour*, and so indeed, in principle, is the situation of every inexperienced child listening to an adult: Daddy is tacitly assumed to be the one who both saw what happened *and* knows what is meant. The constellation of dyadic social reality and control pattern is hence I (4) II (21) III (1) IV (1), and what the son learns *about Mr. Smith* is accordingly less unequivocal than that which is made known to his mother. Notice, however, the truly proleptic feature of the father-to-son conversation: The father, p_1, talks to his son, p_2, on *the assumption that*, or *as if*, he, p_2, already shares his, p_1's, outlook on lawn-mowing and good, conventional Scarsdale life. And this naive pragmatic postulate or primitive faith in one fully shared world is, in some sense, self-fulfilling since the child has indeed to endorse his father's presuppositions in order to make full sense of what he tells him. An essential aspect of *what is achieved by what is said* in such a conversation is thus apparently a subtle transmission of firmly held presuppositions from one generation to another.

CASE 3, p_2 IS MR. SMITH'S PRYING NEIGHBOUR

The encounter between the incidental passer-by p_1 and the pryer p_2 takes place shortly after *both of them have observed* what was going on in Mr. Smith's garden. Let us assume, moreover, that the passer-by p_1 takes it for granted that spouses may sometimes engage in manoeuvres of avoidance *and* that the pryer p_2 is fully familiar with the establishment's conventional perspective on gardening and the good life. There are, thus, no actual constraints upon interchangeability of dialogue roles in the conversation between them. Thus the situation *when p_2 is listening to p_1's* report is very likely constellation I (2) II (1) III (2) IV (1) in Table 1. p_2 assumes correctly that p_1 considers what he has just seen as a manifestation of good citizenship [t in column II, p_1: (p_2 in w_2)], while himself rejecting that presupposition in favour of a specific alternative explanation (f_1 in column I, p_2 in w_2). He is making sense of what p_1 is telling him, though, on p_1's *own premises* [p_1 p_2 in column IV, p_2: (p_1/p_2)]. What happens as the pryer p_2 *understands* what the passer-by p_1 tells him is thus, in a way, that his private world w_2 is temporarily expanded so as to include p_1's private outlook on what happened as a *possibility*. He does not *share* that outlook, however, and his response to the passer-by's story may be:

So you think that Mr. Smith is a nice citizen caring for his garden and his wife and the neighbourhood, eh? I'll tell you something: He grabbed that lawn-mower merely to get away from his wife and make life miserable for Mr. Ifabrumliz, his neighbour, who likes to sleep late!

This switch of dialogue roles implies that the incidental passer-by p_1 is now committed to listen *on p_2's premises*, that is, the pattern of actual and reciprocally assumed control of what is being meant while p_2 is talking is constellation III (2) IV (11) in Table 1. The incidental passer-by will accordingly be very likely, at least if he considers the pryer a credible fellow, to revise the passage about Mr. Smith in repeated performances of his Saturday morning report.

CASE 4, p_2 IS ANOTHER INCIDENTAL PASSER-BY WITH A DIFFERENT PERSPECTIVE ON WHAT MR. SMITH WAS DOING

This case is of the same kind as case 3 with respect to formal aspects, and the situation when p_2 is listening to p_1's report is thus I (2) II (1) III (2) IV (1). We assume also in this case that p_2 is familiar with the establishment's conventional perspective on gardening and the good life, and that p_2 is listening to p_1's story on p_1's own premises.

What happened to p_1 *when listening to the pryer's* response was that, at least temporarily, he had to adopt a composite or dual perspective on what he had seen. The additional 'prying perspective', however, was in that case *already available* as one definite possibility within his pre-established repertory of possible private positions. But let us assume, in this case, that the other passer-by p_2's private world w_2 is, *in some respects*, entirely novel and alien to p_1. Suppose, for instance, that *the deviant style of gardening and the alternative notion of beautification of gardens* (see Figure 1 and account B above) are *entirely unknown to p_1 prior to his encounter with p_2*. Their conversation in that case, after p_1's introductory report, may proceed as follows:

p_2: You are right. Scarsdale is very nice and very conventional, and its snobbishness can indeed be measured in terms of neatly kept lawns. But you are apparently entirely wrong about Mr. Smith. Didn't you notice that his lawn hadn't been mowed for months!

p_1: I think I noticed, now when you mention it . . . But I assumed he had been away from his home for some time . . . Yes, now I remember: I thought he had probably returned late Friday night. That's the reason why he is out at such an early hour, I thought: He is so eager to make the lawn nice and neat-looking again . . . And, by the way, *he also nodded in assent when I remarked that he was out beautifying the garden.*

p_2: But that was precisely what he was doing too, though not in the way you think. He was indeed preparing the ground for another rich crop of long grass and clover blossoms. That's what *I* call beauty, fullgrown grass and sweet-smelling blossoms! But what is *beautification of gardens* to most people here in Scarsdale? Making lawns neat and sterile-looking?

p_1: *Beautification of gardens . . .*

Something very intriguing is possibly happening towards the end of this conversation. p_2 says: '*Beautification of gardens . . .*', and p_1, even at this stage, may be listening, *not* on p_2's but on his own premises. The pattern of communication control as p_1 *starts* listening to p_2's last contribution is in that case temporarily III (2) IV (3), that is, one of *egocentric symmetry* (see Rommetveit 1979). Their conversation may, hence, easily be locked in a frozen ideological conflict: p_1 may persist in making sense of the expression 'beautification' solely in terms of his own particular gardening ideology even when it is clearly meant otherwise by p_2.

The sarcastic flavour of p_2's remark on beautification of gardens in Scarsdale is such, however, that p_1's centration in his own particular position is being undermined. Is p_2 suggesting that beautification of gardens is actually *not* beautification of gardens? What can be meant by 'beautification' then? Who *knows* what is being meant by that expression, p_1 or p_2?

What may happen is thus that a pattern of egocentric symmetry is transformed into *a state of genuine ignorance or uncertainty with respect to assumed control of what is being meant*, to constellation III (2) IV (15) in Table 1. And this genuine state of uncertainty on the part of p_1 is very likely a *sine qua non* as a transient state in the transformation of egocentric symmetry into full interchangeability of dialogue roles, that is, into an oscillation between patterns III (2) IV (1) and III (2) IV (11) strictly determined by *the primary contract of communication control*. p_1's final hesitation after having repeated p_2's 'Beautification of gardens . . .' may thus possibly signal that he is on the verge of engaging in a *genuine dialogue* and hence also, under those particular conditions, on the verge of expanding his private repertory of possible perspectives so as to discover novel aspects of life.

But let us now return to p_1's own introductory Saturday morning report and try to summarize what happens in our four different settings. What is *meant, understood* and *made known* by his utterance '. . . and Mr. Smith was indeed already busy mowing the lawn' when p_1 is engaged in conversation with his wife, with his younger son, with the pryer, and with the 'deviant' passer-by!

The issue of *what is meant* can, of course, be only partially settled, but is in this case indeed greatly simplified by our assumption, as outlined above, that p_1 on every occasion takes it for granted that *the listener p_2's world w_2 in certain essential respects is a duplicate of his own private world w_1*. The only conversation partner who fully *shares* his presupposition that S is R_j while listening to him, however, is *his wife*. Thus, what is meant by p_1 is, in his conversation with his wife, *expressed and understood within the dyadic frame of a perfectly shared social reality*. A significant part of what is meant by the utterance *in all four cases* is accordingly that which is made known *only to his wife*: That Mr. Smith appears to be exceptionally conscientious, good and respectable Scarsdale citizen.

What is meant by p_1 is, as already indicated, hardly fully understood by his young son. It is *understood*, though, by the pryer and the 'deviant' passer-by in the sense that p_1's private interpretation of what went on is comprehended *as a possibility* while they are listening to what he is saying. They persist in viewing the event from their own pre-established positions, however. Hence, part of what is meant *and* understood is perhaps immediately rejected, by the pryer as *an irrelevant interpretation* and by the deviant as *a false belief*. Nothing, in that case, is made known about *what happened in Mr. Smith's garden* beyond what each of them already knows or assumes to be the case. What both of them learn in their conversations with p_1, however, is something about *his private world* w_1 which his wife takes for granted as a perfectly shared social reality while listening to his Saturday morning report.

4   Epilogue: Notes on the Ambiguities of Life, the Autonomy of Texts, and the Construction of States of Human Intersubjectivity

What happens when a tacitly monistic outlook on life is replaced by a consistently pluralistic set of assumptions is that its inherent ambiguities can no longer be evaded by reference to postulated, though inaccessible public meanings of acts and literal meanings of expressions. What is meant by what is said in encounters between different private worlds cannot, therefore, be explicated as *autonomous 'texts'* (see Olson 1977) embedded in unequivocal frameworks of shared propositional knowledge of the world (see Labov 1972, p. 122). Human communication must instead be examined in terms of transformations of dyadic states of social reality under variant conditions of actual and reciprocally assumed *control* of what is being meant.

A person's private world w_1 may be described in terms of a range of sustained presuppositions and potentially available perspectives. The *linguistic* basis for partially and even perfectly shared states of social reality, I have argued, is a repertory of general and partly negotiable drafts of contracts concerning categorization and attribution inherent in ordinary languages. A person's semantic competence may accordingly be conceived of as mastery of potentially shared strategies of categorization and cognitive-emotional perspectives on talked-about states of affairs (Rommetveit 1974, 1978, 1979). Our private worlds are thus by no means solipsistic. They intersect in 'trivial minima' (such as, for example, the publicly identifiable act *mowing the lawn* in a lawn-mowing community), and a particular private world w_1 can be expanded so as to entail, as *experiential possibilities*, aspects of states of affairs that are visible only when those states of affairs are viewed from the positions of other people.

States of nearly perfect intersubjectivity can thus in principle be *temporarily* attained even in encounters between two very different private worlds w_1 and w_2 under conditions of *adequate role-taking in accordance with the primary contract of communication control*. And these conditions are apparently fulfilled when the pryer and the 'deviant' are listening to the incidental passer-by's Saturday morning report. A transient state of nearly perfect intersubjectivity is thus possibly attained *the moment the pryer understands what is meant by the incidental passer-by's remark about Mr. Smith*. Hence, the conversation between them may even result in a partially shared social reality which, in a way, entails two different pre-established perspectives: Their joint solution of the mystery may simply be that Mr. Smith, while avoiding his wife, also made the lawn look neat to good citizens walking by his residence. The former aspect (wife-avoidance) was obviously *invisible* to the incidental passer-by and the latter aspect, making lawn neat-looking, very likely *beyond the very restricted field of vision* of the ardent pryer *prior to their* conversation.

Our casuistic analysis of what happens when two persons engage in discourse may thus serve as a corroboration and further explication of one of William James' profound insights into life in a pluralistic social world. James (1962b, p. 197) maintained: '*You accept my verification of one thing, I yours of another. We trade on each other's truth.*' And such '*trading on each other's truth*' may also generate *states of genuine uncertainty* with respect to what is being meant which, at least under certain conditions, make for transcendence of a person's repertory of pre-established 'meanings'. The moment when a previously unequivocal expression (such as 'beautification of gardens') becomes *ambiguous* may hence be the dawning of a novel aspect of life.

But James (1962a, p. 171) was also concerned with '. . . cases where faith creates its own verification'. And Bateson (1973, p. 285) maintains: 'The living man is bound within a net of epistemological and ontological premises which – regardless of truth or falsity – become partially self-validating for him'. The ultimate meaning of life, to people who confess to the same religious faith, may thus become institutionalized as '*the immanent meaning*' of their sacred religious texts. And, as Olson (1977, p. 275) very cautiously remarks: 'Whether or not all meaning can be made explicit or not is perhaps less critical than the belief that it can . . .'

We have in our analysis of specific conversations examined cases of apparent self-validation and tried to explore under which conditions p_1's presupposition unknowingly may become p_2's belief. These conditions were described in terms of characteristic constellations of dyadic states of belief and patterns of communication control, such as I (4), II (21), III (1), IV (1) in Table 1. The truly proleptic features of the guided tour and the father-to-son conversations, moreover, are distinctive features of 'disguised preaching' in dyadic communication.

And *actual control* of what is meant in terms of, for example, superior knowledge is, of course, greatly enhanced if the camouflaged preacher, whether he appears in the guise of a father telling his son about morning life in Scarsdale or that of a university professor telling his students about rules of discourse, can rely on his audience's faith in the autonomous meaning of his 'text'. Such faith becomes increasingly important the less the audience knows, and it approaches a maximum of importance in a situation in which, for instance, linguistically ignorant social scientists try to make sense of a prestigious and formally very impressive text of linguistic structural analysis.

Other implications of a consistently pluralistic outlook on dyadic human communication have been explored in analysis of 'quasi-dialogues' and cases of 'pluralistic ignorance' (Rommetveit 1979). The issue of *power* in interpersonal relations then becomes in part a question of whose private world, w_1, w_2, or neither of them, is accepted by both persons as a foundation of a temporarily shared social reality when p_1 and p_2 engage in a dialogue. What Berger and Luckmann (1967, p. 38) refer to as *social validation of a person's subjectivity*, moreover, can thus in part be examined in terms of *control of what is being meant* and *faith in a shared world*.

What strikes us in a systematic analysis of Man as engaged in action and communication in a pluralistic social world is his profound dependency upon fellow human beings. As Naess (1975, p. 46) comments in his analysis of Spinoza's ethics: 'A person is part of something, and his personal identity is relational . . . Man exists *in* the personal relations, as a changing centre of interactions in a field of relations.' The student of human communication who abandons his monistic assumptions will accordingly have to redefine his trade in some important respects: To explicate the ambiguities of life will not only be considered a legitimate, but possibly even the most important part of his task. His duty as a scholar is to try to *be precise about* rather than *evade* life's inherent versatility and vagueness. And his uniquely *social scientific perspective* should –

ideally – be that of the participant observer of all varieties of human life who, despite his sophistication, has managed to preserve the naïveté of the child in H. C. Andersen's tale about the emperor's new suit.

References

G. Bateson, 1973, *Steps to an Ecology of Mind*, Suffolk: Palladin

P. L. Berger and T. Luckmann, 1967, *The Social Construction of Reality*, New York: Doubleday

R. M. Blakar and T. B. Pedersen, 1978, 'Control and Self-Confidence as Reflected in Sex-Bound Patterns in Communication: An Experimental Approach', published working paper, Department of Psychology, Oslo University

D. Davidson, 1971, Agency, in: R. Binkley et al. (Eds.), *Agent, Action and Reason*, Toronto: University of Toronto Press

W. Deutsch, 1976, 'Sprachliche Redundanz und Objektidentifikation', published Ph.D. thesis, Marburg University

G. Eckblad, 1977, 'Schemes and Intrinsic Motivation, II. Scheme Theory, A Conceptual Framework for Intrinsically Motivated Behavior', published working paper, Department of Psychology, Bergen University

G. P. Ginsburg (Ed.), 1979, *Emerging Strategies in Social Psychological Research*, London: Wiley

E. Goffman, 1974, *Frame Analysis*, New York: Harper & Row

R. Harré, 1978, 'Accounts, Actions and Meanings – The Practice of Participatory Psychology', in: M. Brenner, P. Marsh and M. Brenner (Eds.), *The Social Contexts of Method*, London: Croom Helm

K. Hundeide, 1978, 'Perspectivity, Intentionality, and Development', published working paper, Department of Psychology, Oslo University

W. James, 1962a, 'The Sentiment of Rationality', in: W. Barrett and H. D. Aiken (Eds.), *Philosophy in the Twentieth Century*, Vol. 1, New York: Random House

W. James, 1962b, 'Pragmatism's Conception of Truth', in: W. Barrett and H. D. Aiken (Eds.), *Philosophy in the Twentieth Century*, Vol. 1, New York: Random House

S. Kripke, 1975, Outline of a Theory of Truth, *Journal of Philosophy*, Vol. 72, pp. 690–716

W. Labov, 1972, 'Rules for Ritual Insults', in: D. Sudnow (Ed.), *Studies in Social Interaction*, New York: Free Press

K. Mannheim, 1952, *Essays on the Sociology of Knowledge*, Oxford: Oxford University Press

H. Menzel, 1978, 'Meaning – Who Needs It?', in: M. Brenner, P. Marsh and M. Brenner (Eds.), *The Social Contexts of Method*, London: Croom Helm

M. Merleau-Ponty, 1962, *Phenomenology of Perception*, London: Routledge & Kegan Paul

M. Minsky, 1975, 'A Framework for Representing Knowledge', in: P. H. Winston (Ed.), *The Psychology of Computer Vision*, New York: McGraw-Hill

A. Naess, 1975, *Freedom, Emotion and Self-Subsistence, The Structure of a Central Part of Spinoza's Ethics*, Oslo: Oslo University Press

D. Olson, 1970, 'Language and Thought, Aspects of a Cognitive Theory of Semantics', *Psychological Review*, Vol. 77, pp. 257–273

D. Olson, 1977, 'From Utterance to Text: The Bias of Language in Speech and Writing', *Harvard Educational Review*, Vol. 47, pp. 257–281

R. Rommetveit, 1974, *On Message Structure, A Framework for the Study of Language and Communication*, London: Wiley

R. Rommetveit, 1978, 'On Negative Rationalism in Scholarly Studies of Verbal Communication and Dynamic Residuals in the Construction of Human Intersubjectivity', in: M. Brenner, P. Marsh and M. Brenner (Eds.), *The Social Contexts of Method*, London: Croom Helm

R. Rommetveit, 1979, 'The Role of Language in the Creation and Transmission of Social Representations', Paper presented at the Colloque sur les Représentations Sociales, Paris, January 8–10

L. D. Ross, T. M. Amabile and J. L. Steinmetz, 1978, 'Social Roles, Social Control, and Bias in Social-Perception Processes', *Journal of Personality and Social Psychology*, Vol. 35, pp. 485–494

R. C. Schank, 1975, *Conceptual Information Processing*, Amsterdam: North Holland

A. Schuetz, 1951, 'Choosing Among Projects of Action', *Philosophical and Phenomenological Research*, Vol. 12, pp. 161–184

J. Searle, 1974, *On Speech Acts*, Cambridge: Cambridge University Press

J. Smedslund, 1969, 'Meanings, Implications, and Universals: Toward a Psychology of Man', *Scandinavian Journal of Psychology*, Vol. 10, pp. 1–15

M. Weber, 1958, *The Protestant Ethic and the Spirit of Capitalism*, New York: Scribner

L. Wittgenstein, 1968, *Philosophical Investigations*, Oxford: Blackwell

Segmenting the Behaviour Stream

PETER COLLETT   *Oxford University*

---

1   *Introductory Remarks*

It used to be said that the man who takes a wife also marries her family. If this is no longer true of matrimony, it is certainly the case with methodology. When the student of human action chooses a method he also commits himself, sometimes unwittingly, to a set of related assumptions about the phenomenon he hopes to understand. In this paper I attempt to make some of these assumptions explicit. I will look at the relative advantages of viewing action as constituted in terms of variables and units, explore the temporal aspect of behaviour and then discuss the repercussions of defining action units in the investigator's, as opposed to the layman's, terms. Finally, I will argue that the proper study of human behaviour should take account, not only of the manner in which actions are produced in time, but also of the ways in which we place constructions on these actions.

2   *Variables versus Units*

The first opposition to be considered is that between variables and units. Duncan (1969) has distinguished two research strategies in the study of behaviour, namely what he calls the 'external variable' and the 'structural' approach. According to Duncan the external variable approach involves the application of traditional psychological methods; it is found wherever the investigator attempts to relate the occurrence of specific behaviour to variables that are intrinsic to those behaviours. The structural approach, on the other hand, involves the isolation of units or segments in the stream of behaviour and the subsequent analysis of their relations within a temporal structure.[1] This strategy, as he puts it, attempts 'to study communication as a tightly organized and self-contained social system, like language'.

This distinction between the external variable and the structural is a useful one, but it fails to capture the essence of what is involved in the two types of approach. It is possible to identify certain structural studies which, because they focus on interpersonal influence, can only properly be termed 'external-structural', which suggests that the notion of externality is redundant to the distinction we require. The crucial difference between the two research strategies mentioned by Duncan may be found in the distinction between those that focus on variable aspects of behaviour and those which are concerned with units. Studies which focus on variables derive their model from the physical sciences (for example, Boyle's Law), while those that concentrate on units take their inspiration from either ethology or linguistics. The distinction is a little like that between the conception of light as wave and light as particle, or, say, the difference between parametric and non-parametric statistics. In the former case, an underlying parameter or continuum is inferred, while, in the latter, it is

1 The idea of a stream was first used by psychologists in connection with thinking. The expression 'stream of thought' is usually attributed to William James (1890), whereas it may, in fact, be found in the earlier work by Alexander Bain (1869), with which James was acquainted. By selecting a fluvial metaphor James drew attention to the continuous and changing quality of consciousness. However, he did not insist, as is sometimes supposed, that thinking is indivisible, only that it is smooth and that individual thoughts 'melt into each other like dissolving views'.

assumed that actions are discontinuous and discrete. Duncan, however, was not particularly inclined towards either the external variable or the structural approach. He felt that both have an important role to play in the study of behaviour and proposed that the two strategies should complement each other. I think there are good reasons for rejecting this bi-partisan solution.

Suppose I move my arm through the air. There is a sense in which it would be impossible to offer an objective description of the separate actions that I have performed. Any attempt to identify the constituents, let alone the boundaries of the actual movement itself, would necessarily arise out of a set of assumptions that I entertain about the nature of such action. In other words, the stream of behaviour is, for all practical purposes, homogenous in time. It is seamless, and it is only by virtue of the segmentations that I impose on it, and the way in which these segments are seen as relating to each other, that it can have any meaning or significance for me. The crucial term here is meaning, and it follows from any attempt to analyse people's meaningful transactions that we must focus on units. The question of who is to designate these units is a matter to which we will return, but, for the moment, the point I wish to make is that any study of social semantics must, of necessity, deal with units, for the simple reason that meanings inhere in units and units in combination. Anyone who doubts this need only consider the parody that would arise from an attempt to treat language parametrically.

In arguing that studies which are addressed to social trans-actions can only deal in units, there are two things that are not being maintained. Firstly, I am not saying that parametric analyses have no place in psychology, only that they cannot hope to play a role in any understanding of the way in which people interact with each other. Secondly, it is not being proposed that there are no underlying variables, only that people's thinking has categorical properties. The sense we make of others involves a conversion of the analogue world into digital information. This point is nicely captured in Hall's

writings on proxemics and, say, the work on phonetic boundaries by Liberman and his colleagues.[2] When Hall (1966) tells
us that there are discrete zones of interpersonal space between
individuals, he is not suggesting that distance is not a variable.
He is merely proposing that the physical continuum is transformed in a set of cultural discontinua or categories, each with
its own function and social purpose. Similarly with the research by Liberman et al. (1957), in which they synthesized a
series of sounds between two adjacent phonemes, in this case
/b/ and /d/. These were presented to subjects who were asked
to identify the sound, and it was discovered that people give
categorical responses. Each sound was judged to be either /b/
or /d/, never something in between or a combination of the
two. This study shows that a physical continuum is transformed into discrete categories and, equally important, it
demonstrates that these units are not, as it were, in the world,
but rather in our construction of the world.[3]

3   Synchronic versus Diachronic

The second distinction is that between synchronic and diachronic. A synchronic study is one which addresses itself to
the relationship between a set of elements at a particular point
in time. The overriding majority of social-psychological
studies are of this type. Whether they involve an analysis of

2 The notion of categoriality is well entrenched in other, non-social areas of
   psychology, especially perception. A nice case in point is Michotte's
   (1963) work on the perception of a causality. Michotte discovered that
   people will make inferences about one object affecting the movement of
   another under certain specific conditions but not others.
3 They are not in the world because different linguistic communities make
   different phonetic distinctions; or rather, this is true for certain parts of the
   vocal spectrum. The selection of some phonemes is arbitrary, while that
   of others is not. For example, Kuhl and Miller (1975) have discovered that
   the chinchilla, which has similar auditory capacities to us, also distinguishes voiced from unvoiced plosives in a categorical fashion, and that
   the voiced-unvoiced boundary of the chinchilla is the same as that for
   humans.

subjective space through the repertory grid or multi-dimensional scaling, the ways in which expressed attitudes cluster into constellations, or the manner in which certain behaviours correlate across persons, they all tend to consider a configuration through one slice of the cake. This is equally true of longitudinal investigations which involve a comparison of configurations at different points in time. These types of studies arise out of particular questions, questions about association and correlation, and they are, therefore, suited to those types of enterprise. But it is also the case that they cannot expand our understanding of the actual process of communication. They cannot do so because, by its very nature, behaviour is diachronic. It is produced in time and made sense of within a temporal dimension. The Swiss linguist, Saussure (1916), provides a rather neat analogy of the difference between synchronic and diachronic analyses. He compares the two types of operation to the ways in which one might examine a plant stem. One way, the synchronic, would be to cut at right angles to the stem, thereby exposing the configuration of the cells. The second, the diachronic, would involve slicing along the length of the stem in order to see how the various strands alter their relations to each other. For Saussure the length of the stem represented time. Just as we can only fully understand the constitution of the stem by cutting it both ways, so too it is necessary to scrutinize behaviour, not only in terms of its structure at any point in time, but also in terms of the ways in which it unfolds, is produced and comprehended in time.

So far, I have raised two arguments, namely that the proper study of communication must adopt a unit approach, and that it needs to examine people's actions as they are temporarily constituted and responded to. These two points are of course first cousins. A unit-type approach cannot be effected without attention to time because units are, so to speak, action-slots in time, and by opting for a diachronic approach we are necessarily drawn into examining the relations between segments of action.

4   *Emic versus Etic*

The third distinction is that between 'emic' and 'etic' descriptions. These terms were coined by Pike (1967) on analogy with phonemic and phonetic. Phonemic descriptions are those which are addressed to the range and structured pattern of sounds within a language, while phonetic descriptions are concerned with the range of sounds that can be produced by the vocal apparatus, that is, those found in human language. Emic refers, therefore, to the set of distinctions that are made by the native, etic to those made by the investigator. Although the difference between these two modes of description has preoccupied linguists and anthropologists, it also has special relevance for social psychologists, particularly those concerned with the analysis of action.

Earlier I proposed that descriptions of people's social transactions should proceed by examining the ways that action segments are combined in time. It follows that any attempt to understand how they make sense of others' behaviour requires description of the ways in which they subjectively construe the combination of action units in time. But this proposal leaves us with a problem, namely how are we to decide who should specify the units. Are we to allow the investigator to designate the segments in a sequence, and are we then to assume that they are the same as those generally identified by people, or should we appeal to their intuitions in order to disclose the properties of their emic systems? Let me illustrate the dilemma.

Birdwhistell (1971) tells us that there are four discrete positions of the eyebrows, lifted brow, lowered brow, knit brow and single brow movement, the suggestion being that, whenever one or both brows move, there are four movements that can be executed. We can see that although the range of possible eyebrow positions is infinite, they may only assume a finite number of positions; and in principle we could support Birdwhistell's contention by assembling a film corpus and then coding off the positions that are assumed. For the purpose of argument let us suppose that Birdwhistell is correct and that we are able to corroborate his suggestion that there are only four discrete positions. What kind of statement would we have made? Well, we would have offered an etic description, because our analysis would have been performed from the point of view of the outsider. Birdwhistell and other students of body movement, however, occasionally make the point that their descriptions are emic. In other words, they are prepared to assume that their discriminations reflect those made by people in the course of their interactions with others.[4] While this could conceivably be the case, such equations of the emic with the etic allow a serious question to go begging and the question is: are people's phenomenal distinctions the same as those of the investigator? This could be settled by taking a leaf out of Liberman's book. Failing a more sophisticated method, we could photograph eyebrows in a variety of positions and have people sort them into categories. We might discover that the number and location of the categories tally with what Birdwhistell has to say. But equally, we could find that they only discriminate, say, three discrete positions. That is, they collapse two of Birdwhistell's etic positions. These two findings would be consistent with each other. On the one hand we would have discovered that people's eyebrows characteristically assume one of four discrete positions (an etic description), while on the other we would have discovered that they only discriminate three out of these four categories (an emic description).

Several points follow from this illustration. First of all, we can see that the emic cannot automatically be recovered, or inferred, from the etic, and there is no sense in pretending that it can. In other pursuits, such as ethology and developmental

4 Birdwhistell's kinesic notation system is sometimes thought to be emically derived, but as he himself says: 'Much of the research that went into the initial isolation of the microkinesic structure was done on behaviour captured on film for slow-motion projection and study. As each new unit was abstracted, it was tested both in multiple universes provided by . . . interactional film and in the direct observational situation' (1971, p. 101). See also Ekman's (1979) recent work on eyebrows.

psychology, the problem is compounded by the fact that the investigator does not have recourse to statements about subjective impressions. But even though the ethologist cannot ask his tame chimpanzee to describe its impressions, he can nevertheless take some comfort from the assumption that it wears a great deal of its response on its skin. In non-humans a greater proportion of the covert is made overt, and this, so we assume, allows us to infer the subjective from the objective when dealing with less sophisticated organisms. But the task of the social psychologist intent on understanding adult humans is complicated by the fact that a great deal of our behaviour involves prevarication. We feel hurt by some slight but choose not to show our feelings, or we hear an irksome acquaintance greet us but decide not to reciprocate. Not only is it the case that our actions have become emancipated from the inner world that occasionally gives rise to them, but at the same time we are capable of disguising our responses to the actions of others. The simplest upshot of all this is that the poor student of human behaviour is doubly pressed. He needs first to devise a means of describing people's actions and then he needs to check that his system conforms to that upheld by those whom he studies.

Earlier on I pointed out that an emic description need not correspond to an etic one. I also suggested that we could happily entertain two divergent descriptions of the same phenomenon in the knowledge that each arose within different terms of reference. The other point that could be made is that we should not be surprised to discover that some of our conventional wisdom about the actions of others and ourselves is less refined than that offered by the investigator who spends hours staring at video-tape or listening to pieces of looped sound tape. We should not be content with anything less than this state of affairs, and it continues to be the responsibility of the social psychologist to show that our actions are more complex than we imagine.

At this point I wish to apply the emic-etic distinction to the study of action in time. I have already noted that the ethologist is in the business of identifying units and their sequential relations, and similar procedures have been applied to the study of young children. In what remains of this paper I intend to discuss some general principles associated with the identification of units within etic and emic frameworks.

When we set about analysing the temporal constitution of a piece of behaviour we are faced with the task of discerning its underlying units. Our task is to identify the segments in the stream of behaviour. The first problem we encounter, which is in itself a version of our overriding concern, is how to bound or bracket the action sequence. It consists very simply in having to decide where to begin and where to end the analysis.[5] It is nicely illustrated in the case of the parting ritual where the investigator finds himself backtracking through the video-tape record in search of the beginning of the sequence. In some cases the problem may be solved because the investigator only possesses a piece of the record while in others it may be circumvented by defining the action in terms of its departure from a stable baseline. For example, in our work in the various motor signs used to signal affirmation and negation in Italy, the onset and termination of the movements are identified in relation to the resting position of the head (Morris et al. 1979).

Once the investigator has managed to identify the outer limits of the sequence that he wishes to analyse his next task is to segment it into units. Several authors have written on the nature of units and the principles underlying their organisation. Pike (1967), for example, identifies what he calls a behavioureme. Birdwhistell (1971) speaks of *kinemes* and their combination into *kinemorphes* and *kinemorphic constructions*. Harris (1964) refers to *actons*, Bjerg (1968) to *agons*, Scheflen

5 The problem of determining the outer temporal limits of an action sequence is similar to the business of identifying the entailments of a contract. Sacks (1963) and Garfinkel (1967) speak of the *et cetera* clause that covers explicit agreements between parties. Just as contracts carry with them certain unspecified understandings, so too the isolation of certain action frames carries with it the understanding that the action continues outside the boundaries of the segment.

(1973) to the *point* and *position* and Barker and Wright (1955) to the *behaviour unit*. By the time one has assembled the full list it is extremely difficult to see whether these various authors are talking about the same or related things.

Let us consider some of the problems that arise in the description of units. The first point I think we need to accept is that there are no natural units of behaviour. The segments that the investigator identifies will depend on his status as observer. Obviously, as a discipline develops, its members are likely to reach greater consensus, and with the introduction of workable notation systems there is the possibility of fairly good agreement among investigators. But such scientific conventions should not be taken to reflect the actual state of affairs in the world. They are, and can be, no more than a convenient means of imposing order on what is observed. There is a branch of philosophy called the philosophy of action which is concerned with just this problem. Their case is represented by Hampshire (1970) who makes the point that there is an indeterminate number of ways of describing the same objective action–sequence, and the mode of description that is selected will invariably depend on the use to which it is to be put. Just as the chef and the dietician are likely to offer quite divergent accounts of the same meal, so too the kind of description offered by the student of behaviour is likely to depend on his point of view, the question he has posed and the type of answer he hopes to extract from his material.

The second point is that even within an established framework we may discover that action units are not as immutable as we would have wished. Phonemes can be identified with reasonable, although apparently not perfect, certainty, and they and morphemes can be permuted in a wide variety of combinations. This type of transposition and juxtaposition facilitates the isolation of such units. Whether this is the case for action is not entirely clear and it still remains to be shown that segments of behaviour retain their formal identity across different contextual frames. Furthermore, it is not always clear what the unit of analysis should be. Goffman

(1976), for example, makes the point that the sentence, that unit dear to grammarians' hearts, is inappropriate for the analysis of conversational material because each speaker may use a variable number in each turn. Equally, the turn itself is an unattractive candidate for the simple reason that the talk during two different turns may function as one interactional unit. Instead he recommends what he calls the move. A move need not correspond to either a sentence or a turn, and, of course, it need not be linguistic in nature.

There are several other issues which are pertinent to any analysis of action. One involves the type of temporal baseline used. Here we could use a real-time or a fixed unit baseline and each may produce quite different models at the stage of analysis. If we use a real-time baseline we need to examine the effects of various time sampling procedures. Hayes et al. (1970) have shown that the frequency with which behaviour is sampled can have dramatic effects on the conclusions that are finally drawn.

The most important issue is that which concerns the background knowledge of the investigator. A strictly formal or non-semantic analysis can do serious damage to one's material. Clarke (1977) makes the point that, just as a librarian would not catalogue books according to their weight, so too the linguist would not dissect talk in terms of sound fluctuations. He would not do so because there may be as many sound minima within words as there are between words. Fodor et al. (1974) have suggested that one of the reasons we think that foreigners speak so quickly is that we cannot detect the pauses that they do not make. The same may apply in the case of action. Units which have quite distinct significance for the actors may be run together, and the unwitting observer may fail to recognize the junctures identified by those who share the code. All this suggests that a parsimonious segmentation cannot be effected without considering the point of view of those who produce and those to whom the action is addressed. It may well be the case that strictly motoric behaviour does not give rise to such problems, but meaningful transactions cannot be adequately handled without some knowledge of the segments and their significance for those involved.

Earlier on we offered the suggestion that etic descriptions may be at variance with emic ones. Since then we touched on some of the problems associated with identifying the terminal units in a sequence. Terminal units can occasionally be subsumed within other higher-order units to the point where the entire sequence is captured under a single node. At this juncture let us now turn to the ways in which we might attempt to uncover an emic description of a sequence. If an etic description is one offered from the investigator's point of view then it follows logically that an emic description is one provided by the native, or, in our case, the subject. The question becomes not so much, what are the units, but what are the units taken to be? This can only be answered by appealing to the intuitions of the subject.

Several methods have been used to explore the way in which people subjectively structure the behaviour of others. Dickman (1963), for example, had his subjects watch a story on film. He then presented them with a chronologically ordered set of cards describing scenes from the story and asked them to group the cards into distinct happenings. He discovered that in some cases a high proportion of his subjects agreed in their designation of the break-points. He also found that, although the subjects agreed upon certain break-points, their consensus over the actual units was rather low. Recently, Newtson (1973) has performed a series of studies along similar lines. But instead of asking his subjects to identify the break-points *post hoc*, he had them watch a film sequence and indicate, by pressing a button connected to a separate event-recorder, the point at which one action began and another ended. Newtson found that subjects produced a variable number of presses depending on the nature of the instructions.

If we consider these two methods we can see that each has its drawbacks, the first because it begs the question of what a subject's break-points and units are; the second because it cannot handle variable response latencies within and between the subjects, and because it loses track of the material to which they have addressed themselves. Recently we have developed a new parsing method which, it is hoped, circumvents some of these criticisms (McPhail and Collett 1978). The subject is asked to view a video-tape sequence, in this case someone entering the room, having coffee, performing various chores and then leaving. The subject is instructed to press a button which places a mark on the sound track of the video-tape whenever he sees the slightest change in action. Once he has viewed the sequence and placed his marks the video-tape is played back to him. On this occasion he hears his button presses and is asked to provide a description of the segment which he had identified on first viewing. This procedure gives us a list of action glosses which are recorded by the investigator. The subject is then asked to group the glosses, preferably into pairs and to work up through the groupings until all the glosses are subtended under a single node. In this way we are able to derive a record of the junctures he identified, his labels for each of the segments, and the way in which he sees the segments forming higher-order units.

Instead of selecting the segments in advance, like Dickman (1963), we have made the issue of utilization problematic, and allowed each subject to nominate his own junctures and segments. And instead of analysing subjects' marks in real time we have compared segments via their glosses. This enables us to derive a common emic baseline for a group of subjects, that is, it enables us to record the marks provided by each subject against a baseline defined by himself and others. We find that there are certain junctures which are identified more frequently than others, and that irrespective of the fineness of their discriminations people locate the boundaries of suprasegmental units in roughly the same place in the sequence. What is interesting is that these suprasegmental junctures occur within definite boundaries or 'transitional envelopes' and that certain acts are identified more readily than others as points of suprasegment onset and termination.

There are at least two types of method that can be used in order to analyse the constructions that people place on on-going behaviour. Having asked someone to view an action sequence we can either require him to identify the units while he is watching it or have him report on the units afterwards. Each procedure has its limitations; the former because it demands that the subject perform two tasks simultaneously, the latter because it relies on perfect recall. Furthermore, both methods remove the process of subjective construction from the interactive context within which it normally occurs. When we endeavour to make sense of someone else they are usually present, and in most instances doing the same. In these circumstances we seldom monitor others as an end in itself. We do not pursue knowledge for its own sake, but rather as a means to steering our own actions. Kendon (1976) has gone some way towards meeting the criticisms. He has devised a method whereby the subject is required to watch and then repeat a sequence of actions performed by the experimenter. Kendon finds that subjects impose definite limits on what they take to be the action. For example, when the experimenter performs a finger exercise and completes the sequence by placing his hands on his knees, most subjects repeat the exercise but not the terminal resting posture of the hands. This demonstrates that we have quite set opinions about the bounded character of actions. Some are seen as being bracketed together, others as being outside the sequence. Whether or not this method promises to disclose other important aspects of subjective construction remains to be seen. It certainly cannot reveal the hierarchical process of segmentation within the sequence of acts being mimed, and like other role-playing procedures, it may not be able to distinguish an inability to decode complex sequences from an inability to encode these sequences correctly.

A rather different, but related, approach to the issue of action segmentation may be found in a piece of research reported by Worth and Adair (1972). In 1966, the authors, together with Robert Chalfen, spent several weeks in a

Navaho community teaching a selected group of men and women how to use motion picture cameras. The idea was to explore the ways in which an entirely different ethnic group might impose its view of the world on to film. Six Navaho were taught how to use the cameras and editing facilities and each was then allowed to choose his or her own subject and make a short film.

The investigators concentrated on their students' selection of topics and discovered that they had clear notions of what constituted a proper theme. It emerged that the narrative style of the Navaho films, and the way they composed and juxta-posed their shots, was quite different from conventional cinematography. They found, for example, that the films were more concerned with movement, especially walking, and that there were few close-ups of the face. The former, it was suggested, reflects a cultural preoccupation with the sheer time it takes to get around, the latter a tacit understanding regarding invasion of privacy. Furthermore, the Navaho entertained quite distinct notions about how one action leads to another. Established film technique demands that when sequences depicting the same sequence of action are spliced together, they be joined 'in parallel', so that the action in one shot follows immediately on the one preceding. But instead the Navaho used the 'jump-cuts' which, to Western eyes, gives the impression of discontinuity. This the authors explained in terms of the Navaho conception of time.

The idea of using film to uncover cultural assumptions about action and movement is certainly original (the closest attempt we find to this is the analysis of children's films by Lidstone and McIntosh 1970). But from the psychologist's point of view this type of procedure stands in danger of being impressionistic. In their book, Worth and Adair go to great lengths to discount any explanation of Navaho film techniques, in terms of their inability to master the medium, but they fail to address themselves to the equally important question (which has often been debated) as to whether artistic creations, films included, actually reflect the artist's constructions about the world or merely conventional ways of viewing the world. The authors might persuade us, for example, that the Navaho use of the jump-cut is intentional, but they are less convincing in their suggestions that this tells us something about how the Navaho think when they are not making films.

I have already identified several problems associated with emic analysis of action sequences. Beyond these, there are other issues which deserve a mention. The first is that all action is multi-channel, and although various modalities can be isolated and handled within an etic framework, this is less so within an emic analysis. The patient investigator will always be able to discern more than the hurried subject who must reach a decision without the benefit of play-back facilities. Furthermore, as noted, the kinds of units that are identified in an etic description will inevitably depend on the purpose underlying that description. It seems just as likely that the experimental instructions and the disposition and interest of the subject, not to mention the sense that he makes of the study, will affect the type of criteria he brings to bear.

The nature of the material being gathered needs to be seriously considered. We assume all along that when someone observes the actions of another he automatically segments the stream into units, and so on. We also assume that by asking him to parse the sequence for us we somehow manage to externalise this subjective process. We are happy to assume that the segmentations he offers us within the confines of our study are probably those that he would have identified elsewhere. But here, as in other simulated interactions, it is important to remember that this assumption cannot be supported. Our subjects are often cast in the role of third party to the interaction. They come to the material cold and in most cases never experience those feelings that are aroused in the real situation.

5   *Conclusion*

The ways in which people segment and make sense of the actions of others represents an important area of study, one which we are likely to pursue for a long time to come. It is to be expected that in the early stages of the enterprise we should encounter serious theoretical and methodological problems. Some of these may prove to be intractable. They may arise out of our very attempts to interfere with the process whereby people make sense of behaviour. But undoubtedly there are others which, through the exercise of imagination and a proper respect for our subject matter, we will be able to solve.

References

A. Bain, 1859, *The Emotions and the Will*, London: J. W. Parker & Sons

R. G. Barker and H. F. Wright, 1955, *Midwest and Its Children*, New York: Harper & Row

R. Birdwhistell, 1971, *Kinesics and Context*, London: Allen Lane

K. Bjerg, 1968, 'Interplay Analysis', *Acta Psychologica*, Vol. 28, pp. 201–245

D. D. Clarke, 1977, 'Rules and Sequences in Conversation', in: P. Collett (Ed.), *Social Rules and Social Behaviour*, Oxford: Blackwell

H. R. Dickman, 1963, 'The Perception of Behavioural Units', in: R. G. Barker (Ed.), *The Stream of Behaviour*, New York: Appleton-Century-Crofts

S. Duncan, 1969, 'Nonverbal Communication', *Psychological Bulletin*, Vol. 72, pp. 118–137

P. Ekman, 1979, 'About Brows: Emotional and Conversational Signals', in: J. Aschoff, M. von Cranach, I. Eibl-Eibersfeldt and W. Lepenies (Eds.), *Human Ethology*, London: Cambridge University Press

J. A. Fodor, T. G. Bever and M. F. Garrett, 1974, *The Psychology of Language*, New York: MacGraw-Hill

H. Garfinkel, 1967, *Studies in Ethnomethodology*, Englewood Cliffs, N.J.: Prentice-Hall

E. Goffman, 1976, *Replies and Responses, Language in Society, Vol. 5*, pp. 257–313

E. T. Hall, 1966, *The Hidden Dimension*, New York: Doubleday

S. Hampshire, 1970, *Thought and Action*, London: Chatto & Windus

M. Harris, 1964, *The Nature of Cultural Things*, New York: Random House

D. P. Hayes, L. Meltzer and G. Wolf, 1970, 'Substantive Conclusions are Dependent upon Techniques of Measurement', *Behavioural Science*, Vol. 15, pp. 265–268

W. James, 1890, *The Principles of Psychology*, New York: Henry Holt

A. Kendon, 1976, 'Differential Perception and Attentional Frame in Face-to-Face Interaction', paper presented at the 75th annual meeting of the American Anthropological Association, Washington, D.C.

P. K. Kuhl and J. D. Miller, 1975, 'Speech Perception by the Chinchilla: The Voiced-Voiceless Distinction in Alveolar Plosive Consonants', *Science*, Vol. 190, pp. 69–72

A. M. Liberman, K. C. Harris, M. S. Hoffman and B. C. Griffith, 1957, 'The Discrimination of Speech Sounds within and across Phoneme Boundaries', *Journal of Experimental Psychology*, Vol. 54, pp. 358–368

J. Lidstone and D. McIntosh, 1970, *Children as Filmmakers*, New York: Van Nostrand Reinhold

J. Lyons, 1956, 'The Perception of Human Actions', *Journal of General Psychology*, Vol. 54, pp. 45–55

D. Morris, P. Collett, P. Marsh and M. O'Shaughnessy, 1979, *Gestures: Their Origins and Distribution*, London: Jonathan Cape

P. McPhail and P. Collett, 1978, 'Parsing and the Perception of Behavioural Units', unpublished paper, Oxford University

A. Michotte, 1963, *The Perception of Causality*, London: Methuen

D. Newtson, 1973, 'Attribution and the Unit of Perception of Ongoing Behaviour', *Journal of Personality and Social Psychology*, Vol. 28, pp. 28–38

K. Pike, 1967, *Language in Relation to a Unified Theory of the Structure of Human Behaviour*, The Hague: Mouton

H. Sacks, 1963, 'On Sociological Description', *Berkeley Journal of Sociology*, Vol. 8, pp. 1–16

F. de Saussure, 1916, *Cours de Linguistique Générale*, Paris: Payot

A. Scheflen, 1973, *How Behaviour Means*, New York: Gordon and Breach

S. Worth and J. Adair, 1972, *Through Navaho Eyes: An Exploration in Film Communication and Anthropology*, Bloomington: Indiana University Press

An Analysis of Communicative Action

JENS ALLWOOD   *University of Gothenburg*

1 *Introduction*

This paper has a double purpose. On the one hand, I want to discuss some properties of communicative action and try to state some of the components in a model of communication. On the other hand, I want to try to show how these properties and components can be used to give an analysis of the verbs of communication as a semantic field.

I use the label 'verbs of communication' to designate verbs of the following type: *warn, admit, threaten, state, deny, request, guess* and *assert*. All of these are verbs which refer to some aspect of an interaction between persons which at least partly involves communication. The term 'verbs of communication' has been chosen rather than the otherwise common term 'speech act verbs' since those aspects of communication to which the verbs refer are far from always connected with speech. One can quite well warn, threaten, request, reject and order without using speech or even gestures with conventional meaning. Without any set conventional significance, a fist raised spontaneously as though to strike can by virtue of its natural connections with anger and pain be quite sufficient to threaten somebody.

Before I continue I would like to say a few words about the method I use in order to achieve the two purposes I have mentioned above. I think the method illustrates quite well a common procedure among linguists which can be called the linguistic phenomenological observational method. The purpose of this method is to make explicit as much as possible of one's intuitive common sense knowledge about a certain phenomenon. In this case, the phenomenon in question is communication. At least the following stages can be distinguished analytically in the application of this method:

1. I am interested in communication and want to know something more precise and explicit about this phenomenon. I increase my insights by:

(i) analysing the meaning of a subset of all the expressions of everyday language which refer to aspects of communicative activities,

(ii) trying to become conscious of my own ideas concerning how one communicates,

(iii) making unsystematic observations of how people I meet conduct themselves in order to communicate.

2. I start to put together my insights from these three sources of knowledge and construct a tentative model for certain aspects of what it is to communicate.

3. I start to test and extend my model by:

(i) sharpening my intuitions about communicative activities, by formalizing or quantifying aspects of the model or by providing explicit or operational definitions of certain concepts,

(ii) making more systematic observations of the communication of others. Both non-interfering observation and experimental observation can be used here,

(iii) last, but not least, exposing my model to renewed conceptual testing by taking more of the expressions of everyday language for communicative activities into account and by seeing whether what I know about the meaning of these words matches the underlying parameters for communication with which I work in my model.

4. One or more of these steps is repeated, yielding, first, a better understanding of communication and, secondly, a better lexical analysis of the terms of communication in everyday language.

Thus, the methodology espoused is a very pluralistic one, making simultaneous use of experimentation, observation, formalization, lexical analysis and also computer simulation. As far as I can see there is no evidence to indicate that these methods may not be combined. On the contrary, a methodological pluralism of this type seems to be supported by two underlying assumptions which, to me, seem fruitful in the study of language and communication. The first is that scientific thinking differs from everyday thinking only by gradual refinement, and the other is that there is no sharp distinction to be drawn between meaning and belief.[1] These two assumptions are quite in harmony with a phenomeno-logically based investigation if one allows a place for the scientific refinement of intuition, i.e., no ontological chasm is imposed between the world of common sense reality and the analysis and explanation of phenomena in this world. The assumption concerning the relationship between meaning and belief allows an investigation of common sense beliefs starting in language, i.e., no clear line is drawn between lexical analysis and an analysis of the phenomena being designated by the linguistic expressions.

The analysis presented in this paper is at a relatively early stage in the research programme, which has been outlined above, and has been carried out entirely within the confines of the above-mentioned linguistic phenomenological observa-tional method. The later stages of more explicit formalization and experimentation have not yet been attempted. However, I think the analysis presented here has some value in that it opens a fruitful but infrequently utilized perspective on lin-guistic communication to linguists and others interested in communication.

1 See Quine (1960) for an elaborate defence of this view.

2   Communication as Action and Cooperation

The fundamental traits of this perspective are arrived at by viewing communication as a type of action and cooperation. Action should here be perceived as intentional behaviour directed towards a certain goal. Behaviour which is not intentional, as, for example, patellar reflexes or breathing, is therefore not viewed as action.[2]

In order to investigate the factors which are relevant for our conception of a certain type of action, it is often helpful to study the 'felicity conditions' of the action concerned; that is to say those conditions which have to be met so that the action may be considered ideally felicitous.

Intuitions about ideal felicity are perhaps hard to swallow for those with a positivistic inclination, but to some extent such intuitions can be justified by attempts at behaving infelicitously with regard to the conditions given below. The reactions of other persons should then provide indirect support for the existence of the conditions if the intuitions are correct.

Below I list some of the conditions which a communicative action must meet in order to be felicitous. Some of these conditions are not unique to communicative actions but apply to action in general.

(i) Intentionality and voluntariness: The behaviour should be voluntary and intentional. Within the framework of this paper those intentions which are connected with communication are of special interest and they will therefore be treated below in section 4.

(ii) Rationality: The action should be 'adequate', i.e., as effective and efficient as possible and 'competent',[3] i.e., should only be performed if there is a likelihood of success. Actions which are not intentional and rational in the sense intended

---

2 For a more thorough analysis of the relation between action and behaviour see Allwood (1976, Chapter 2).

3 The concept of adequacy and competence are presented more carefully in Allwood (1976, Chapter 5).

here are likely to be seen as irrational or even irresponsible, and can be subject to social sanctions, thus giving some support for the status of rationality and intentionality as felicity conditions.

(iii) Ethical considerations: Perhaps the most important ethical requirement of communication is genuineness. Senders should possess those feelings, attitudes or intentions which are usually connected with the behaviour of the sender on natural or conventional grounds by a receiver. For example, my questions should express my desire for information and my statements should express what I believe to be true. Here, common sanctions against dishonesty and deceit provide support for genuineness as a condition of felicity. But there are also ethical considerations which bear on communication. In general, the consequences of the so-called 'golden rule' – Do unto others what you would have them do unto you – seems to apply with as great a force to communicative behaviour as to other behaviour. An analysis of the forms of politeness in ordinary language provides some illustration of this.[4]

(iv) The form of the behaviour: Communicative behaviour should be conventionally correct with regard to (a) the correspondence between units of expression and desired content (lexical conventions)[5] and (b) the joining together of units of expression to form bigger units (syntax). Furthermore, the behaviour must sometimes possess other traits, as, for example, a certain speed or strength of movement. In general, one can view the form of the behaviour as a result of the co-ordination of sequential and simultaneous aspects of behaviour.

(v) Relation to context: The behaviour should be adapted to context with regard to both its external form and to the content it expresses (e.g., feelings, attitudes, subject matter or intentions to affect). Certain contents can only be expressed in certain contexts.

4 See Aijmer (1977) and Brown and Levinson (1978). In both these papers it becomes clear that ethics and rationality play a role in politeness.
5 Expression and content are here used in the sense of Hjelmslev (1943).

(vi) Success: In order to be felicitous the purpose of an action must be achieved. For a communicative action this usually means that a sender, by transferring information to a receiver, is able to affect the receiver in the way he had intended. For some communicative actions, however, the main purpose seems to be to achieve a certain social effect. Paradigm examples of this are communicative actions which are performed with the help of institutionalized performative expressions of the type *I baptize* or *I excommunicate.*

By contemplating these six types of felicity conditions and possibly some more we arrive at a host of relevant facts and conclusions about communicative actions. Some of these conclusions seem to me especially important and will therefore be discussed below.

3   Criteria of Communicative Action

The first conclusion concerns the criteria we use to identify a certain communicative action or analogously the criteria we use to determine the correct application of a certain term of communicative action. These criteria cannot be identical to the felicity conditions since an action can very well occur without being completely felicitous. One can for example give an order which is ignored or warn somebody without having intended to do so. The order and the warning are not ideally felicitous but can in spite of this be said to have occurred.

How should the identification criteria of a communicative action be characterized? (If one preferred to see matters from a purely linguistic perspective one could ask here: How should the application criteria of a certain term of communication be characterized?) Unfortunately, it does not seem to be possible to give a simple answer to any of these two variants of the question. There seem to be at least four different factors which can be used to identify a certain action. Furthermore, it seems to hold that each of the four factors is sufficient without it being true that any one of these factors is necessary to identify certain actions.

I think this laxness with regard to which factors can be used to identify a communicative action is connected with a lack of clarity in our ordinary concept of action, i.e., it is not clear with respect to ordinary actions and action-terminology what the essential properties of an action are supposed to be. It is possible to speculate that this is one of the reasons behind disagreements between behaviouristic and mentalistic accounts of action. We have intuitions about action which support both types of analysis. As we will see, one of the consequences of this lack of clarity in our ordinary concept of action is that several of the verbs of communication can be claimed to be ambiguous.

The four factors which most commonly seem to be used to identify behaviour as a certain type of action are:
(i) the intentional phenomena governing the behaviour,
(ii) the form of the behaviour (conventional or non-conventional),
(iii) the result which is achieved through the behaviour,
(iv) the context in which the behaviour occurs.

As we see, these four factors of identification are related to the felicity conditions (i), (iv), (vi) and (v). This is what one should expect since an ideal occurrence of an action should be a special case of the general occurrence of that action, i.e., an action does not need to be felicitous to occur.

It should also be made clear that the four factors are criteria of identification but not necessarily of identity.[6] They are properties which we use to ascertain the presence of a certain phenomenon but they are not necessarily, therefore, the properties of the phenomenon which give it its identity. For example, the context sometimes makes it possible for us to identify an action without it being true that the context is an essential property of the action itself.

6 The utility of this distinction has been explored in Ballmer (1976) in terms of a distinction between ontic and epistemic criteria. However, the philosophical problem of deciding whether or not proposed ontic criteria really make up a subset of the possible epistemic criteria remains.

The first type of identification is dependent on the intentions and purposes an agent is attributing to his behaviour irrespective of whether these are achieved or not. This type of identification can, therefore, be used before the purpose that a certain action is intended to achieve has been achieved. A carpenter can, for example, be said to be producing a chair before it is finished.

The form of the behaviour is used for identification especially when the behaviour follows a conventional pattern. For example a rhetorical question can be said to be a question by virtue of its conventional form even if it is not at all intended as a question but rather as a statement.

The third type of identification uses the actual result of the behaviour and does not at all need to consider the kind of action that an agent is intending to perform. For example, a farmer is cultivating his land in the most modern way with chemical fertilizers and insecticides in order to get as big a harvest as possible. One of the results of his activities is environmental pollution. It now seems to be in accordance with normal linguistic usage to claim that what the farmer is doing is to pollute the environment. An identification of action of this third type thus relies completely on the interpretation that an observer or the agent himself can give of the actual effects of a certain behaviour, irrespective of whether this interpretation corresponds to the real intentions of the agent.

The fourth type of identification makes it possible to identify a certain type of behaviour by using the context within which it occurs. Identifying something as an *answer* illustrates this. It seems possible to consider any verbal utterance which follows a question as an answer. For example sentence (2) below, despite its irrelevance, could be said to be an answer to sentence (1), since sentence (1) is a question.

(1) What time is it?
(2) I have a stomach ache.

There are, of course, other more restricted notions of answering for which more than 'just following a question' would be required. Notice here how the different notions of answering illustrate the importance of context for identity and identification. With a very lax notion of *answer*, the question-context would be sufficient to allow any following verbal utterance to be called an answer. If, in addition, one claimed that something like a question was necessary for the occurrence of an answer – an answer presupposes something to be answered (a problem or a question) – the tie between a question and a subsequent verbal utterance with regard to its status as an answer would be analytic. The question-context would then be one of the identity-requirements for lax answers as well as an identification criterion. However, this would not be the case with a more substantial notion of *answer*, where a question could help to identify a certain verbal utterance as an answer thereby giving the utterance its identity.

The four criteria of identification which have just been mentioned clearly differ in epistemological status. While all four criteria are, in principle, available to the agent performing the action to be identified, only the latter three are available to an outside observer. As is well known this provides one of the strongest motivating forces for those who hold that an inter-subjective account of human action can only be given in behavioural terms. But since it seems very difficult if not impossible to give an interesting account of human action in non-intentional terms, I think, intentionality is a phenomenon we must accept. Intentionality seems to have not only a special epistemological status but also a special ontological status with regard to human action (see von Wright 1971).

Thus, as observers, we must accept the double task of finding identification criteria both for actions and for intentions, while as performing agents our intentions are at least sometimes, but by no means always, directly available. To the extent that intentions can have a low degree of consciousness, or may even be subconscious, the agent will have an identification problem which is similar to that of the observer.

Let me now return to the four proposed factors in order to illustrate how, on the one hand, they can be used to provide an explanation of how a sentence out of context can be regarded as several clearly differentiated communicative actions,[7] and, on the other, how many verbs of communication can be claimed to exhibit a systematic ambiguity with regard to them. As an illustration of the first phenomenon we consider sentence (3) below (context free).

(3) It is slippery outside.

Many different intentions could be associated with the use of (3), for example the intention to warn or to inform. Using the type of identification relying on intention, (3) will then be a *warning* or a *statement*. If we use instead the conventional form of the sentence – the indicative – we may want to classify the sentence as a *statement*. If we use the reaction which could have been aroused in some receiver upon hearing the sentence we might choose instead to say that the sentence was used to *frighten* the receiver. Finally, we could quite well classify the sentence as an *answer* if it occurred after a question.

As an illustration of the second phenomenon we will consider a certain type of systematic ambiguity in the verbs of communication which is produced because the obscurity in our concept of action arises especially often with regard to a result interpretation and an intention interpretation. Consider the sentences (4) and (5) below.

(4) I warned Bill but he did not even hear me.

(5) I warned Bill without intending to do so.

In (4) it is my intention to warn Bill which gives me the right to claim that I have warned him. In (5) it is the fact that the result of my action was that Bill was warned which gives me the same right.

4   *Intentionality*

Very much of our thinking about action and communication presupposes the notion of intentionality. In the discussion

---

7 For the reader who is acquainted with the linguistic literature of the last twenty years there should be no difficulties in remembering a host of examples of this type. See especially those examples which have been discussed in connection with the so-called performative hypothesis.

above I have certainly taken intentionality to be perhaps the most important notion, even if I admit that not all traits of our common sense thinking about action and communication point to this. However, it seems important to study in a little more detail how intentionality plays a role in communication. Below, therefore, I will outline what seem to me to be some of the most crucial features of intentionality in communication.[8]

First, there is the concept of a communicative act itself. I would like to define a *communicative act* as an *occurrence of behaviour* connected with a *parcel of communicative intentions*. Maybe the first thing to note about this definition is that it allows a communicative act to be associated with several different intentions, i.e., with a parcel of intentions. Some consideration of the following example of a dialogue or of other, similar, examples will make it clear that such multi-intentionality is the normal case in communication.

(6) A: Stop flirting with my wife.
    B: I've got something in my eye.
    A: I know you are lying.

We see here that there are many ways of construing A's first remark. For example, it could be a request and an accusation. B's first remark qualifies as a statement, an extenuation and an explanation. A's second remark could be a statement, an objection and a renewed accusation. The point here is that many so-called speech act labels fit one and the same communicative act simultaneously. There are at least two reasons for this. One has already been discussed above. The ordinary concept of action makes it possible for an observer to classify an utterance from many different points of view, some of them having nothing to do with intentions, and we will see in section 5 how the semantics of communicative expressions help to preserve this possibility by making the perspective through which a certain communicative action is designated a

8 A more detailed argument about some of the features can be found in Allwood (1976).

part of the meaning of the expression.

The other reason is that, even if we view a communicative act from a wholly intentional perspective, the same act can be compatible with many different intentions. For example, the intentions to state, object, and accuse are all compatible with A's second utterance. To the extent that the multiple of compatible intentions is not just a product of the observer's interpretation, the agent can then be said to have several different intentions associated with one and the same communicative act.

Logically, mutually compatible intentions associated with one act of behaviour can be structured in two ways. They can be subordinate to each other, as when I state in order to object, or coordinate, as when I simultaneously object and accuse. Parcels of intentions are thus assumed to be complex structures of mutually compatible intentions which are either coordinate or subordinate. It is also possible that a parcel of intentions could contain incompatible intentions but such intentions would then be associated with seemingly irrational behaviour.

Let me now continue by taking a look at the three major types of intentionality which, I suggest, are connected with communication.

I

First there are intentions connected with the *content communicated.* I suggest that the following three dimensions of content are useful to consider.

The expressive dimension: By the expressive content of a communicative act is meant the information a sender gives about his *physical* and *social* identity and the information he gives about his *emotions* and *attitudes.* Both interpersonal and cognitive attitudes are meant to be included, where cognitive attitudes are such things as beliefs, desires and hopes. Thus, the expressive content of a communicative act is not always intentional since it is easy to see that one could betray one's emotions, attitudes, social and physical status unintentionally. But they could also be communicated intentionally. To the extent that a sender betrays this type of information unintentionally to a receiver, he functions as a natural sign.[9] The expressive dimension of content thus encompasses most of the information that a sender expresses in his communicative acts. However, there are two types of information which seem important to me, which are not included in the expressive dimension. They are both, of course, also expressed in some sense by the sender, but play a sufficiently independent role to merit attention as separate dimensions of content.

The evocative dimension: The first of these dimensions is the evocative dimension. By *evoking* in this context I mean the intention to influence another person through communication. In communicating we normally intend to influence other persons in many different respects. At the very least we want them to notice, *apprehend* or attend to some information. But very commonly we also want to influence their *understanding, emotions, attitudes* (including beliefs) and *behaviour*. Sometimes we want to influence other persons in several ways simultaneously. For example, if I make an objection I might intend the other person, first, to notice a certain fact, secondly, to understand that the fact contradicts a belief he has expressed, thirdly, to change his belief, and, fourthly, to admire my acumen. Thus, it is easy to see how evocative intentions can be hierarchically embedded in each other in the accordion-like fashion described above.

The obligative dimension: The obligative dimension is intended to capture what I take to be the most important intuition behind Austin's (1962) notion of performative utterances. The intuition is that social obligations are created by communication. Communicative acts commit you to social consequ-

9 See Grice (1975) for a discussion of the concepts of natural and non-natural meaning.

ences. Some of these social consequences are connected with communication by strong conventional ties; some are not. Sentence moods such as the indicative, the interrogative and the imperative and institutionalized performatives provide examples of the conventionally created obligations I have in mind.

It is important to stress that the expressive, evocative and obligative dimensions of content are only distinct analytically and that, *de facto*, they always occur together in one and the same act. Let me illustrate this by analysing the dimensions of content of an indicative sentence used as a statement.

(7) It's five o'clock.

The expressive dimension of the content of the act performed by (7) is an attempt to express one of the sender's beliefs. The evocative dimension of the act is an attempt to influence the receiver's system of beliefs and the obligative dimension of the act is an attempt to take responsibility for a certain representation of reality. Thus, one makes a statement in order to take responsibility for an expressed belief which one intends the receiver to accept as his own.

II

But the content communicated is only one of the intentional phenomena that seem to play a role in communication. A different type of intentionality is associated with what I would like to call *communicative status*. Under this heading I want to discuss two types of phenomena.

Communicative awareness: A sender can transmit information with varying degrees of intentionality. This variation in the degree of intentionality I refer to as communicative awareness.

Although communicative awareness is a matter of degree, I would like to suggest that it is useful to distinguish the following three stages.

A   Indication: A sender functions as an *indicator* of information if he has no intention of transmitting the information an observer picks up from him at all, i.e., he functions as a natural sign.

B   Displaying: A sender is displaying information if he acts in order to make a receiver aware of the information.

C   Signalling: A sender signals information if he intends that the receiver should apprehend the information and further realize that it is displayed to him by the sender.

Indication is the level of no communicative awareness. Displaying is the lowest stage of communicative awareness where the sender is trying to bring something to a receiver's attention. It is only with signalling that we reach what I would claim to be normal communicative awareness, where a receiver is intended to be aware that a certain sender is communicating to him. This is the type of communicative awareness I think we find in normal linguistic communication.

Even though these distinctions might seem simple they have sometimes been overlooked. Thus, in Bühler (1934) both an instinctive reflexive reaction and the utterance *I am in pain* as responses to the infliction of pain would be classed as examples of what Bühler called the symptom[10] function. In the present framework the reflexive reaction would be classified as an expressive indication of emotion while the utterance would be classified as an expressive signal of belief (and possibly also of emotion). The differences and similarities between the two responses in both communicative status and content would thus be brought out more clearly.

Prominence of information: The second phenomenon relating to communicative status that I would like to discuss is prominence of information. By this term is meant the news-value, importance or interest that the various parts of an utterance

10 In Bühler (1934) the following three main functions of linguistic communication are given: 1. The symptom function – information pertaining to the speaker. 2. The symbol function – information pertaining to the world. 3. The signal function – information pertaining to the hearer.

have in relation to each other. Some information is regarded by the speaker as more important. This is, therefore, put in the foreground by means such as word order, intonation or special morphemes. Other information is seen as less important. This is kept in the background by similar means. Often terms such as *focus* and *comment* or *theme* are used to refer to parts or all of the information which is foregrounded. Terms such as *presupposed, topic* or *theme* have been used for that information which is in the background.

It is possible that there is a relation between communicative awareness and prominence of information, so that the information which is foregrounded is the information of which one has the greatest degree of awareness.

III

Besides content and communicative status there is a third type of intentionality involved in communication which I would like to refer to as *instrumental*. Instrumental intentionality is what connects the various types of content and communicative status with overt behaviour. The connection is achieved through a successive integration of simultaneous and sequential verbal and non-verbal elements of behaviour. On the verbal side the three main parameters are word order, morphology and prosody. On the non-verbal side there are movements of the head, face, shoulders, arms, hands and feet, non-verbal sounds such as grunts, snorts and hisses and finally various effects of touch, smell, taste and spatial positioning.

Thus, to summarize, I suggest that there are three main types of intentionality involved in communication: the first having to do with content, the second with communicative status and the third with instrumentality. There are three main dimensions of content: expression, evocation and obligation and there are two aspects of communicative status: communicative awareness and prominence of information.

Now I would like to make some brief comments about how this account of communicative intentionality compares with Bühler's account of speech functions, Austin's account of the locutionary, illocutionary and perlocutionary dimensions of meaning and Grice's account of non-natural meaning and conversational maxims. (For more detailed arguments in support of several of these comments see Allwood (1976, 1977).)

In Bühler's account of speech functions, what I have called communicative status and the obligative dimension of content are not considered. Bühler's functions (see footnote 10) relate in a more general fashion to the speaker, hearer and subject matter than is the case in my analysis. In one respect I have been more general than Bühler. I have lumped his symbol and sympton functions into one category – the expressive dimension – since it seems to me that the symbol function is always mediated by the sender's beliefs and attitudes.

In comparison with Austin's account of meaning, perhaps the most noticeable difference is that his central notion – illocutionary force – is in my account split up into the three dimensions of expression, evocation and obligation. His notion of perlocution, at least in my interpretation of this concept, very closely corresponds to what I would call the actually evoked response. Locutionary meaning has not been treated in the account so far provided but would be dealt with in the context of how various dimensions of content are codified as conventional meaning. In Austin's, just as in Bühler's, account there is no treatment of what I have called communicative status.

With regard to Grice, his ideas about the notion of non-natural meaning have been, perhaps, the most important source of inspiration in developing the concept of communicative awareness. An important difference between my account and Grice's is that the problem of conventional meaning has explicitly been left out of my discussion. Finally, I have also drawn upon Grice's ideas about conversational maxims in the discussion of felicity conditions above.

In closing this section I would like briefly to remark on the

relationship between felicity conditions, identification/
identity criteria and the intentional parameters of a communicative act that I have discussed above. The six mentioned
felicity considerations are intentionality and voluntariness,
rationality, ethical considerations, form of the behaviour,
relation to context and success. The four suggested identification criteria are intentionality, form of the behaviour,
achieved result and contextual cues. If one wants a distinction
between criteria that identify and criteria that give identity, it
seems that the three first identification criteria would also be
acceptable as identity criteria.

All but two of the felicity conditions, namely, rationality
and ethics, have been made criteria of identification. It is
possible that these two types of condition will also be needed
as identification criteria in a more extended analysis. For
example, it seems difficult to do justice to the difference
between threatening and promising without bringing in ethical considerations. One commits oneself to something which
is in the interest of a receiver by promising him something, but
one commits oneself to something which is against his interests by threatening him. Thus, to determine whether a certain
communicative act is to count as a promise or a threat, we have
to determine whether the action a sender commits himself to is
in the receiver's best interest[11] or not.

As for the intentional parameters mentioned, they are all, of
course, related to intentionality. But they are also, in so far as
they are connected with achieved purposes, related to result,
where the result can be both of a social institutional kind and of
a more private kind. Instrumental intentionality is particularly
closely related to the form of behaviour and to the way in
which behaviour is contextually adapted. In fact, with regard
to the relationship between external behaviour and intentionality one could say that behavioural commands are hierarchically organised from content by way of communicative status

---

11 I leave aside the problem of whether what is relevant is actual best
  interests or the interests sender and receiver take to be their best interests.

to instrumental intentionality, which then determines the external form of behaviour.

5   The Semantic Parameters of Verbs of Communication

Another conclusion which a study of the felicity conditions of communicative action seems to justify can perhaps be expressed in the following manner. Verbs of communication do not usually refer to a communicative action *in toto* but rather they could be said to refer to certain definite aspects of a communicative action from a certain perspective.[12]

The aspects of communicative actions which seem to be relevant for capturing the referential orientation of the verbs of communication are all related to the felicity conditions, identification criteria and intentional parameters. Below, I will exemplify how these aspects can be used to organize a semantic field for the verbs of communication. The fact that the aspects can be used in this way provides confirmation that they play an important role in our conception of communication. They can be used as semantic parameters in a conceptual field where verbs of communication are organized according to their referential orientation and they can be used as components in the model of communicative action which I have tried to outline above.

The semantic parameters should be regarded as features of the meaning of the verb rather than as class labels for a class of verbs. In other words, one verb will be related to several of the semantic parameters. Often one parameter will be more central than the others. This is the aspect of a communicative act which the verb primarily designates. But there will always be contexts in which the verb can be made to designate other aspects. If such other aspects seem relevant the verb will be listed several times. The list of semantic parameters is not exhaustive. This also applies to the verbs[13] which are men-

12 For a similar view of verbs as perspective inducing see Fillmore (1977).
13 As a source for verbs I have used the Merriam Webster Dictionary (Webster 1964).

tioned in connection with the various parameters. The purpose of the account is exemplification.

A   THE INSTRUMENTAL BEHAVIOURAL PARAMETER

Here we find verbs which are primarily oriented towards the external behavioural side of communication. The verbs are oriented towards both conventionally and non-conventionally regulated aspects of the organization of the behaviour.

(i) *Purely phonetic orientation*: whistle, lisp, mutter, mumble, snort, sniff, sigh, grunt, gasp, gurgle (and, bridging the gap to the animal kingdom, bark and neigh).

(ii) *Linguistic phonetic orientation*: shout, whisper, bellow, scream.

(iii) *Syntactic orientation*: state, question, request. The verbs are taken here to indicate the mood-forms indicative, interrogative and imperative, which in the paradigm cases are connected with the communicative acts designated by the verbs. The verbs will appear again below under other semantic parameters, since their referential orientation is by no means limited to syntactic organization.

(iv) *Orientation to lack of organization*: babble, stammer, chatter, stutter, prattle.

B   THE PARAMETER OF INFORMATION ORGANIZATION

The verbs which have been related to this parameter have all to do with the way the information is organized, either in terms of logical relations or in terms of prominence of information. Almost all of the verbs function as technical terms in linguistics. Refer, predicate, stress, emphasize, focus, presuppose, imply, entail, suggest, hint, highlight, indicate.

C   THE EXPRESSIVE PARAMETER

The verbs which are related to this parameter denote actions which charateristically express a certain emotion or attitude.[14] However, many verbs which are listed under this category are not primarily oriented towards an expressive aspect. This is due to the fact that emotions and attitudes seldom seem to be used to identify an action. Maybe this is because the relation between external behaviour and emotion or attitude is not one to one. One and the same behaviour can express several different emotions or attitudes and a certain emotion or attitude can be expressed through several different types of behaviour. Below are a number of examples of how emotional states or attitudes can be associated with characteristic expressive actions or expressive types of behaviour.

Fatigue:	yawn, sigh
Dissatisfaction:	groan, whimper, swear, complain, grumble
Sorrow:	cry, wail, sigh
Belief:	state, assert, claim
Curiosity:	question, enquire
Wish:	order, request, beseech
Dislike:	accuse, blame, criticize, condemn

D   THE EVOCATIVE PARAMETER

The verbs which can be related to this parameter fall into two groups: first, those verbs which are oriented towards a *result* – an actually evoked reaction in the receiver, irrespective of whether this reaction was intended or not, and, secondly, those verbs which are more oriented towards the *intention to affect* a receiver, irrespective of whether the receiver is affected or not. The result verbs have much in common with Austin's perlocutionary verbs, but the status of the second group is more uncertain in relation to Austin's framework. For the second group of verbs it holds that the relation between a communicative action and an evoked reaction is not one to

14 Actions which manifest physical or social characteristics have been left out for convenience. Further, expressively relevant activity which is not acoustic, such as blushing, has also been omitted.

one. A certain reaction can be evoked by many different communicative actions and a certain communicative action can give rise to many different reactions. Just as with the expressive aspect, this has as a consequence that many verbs can be related to several different evoked reactions. It is also possible, even if not necessary, for result verbs to be used about intentional actions and for verbs with an intentional orientation to be used about achieved results.

1. *Result verbs – orientation towards actually evoked reaction:*
Irritate, surprise, astound, shock, anger, frighten, scare, convince.

2. *Verbs with orientation towards intended reaction:*

Evocation of belief:	state, assert, lie
Evocation of admiration:	boast
Evocation of informative answer:	question, interrogate
Evocation of irritation:	tease, irritate
Evocation of alertness to danger:	warn, threaten

E THE OBLIGATING PARAMETER

The verbs connected with this parameter all designate actions which create social obligations. Most of these occur in institutionalized contexts but some occur in everyday life.

Judicial:	accuse, sentence, testify, appeal
Religious:	bless, baptize, excommunicate, swear
Everyday:	state, recommend, ask, request, advise

F THE CONTEXTUAL ORIENTATION PARAMETER

Verbs which are connected with this parameter denote communicative acts whose occurrence is bound to very specific contexts. The notion of context is taken in a wide sense to include both the sender's and the receiver's history of interaction, the physical and social environment and those beliefs of the sender and the receiver which can influence their communication. Some typical examples of contexts are given below.

(i) *Discourse context:*

Preceding argument: draw a conclusion, conclude

Preceding discourse: repeat, quote

Preceding suggestion: approve, accept, reject

(ii) *Presupposition and expectations:*

Negatively evaluated action on the part of the speaker: apologize

Negatively evaluated action on the part of the hearer: blame, accuse

Sensitive content: confide

Superior social status: command, order

(iii) *Physical surroundings:* show, point

6   Conclusion

By reflecting on the felicity conditions of communicative actions and the application criteria for verbs of communication, I have tried to draw conclusions about the criteria we use to identify communicative actions, on the one hand, and about what fundamental dimensions there are underlying communicative actions, especially with regard to intentionality, on the other. I have used these dimensions to sketch how the semantic field of verbs of communication could be analysed. The paper as a whole can be seen as an attempt to show how an analysis of communicative acts based on observation and conceptual analysis can be combined with a lexical analysis of the verbs of communication. I think that such attempts are important if one wants a correct picture of communication, since they allow one to tap the enormous sources of implicit knowledge we have about everyday communication from a very natural starting point – our intuitions about everyday linguistic expressions for communication. We should not neglect to make use of this implicit knowledge before we start hypotheses which are worth while investigating before one starts rigid formalization or empirical surveys.

References

K. Aijmer, 1977, 'Acts of Deference and Authority', *Gothenburg Papers in Theoretical Linguistics, No. 34*, Department of Linguistics, University of Gothenburg

J. Allwood, 1976, 'Linguistic Communication as Action and Co-operation', Department of Linguistics, University of Gothenburg

J. Allwood, 1977, 'A Critical Look at Speechact Theory', in: O. Dahl (Ed.), *Logic, Pragmatics and Grammar*, Department of Linguistics, University of Gothenburg

J. L. Austin, 1962, *How to do Things with Words*, Oxford: Oxford University Press

T. Ballmer, 1976, 'Problems of the Classification of Speechacts', unpublished paper, Ruhr University, Bochum

P. Brown and S. Levinson, 1978, 'Universals in Language Usage: Politeness Phenomena', in: E. N. Goody (Ed.), *Questions and Politeness*, London: Cambridge University Press

K. Bühler, 1934, *Sprachtheorie*, Jena: Fischer Verlag

C. Fillmore, 1977, 'The Case for Case Reopened', in: Cole and Sadock (Eds.), *Syntax and Semantics 8*, London: Academic Press

H. P. Grice, 1975, 'Logic and Conversation', in: P. Cole and J. L. Morgan (Eds.), *Syntax and Semantics*, Vol. 3, *Speech Acts*, New York: Academic Press

V. W. O. Quine, 1960, *Word and Object*, Cambridge, Mass.: MIT Press

G. H. von Wright, 1971, *Explanation and Understanding*, London: Routledge & Kegan Paul

M. Webster, 1964, *The New Merriam Webster Pocket Dictionary*, New York: Simon and Schuster

A Framework for the Analysis of Natural Discourse

MARGA KRECKEL *Oxford University*

1   *The Research Problem*

Verbal exchanges are usually not a series of disconnected remarks, but appear in the form of organized sequences of utterances achieved through the cooperation of the speakers. Cooperation is, as Grice (1975) has pointed out, a necessary condition for discourse geared towards effective communication. In his widely quoted article 'Logic and Conversation' he specifies, what he terms the 'cooperation principle', by four maxims:

(1) *Maxim of Quantity*. Make your contribution as informative as required, but not more informative than is required.

(2) *Maxim of Quality*. Try to make your contribution one that is true. That is, do not say anything you believe to be false or for which you lack adequate evidence.

(3) *Maxim of Relation*. Make your contribution relevant to the aims of the ongoing conversation.

(4) *Maxim of Manner*. Be clear. Try to avoid obscurity, ambiguity, wordiness, and disorderliness in your use of language.

The power of these four maxims can be demonstrated by the following exchange:

A: Will you come for dinner tonight?

B: I think, I have work to do.

If speaker A assumes that B's utterance is informative, true, relevant and clear, he will accept it as an answer to his question, unless there is a good reason for him not to do so, for example, A's suspicion that B is pretending to be busy in order to avoid the invitation.

For the purposes of empirical research, the maxim of quality will have to be considered as a separate case, since the question of whether a speaker tells the truth or is successfully deceiving the hearer is not easily amenable to empirical investigation. Each of the three remaining maxims may be verbally realized in a variety of forms. I postulate that varying degrees of shared knowledge between communicants play a key role in determining which empirical form each of the three maxims will take in a specific situation of communication.

This point may be illustrated by means of a hypothetical continuum with a Chinese and a Peruvian conversing in English at the one extreme, two middle-class Englishmen having just been introduced in the middle position, and an English family having lived together for twenty years at the opposite pole. *Speakers* in these three constellations will obviously have to vary the amount of information (maxim of quantity) and their effort at trying to be relevant (maxim of relation) and clear (maxim of manner). For *hearers* the information available will have different degrees of prominence, depending on their location on the continuum. For example, the Chinese or the Peruvian listener will have to monitor closely all the extra- and intralinguistic cues available in order to make sense of the interaction. The English addressee, on the other hand, will be able to distinguish between varying degrees of communicative value, that is, intra- and extralinguistic information pertaining to the English middle-class culture, such as style of clothes, accent or verbal mannerisms, which once identified, will be of marginal informational importance in comparison to, say, last night's government defeat in the House of Commons. Family members, finally, will depend on very few cues in their private interaction since most of the verbal and nonverbal characteristics of each individual are familiar to them and therefore essentially redundant.

From these hypothetical examples one may deduce that the better interactors know each other, the less explicit a speaker has to be in order to be understood, and the less carefully a hearer has to monitor the available information in order to make sense of what has been intentionally or unintentionally transmitted. Dahl (1976) has named this phenomenon the 'laziness principle'. It reads: 'Omit everything that the addressee can figure out by himself'. For the addressee this principle could be expanded into: 'Ignore everything that you know already.' Inherent in this principle is the danger of exaggeration. For instance, two friends of mine, husband and wife, communicate predominantly in half-sentences. This results in occasional misunderstandings when the reduction of information is carried too far.

At first glance, the contention outlined above seems counter-intuitive. Is it not the case that the deepest misunderstandings occur between people who are closest to each other? In order to account for this widespread experience one has to introduce at least two aspects to the emotional assessment of interaction: (a) expectations with respect to mutual understanding and (b) tolerance of frustration. In other words, the better people know each other, the more they expect complete understanding, an ideal which is never achieved, however, and the greater the frustration if the interaction does not live up to it. Conversely, the less people know each other, the lower the level of expectation and the higher the tolerance of frustration. This may account for the occasional experience of 'perfect' understanding between complete strangers. Hence, the emotional appraisal of what is going on in communication need not reflect the actual understanding achieved.

This becomes even more obvious if one takes into account that what is said, or, for that matter, done, cannot usually be taken literally, but must be interpreted in the light of the respective background knowledge of the users. A good illustration of this fact is the standard joking reference to a 'ten-minute job' between two motorcycle-repairing friends. For *them* this expression signifies that a piece of work will take more than a week and will cost more than the motorcycle is worth, whereas for the *uninitiated outsider* this expression implies a job which takes ten minutes. These inside interpretations based on shared knowledge operate not only on the verbal but also on the nonverbal level. The latter can be illustrated by instances in which two male colleagues of mine, one excelling in one-handed press-ups, the other in swimming, will, in competitive situations, mimic press-ups or swimming movements in order to demonstrate their respective potency to one another, movements which must be taken *literally* by outsiders who lack this shared knowledge.

One of the main contentions in this paper will be, first, that a high degree of shared knowledge is a necessary precondition for relatively unambiguous understanding, and, secondly, that shared knowledge increases the likelihood of communicants relying on the same cues when they encode and decode communicative behaviour. Until now, social scientists have refrained from the empirical analysis of the cues used by communicants in the process of encoding and decoding knowledge about the world. It has been generally assumed that such an attempt is premature, if not futile. One of the aims of this paper is to suggest a way to approaching this problem. With this perspective in mind I will discuss, first, the preconditions which empirical material must meet in order to be useful for the investigation of the questions outlined above. Secondly, I will present a conceptual framework within which these problems can be addressed. Thirdly, I will introduce a procedure that lends itself to the empirical analysis of encoded knowledge and of the cues used in decoding.

2 Material

Recorded material of natural interaction based on a high level of shared knowledge is difficult to obtain. In 'The Study of

Language in its Social Context' Labov (1972) pointed out that in the literature there was then only one quantitative study of a self-selected, naturally formed group, namely his study in south-central Harlem (Labov et al. 1968). The data were collected by means of participant observation. 'There was no obvious constraint in these group sessions; the adolescents behaved much as usual, the most of the interaction – physical and verbal – took place between the members. As a result, the effect of systematic observation was reduced to a minimum . . .' (Labov et al. 1968, p. 210). He concluded by hoping that similar studies would be conducted in the near future. According to Labov, empirical material of this kind minimizes the 'observer's paradox', that of trying to find out how people interact when they are not being systematically observed, while data can only be obtained through systematic observation. However, by (a) acquiring additional material to supplement the observational data, by (b) concentrating on situations where the attention of interactors is diverted from the recording process, and by (c) considering situations which involve strong emotions between participants, the influence of the observer upon the interaction can be reduced. Even here, as Labov has emphasized, there is no perfect way out of this dilemma, since candid recordings (even if they are possible to make and ethically permissible) tend to be of such poor quality that they are unsuitable for further analysis.

The material I happened to obtain meets all of Labov's criteria for 'good data':

(1) It consists of the recorded everyday interaction of a working-class family. The family was filmed day after day for a period of four months by a professional team from the BBC (part of the material was transmitted in 1974 in 12 episodes as the BBC documentary 'The Family'). Consent for using the recordings for my purpose was given retrospectively.

(2) Members of the family were interviewed by myself, thus yielding a large quantity of back-ground material (criterion a);

(3) During the recording of the family, existentially important events, such as marriage and moving house, took place which

involved strong emotions (criterion c) and diverted attention from the filming (criterion b).[1]

In view of the observer's paradox I do not suggest that the recordings of the working-class family correspond exactly to what family members would have done in the complete privacy of their home. Generally speaking one might expect the behaviour to be biased towards the formal end of the repertoire. But considering the reactions of the British public, who accused the family of 'foul language' and 'offensive behaviour', any such bias cannot have been too pronounced.

Spontaneous interaction of a private kind recorded in a natural setting is an essential precondition for the investigation of the research problem outlined in the introduction. The development of a particular approach fitting these questions was only rendered possible through the availability of these data.

3   Description and Definition of Practical Codes

The research question implied above is one concerning the relationship between signs and their users. Signs are symbolic entities constituted by the interplay between units of two planes:

(1) Units of the plane of expression (for example, sounds or gestures), that is, *expressive units* or signifiants, and:
(2) Units of the plane of meaning, that is, *semantic units* or signifies.[2]

A sign is realized by the mapping of at least one semantic unit onto an expressive one. This mapping process is anchored in cultural and/or subcultural conventions, that is, it varies

1 This material is used here only for illustrative purposes in the development of a suitable approach for its investigation; a detailed analysis *sui generis* is presented elsewhere (see Kreckel 1979).
2 A more detailed conceptual analysis of signs and codes can be found elsewhere (see Kreckel 1978a, b).

over time and geographically. Both the relationship between units of the two planes and the concept of convention can be clarified by the following example: Consider three expressive units, the English 'honour', the French 'honeur' and the German 'Ehre'. Here we are not only dealing with three different expressive units mapped onto the same semantic entity, but with three *different* expressive units standing for at least three *different* semantic units constituting three *different* signs. For example, the semantic unit corresponding to the expressive unit 'honour' varies when used by a 19th century English royalist or by a 20th century English anarchist. Furthermore, these two semantic units have little in common with the semantic counterparts of the 'honeur' of a French troubadour of the 13th century or the 'Ehre' of a 20th century German football player. Even if the most up-to-date dictionary definitions of the English 'honour', the French 'honeur', and the German 'Ehre' were similar, the way each expressive unit is *used* and the sign it constitutes depends on cultural and subcultural conventions subject to historical change.

These examples highlight an additional fact, namely that signs *do not exist in isolation*. Just as the semantic correlate of the 'honeur' of a French troubadour was created and defined by a whole *system of meanings*, so the particular expressive unit 'honeur' was part of an *expressive system* characteristic for this particular subculture. That is, the specific combination of a meaning-system and an expressive system constitutes the specific *code* of the French troubadour of a certain epoch. For this code, acquired through the *practical experience* of being a troubadour, that is, living the life of a troubadour at a certain time, I introduce the term *practical code*.

4   Problems of Unitization

As indicated with the aid of examples like 'honour' and the 'ten-minute job', the expressive plane can be subdivided into different *forms*. The preference for a particular form is dependent on the theoretical and empirical interest of the research worker. If communication is seen as a vehicle for conveying messages, a form corresponding to a message seems to be the most appropriate one. Linguists like Halliday, interested in the study of natural conversational English, not only equate one message with one unit of information (semantic plane), they also maintain that one message corresponds in principle to one clause or one tone-unit (expressive plane). In order to understand the relationship between these different elements, I will discuss them in more detail.

Halliday (1976) defines *tone-units* as melodic units made up of specific pitch contours. They break up the stretch of discourse into chunks of messages. Laver (1970) suggests that they are the fundamental units of neural encoding. He arrives at this conclusion from his findings which indicate that slips of the tongue rarely cross tone-unit boundaries. However, tone-unit boundaries are not only determined by prosodic features. Both Halliday (1976) and Crystal (1975) emphasize the syntactic basis of tone-units. Halliday, discussing the relationship between the different elements, points out that the 'distribution into information units . . . represents the speaker's organization of discourse into message blocks . . . (and) the number of information units in a discourse tends to be roughly equal to the number of clauses, if one includes dependent clauses' (1976, pp. 175–176). And he adds: 'One clause is one tone group (= tone-unit) unless there is a good reason for it to be otherwise' (1976, p. 216). For Crystal (1975, p. 15) it is, at the moment, 'an open question whether the tone-unit is best described with reference to the unit sentence or to some other unit e.g. clause'. He specifies: '. . . if a sentence consists of one clause; and if this clause consists maximally of the elements Subject+Verb+Complement and/or Object, with one optional Adverb, in this order; and if each of the elements S, C, O or A is expounded by a simple nominal group: then the sentence will have a single tone-unit. This is considered to be the basic pattern.' (p. 16) In his detailed analysis of a corpus of some eight hours of informal, spontaneous conversation he arrives at the conclusion that 'clauses and sentences are the units of organization for relatively informal, fluent discourse.' (p. 22)

Considering these quotations one can argue that the two criteria for tone-unit boundaries are syntactic and prosodic ones. For my purposes here, therefore, the unit of analysis can be determined as a tone-unit defined as a clause which is not interrupted by a pause.

In view of the passages cited above it seems that a clause might provide just as reliable a unit of analysis as a tone-unit. A clause would have the advantage of being an unambiguous unit when only written transcripts of discourse are available. However, I feel that the tone-unit, being the block or unit of particular meaning the *speaker wishes to convey* (see Halliday 1976), corresponds more closely to my research interest in how messages are encoded within discourse, or more specifically, within practical codes.

This concern with the speaker's own encoding expressed by tone-units rather than clauses may be clarified by reference to a short extract from the recordings of the working-class family:

M: //You never told me you'd never marry me//that's what told Mum//
T: //I see . .//that's it . .//We've had this out with your Mum already, love//I didn't say I wouldn't marry you//[3]

The same dialogue could be subdivided by the speaker into different tone-units, the most obvious example being a separate tone-unit for the vocative 'love', indicated by a pause. Equally well one could imagine a further subdivision of the first tone-unit: //You never told me//you'd never marry me//. Both Halliday and Crystal stress that the more formal the speech, the more clauses tend to be divided into a number of tone-units, because they are rather long and full of information.

3 Tone-unit boundaries are symbolized by double slashes.

This brief discussion of tone-units leaves three questions unanswered:

(1) Which message or messages are conveyed by a tone-unit, that is, which signs are created by the mapping of tone-units onto messages?

(2) Is the message character of a specific tone-unit different for participants who interact within the *same* practical code (insiders) as for outside observers who cannot resort to a shared practical code? Or more simply, do insiders and outsiders use different signs?

(3) On which cues do insiders and/or outsiders rely in constituting signs, that is, in assigning a message or messages to a tone-unit?

5   *Structural Properties of Signs*

I have pointed out that tone-units represent the speaker's organization of discourse into message blocks. Within each tone-unit there is one point of prominence, representing the speaker's choice of information focus (very rarely are there two points of prominence, see Halliday 1976). The information focus is realized as phonological prominence or as *focal stress*,[4] indicated by features of loudness, the most extreme pitch within the tone-unit, or length of tonic segment. The stressed lexical item, that is, the tonic segment, within a tone-unit is (according to Halliday and other linguists) what the speaker treats as *new*. The remaining unstressed lexical items are treated, in contrast, as *given*. The terms 'new' and 'given' need not coincide with what was previously mentioned or not mentioned. Rather it corresponds to the speaker's personal assignment of the status 'new' and 'given' to elements of the tone-unit. The differences in allocation of

4 Brazil (1978) uses the term 'tonic' for focal stress. His analysis of intonation patterns is predominantly concerned with the semantic interpretation of different tones used within discourse, an emphasis which is not adopted here.

focal stress, indicated by underlining, can be illustrated in the following example:

(1) //*John* flew to Paris//
(2) //John *flew* to Paris//
(3) //John flew to *Paris*//

In assigning focal stress respectively to 'John', 'flew' and 'Paris' the speaker emphasizes what he considers to be *new* information. The remainder is treated as *given* except for tone-unit (3) where the information focus is on the last lexical item. Quirk and Greenbaum (1973) stress that information focus on the final lexical item in a tone-unit corresponds to normal stress, thus practically constituting an *unmarked* focus. In the unmarked case the remaining item will not have the status of 'given'; rather it is experienced as 'new' due to the cumulative increase in information within a tone-unit.

To sum up, I have described how the speaker breaks up ongoing discourse into message blocks which take the form of tone-units. Except for unmarked instances, he assigns the status of 'new' and 'given' to elements of the tone-unit. 'New' represents the speaker's personal choice of emphasis. It need not correspond to 'what was not mentioned previously'. 'Given' is treated by the sender as recoverable from other extra- and intralinguistic sources, where 'intralinguistic' refers to material previously mentioned in the discourse and 'extralinguistic' refers to the wider social and physical context of a discourse, and to the context of experience on the part of the participants (such as shared knowledge).

I have argued that tone-units carrying specific messages constitute specific signs. Furthermore, it was pointed out that signs are created in relation to other signs within a specific linguistic system: within practical codes. If signs are constituted within specific codes one can assume that they possess *structural properties* which ensure the interrelationship between signs (= inter-unit-structure) and guarantee the individual characteristics of particular signs (= intra-unit-structure).

It is one of my contentions that the character of specific signs is predominantly determined by their *intra-unit-structure* or, more specifically, by their appearing as 'new'. Returning to the previous example, one might interpret //*John* flew to Paris// as 'accusation' (implying, for example, John flew to Paris without Jill), //John *flew* to Paris// as 'reproach' (he spent more money flying than if he had taken a train), and //John flew to *Paris*// as 'affirmation' (John flew to Paris and not to Stockholm). Hence, I would like to claim that the constitution of a tone-unit as a specific sign will depend predominantly on the element with tonic prominence, that is, the element which is treated as 'new' by the speaker.

I stressed previously that the speaker assigns the status of 'given' to those elements of the tone-units which he expects to be recoverable from extra- and intralinguistic sources of information. Extralinguistic sources are either of an observable nature, such as the physical surrounding and the presence of other persons, or of an unobservable one, such as shared knowledge. Intralinguistic sources, on the other hand, are directly accessible within discourse, an access which can be enhanced by detailed linguistic analysis. The analytic devices used for this analysis have been discussed recently in textlinguistics under the heading of *cohesion*. According to Halliday and Hassan (1976, p. 4) '. . . cohesion occurs where the *interpretation* of some element in the discourse is dependent on that of another. The one *presupposes* the other, in the sense that it cannot be effectively decoded except by recourse to it.' They also point out that cohesion is expressed partly through vocabulary and partly through grammar. (An extensive discussion of grammatical and lexical cohesion can be found in their book.) For present purposes, I want primarily to emphasize that intralinguistic cohesive relations provide the *inter-unit-structure* which, together with the *intra-unit-structure* discussed above, constitutes signs within discourse.

Bearing both inter- and intra-unit-structure in mind, consider the following two exchanges. The first dialogue is taken directly from the interaction of the working-class family, while the second one has been arranged to underline my contention.

(1.1) T://I didn't say I *wouldn't* marry you//
(1.2) M://Nobody bloody includes *me*//
(1.3) T://I *said*//I didn't fancy getting married just at the moment//

(2.1) T://I *said*//I didn't fancy getting married just at the *moment*//
(2.2) M://That is a *poor* excuse, I'm afraid//and if you *can't* come up with something better than that//then you know what to *do*//
(2.3) T://*I* didn't say I wouldn't marry you//

Comparing the two lexically identical tone-units (1.1) and (2.3), it becomes apparent that their message character has changed due to the differences in focal stress (intra-unit-structure) and sequential position, which produces different cohesive relations (inter-unit-structure). Whereas (1.1) can be read as 'defense', (2.3) might be interpreted as 'denial'. A comparison between (1.3) and (2.1) again lexically identical, reveals changes in message character as well: (1.3) might be perceived by the hearer as 'refusal' and (2.1) as an 'excuse'. Thus, lexically identical units embedded in different sequences of tone-units and displaying a different distribution of 'new' and 'given' will, first, constitute different expressive units, secondly, correspond to different semantic units, and, thirdly, produce different signs.

6   Functional Properties of Signs

In addition to possessing specific structural properties, a sign can fulfil different functions. A sign like 'excuse' can stand for the speaker's own personal experience (expressive function), it can be used for regulating relationships (interactive function), or it can figure as an introduction to a subsequent request (positional function).[5] Let me now discuss these functions of signs in more detail.

In using language, individuals express personal ideas, feelings and other experiences. The experiential content conveyed by utterances which reflects the speaker's own world corresponds to the *expressive function*. In discussing practical codes I have begun with the assumption, however, that most interchanges between communicants are based on shared knowledge. Conveying shared information has less an expressive than a *relationship-regulating* or *interactive function*. This function can be realized optimally if communicants use the same practical code, that is, if the conventions for interpreting another person's utterances are equally well-known to all participants. In the above example, where M and T are discussing marriage, we can assume, first, that both are using the same practical code, for they have been living together for three years. Secondly, we know (from the video-recordings) that both have argued about marriage in a similar way a number of times. Thirdly, we can therefore conclude that the function of this exchange is one of regulating, that is, changing and/or confirming their relationship. On M's part the emphasis seems to be on *changing*, for she is 'accusing' him of not wanting to marry her. For T the *confirming* seems to dominate, since he is 'justifying' and 'defending' himself.

This example leads us to the last, the *positional function*. In introducing the topic of 'marriage', M might try to 'convince' T that he should marry her. In order to execute this superordinate goal she might 'initiate' a conversation, 'state' certain conditions, and so on, while T may 'respond' to her initiative and try to 'terminate' the conversation. This implies that the *interactive* function of 'accusing' can have the *positional* function of 'initiating' a talk, with the aim of 'getting him to marry her'.

For the analyst of discourse the two structural (the intra- and

5 Habermas (1976) discussed the expressive and interactive functions of signs; I have added the positional function.

inter-unit-structure) and the three functional properties of signs have different empirical status. Given advances in linguistic science, the structural properties of signs are *quantitatively analysable* in terms of systems of tonality (= tone-unit boundaries) and tonicity (= focal stress), and by techniques of grammatical and lexical cohesion. The three functional dimensions, in comparison, are mainly *subject to interpretation*, as they rely on the identification of meanings inherent in messages.

The main characteristics of a sign considered in this paper can be summarized in the following form:

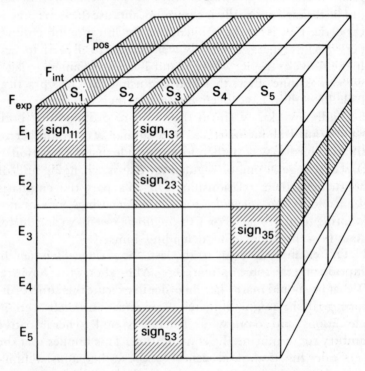

where

E_n = expressive unit or tone-unit, quantitatively analysable in terms of (a) lexical terms, (b) intra-unit-structure, that is, systems of tonality and tonicity, and (c) inter-unit-structure, that is, lexical and grammatical cohesion;

S_n = semantic unit or message dependent on functional use within a specific practical code, subject to interpretation;

sign = $E_i S_j$;

F_{exp} = expressive function;

F_{int} = interactive function;

F_{pos} = positional function.

The graph is designed to highlight the following points:

(1) A specific expressive unit E_i can have any number of semantic correlates S_n, constituting different signs $E_i S_n$. This relationship is reversible, implying that a specific semantic unit S_j can be mapped onto different expressive units E_n, thus producing different signs $E_n S_j$.

(2) Particular combinations $S_1 E_1$ or $S_3 E_5$ generating particular signs are part of particular codes. This point can be illustrated by Eco's (1971) example of the 'whale':

(a) E_3 'whale' plus, S_1 'fish' = sign $E_3 S_1$ (code of mediaeval natural science);

(b) E_3 'whale' plus S_2 'evil = sign $E_3 S_2$ (code of the Bible);

(c) E_3 'whale' plus S_5 'mammal' = sign $E_3 S_5$ (code of 20th century natural science).

Naturally, the example is in reality more complicated, for the expressive unit 'whale' cannot be considered to be a constant. We have to assume that (a) was issued in mediaeval Latin forming, for example, $E_1 S_1$, (b) in Greek forming, for example, $E_5 S_3$, and (c) in any standardized language of the 20th century.

(3) Codes are, as we have seen, acquired through practical use, that is, in interaction with the social and physical environment (see example of the troubadour of the 13th century above).

(4) Signs can be used on a micro- or a macro-level; on the *micro-level*, signs are vehicles used by communicants to express their own personal world (expressive function) *and* to

regulate relationships (interactive function). On a *macro-level* signs fulfil, in addition, a positional function in contributing to superordinate units.

7   *Implications for Empirical Research*

In stating the research problem I have pointed out that Grice's maxims of quantity, relation and manner will have different consequences for speakers and hearers who share a large body of knowledge, like the members of the working-class family mentioned, and for speakers and hearers who cannot resort to shared knowledge established in direct interaction. The extended version of Dahl's 'laziness principle' summarizes this state of affairs. Furthermore, I advanced the expectation that family members encode their shared knowledge in a way which makes it accurately decodable for other family members, and *only* for family members. This implies that a great deal of shared knowledge will (a) be omitted, like the layout of the house, (b) alluded to, like last night's conversation, (c) mentioned, and (d) emphasized. For insiders one can thus assume accepted practices or conventions as to which aspects of shared knowledge have to be mentioned or emphasized and which aspects can be alluded to or omitted. This entails, for the participants, equally well established practices of how to express this knowledge within the practical code of the family. Strangers or outside observers are not in the same privileged position. For them the information available is of very different prominence.

In order to be able to investigate empirically the distribution of shared knowledge I have introduced an analytical procedure originally developed in linguistics. This procedure enables the research worker (a) to segment the continuous stream of discourse into tone-units corresponding to the speaker's distribution of messages, (b) to analyse tone-units in terms of the distribution of knowledge encoded in them (intra-unit-structure), and (c) to investigate the cohesive forces between tone-units (inter-unit-structure).

With the aid of examples from recordings of the everyday interaction of a particular working-class family I have tried to indicate that both intra- and inter-unit-structure contribute essentially to the interpretation of the tone-unit in terms of signs or communicative acts, as they are elements of practical codes. In other words, I assumed that shift of focal stress within tone-units and changes in the cohesive forces between tone-units will lead to the formation of different signs and, thus, of different communicative acts.

Since distribution of 'new' and 'given' is only accurately decodable for insiders who can complement the intra-linguistic information by their extra-linguistic knowledge, one might expect that both intra- and inter-unit-structure will enable insiders to interpret sequences of tone-units in the same way and, thus, to form the same or similar communicative acts. Outside observers who have to rely solely on what is mentioned are expected to arrive at interpretations which overlap only marginally with the interpretations of other outsiders or of the family members themselves. The procedure of analysing how the distribution of knowledge contributes to the interpretation of speech and to the formation of communicative acts, as suggested here, can only be tested, therefore, first, if several family members and several outside observers interpret the same extracts from the recorded family interaction with respect to underlying messages, and secondly, if interpretations within and between those two groups are compared, and, thirdly, if these interpretations are related to the structure of knowledge encoded in the tone-units. An empirical analysis following these lines of enquiry has been carried out and is reported elsewhere (see Kreckel 1979), as this transcends the aims of this paper.

References

D. Brazil, 1978, *Discourse Intonation II*, *Discourse Analysis Monographs*, No. 2, English Language Research, University of Birmingham

D. Crystal, 1975, *The English Tone of Voice*, London: Arnold

D. Dahl, 1976, 'What is New Information?,' in: N. E. Enkvist and V. Kohonen (Eds.), *Reports on Text Linguistics: Approaches to Word Order*, Abo

U. Eco, 1971, *Einführung in die Semiotik*, Munchen: Wilhelm Fink Verlag

H. P. Grice, 1975, 'Logic and Conversation,' in: P. Cole and J. L. Morgan (Eds.), *Syntax and Semantics, Vol. 3, Speech Acts*, New York: Academic Press

J. Habermas, 1976, 'Some Distinctions in Universal Pragmatics', *Theory and Society*, Vol. 3, pp. 155–167

M. A. K. Halliday, 1976, *System and Function in Language: Selected Papers*, London: Oxford University Press

M. A. K. Halliday and R. Hassan, 1976, *Cohesion in English*, London: Longman

M. Kreckel, 1978a, 'Private versus Public Code: A Conceptual Analysis of the Phenomenon of Code-Switching,' *Research Film – Le film de Reserche – Forschungsfilm*, Vol. 9, pp. 445–463

M. Kreckel, 1978b, 'Communicative Acts: A Semiological Approach to the Empirical Analysis of Filmed Interaction,' *Semiotica*, Vol. 24

M. Kreckel, 1979, 'Communicative Acts and Shared Knowledge: A Conceptual Framework and its Empirical Application,' paper prepared for the conference on 'The Organization of Human Action: Theory and Empirical Findings,' Paris, 12–15 January

W. Labov, 1972, *Sociolinguistic Patterns*, Oxford: Blackwell

W. Labov, P. Cohen, C. Robins and J. Lewis, 1968, 'A Study of the Non-Standard English of Negro and Puerto-Rican speakers in New York City, Final Report,' *Cooperative Research Project 3288*, 2 Vols: Philadelphia, Pa.: U.S. Regional Survey

J. Laver, 1970, 'The Production of Speech', in: J. Lyons (Ed.), *New Horizons in Linguistics*, Harmondsworth:Penguin

R. Quirk and S. Greenbaum, 1973, *A University Grammar of English*, London: Longman

Psychopathology and Familial Communication

ROLV MIKKEL BLAKAR   *Oslo University**

1 Introduction

During the last two decades, studies of communication and interaction in the families of schizophrenics have been given particular attention. A number of phenomena considered typical of communication in such families have been described, for example, the double-bind phenomenon (Bateson et al. 1956), pseudo-mutuality (Wynne et al. 1958) and marital schism and marital skew (Lidz et al. 1957). It is not always clear whether these (and other) phenomena are to be understood as a *cause* of schizophrenia in a family member, or as its *product* (Mishler and Waxler 1965). However, the double-bind situation is readily offered as one of a series of preconditions for the development of schizophrenia (Bateson 1960; Bateson et al. 1962). The above phenomena all deal with *communication*

* During the period of 6–8 years while the research was conducted which this paper addresses, many people have made valuable contributions. To list them all is impossible. The development of the project, however, owes much to Ragnar Rommetveit and Hilde Eileen Nafstad so that I wish to thank them in particular. Olav Skardal and Astri Heen Wold provided valuable comments on an earlier version of the present paper.

   This research project has been supported by the Norwegian Council of Social Science and the Humanities.

between members of the schizophrenic's family. For example, Ruesch and Bateson (1951, p. 79) claimed that psychopathology has to be defined *in terms of* 'disturbances of communication'.

This re-definition of psychopathology in the early fifties initiated much research. (For a comprehensive and also critical review see Riskin and Faunce 1972.[1]) However, the research did not demonstrate unequivocal differences in the communication of families with schizophrenic members as against families containing members with other types of psychopathology or normal control families. One of the pioneers of the field, Jay Haley (1972, p. 36), concluded in a review of this type of research: 'The evidence for a difference between the normal family and a family containing a patient member is *no more than indicative.*' (My italics) The optimistic mood which characterized the field in the sixties (see Handel 1967; Mishler and Waxler 1965) has subsequently given way to a more pessimistic and critical attitude (see Haley 1972; Riskin and Faunce 1972; Blakar 1976, 1978a, b).

The lack of progress has been ascribed either to a lack of adequate methods (Haley 1972) or to a lack of 'intermediate concepts' connecting observable phenomena to the superordinate concepts used in theorizing about families with deviant members (Riskin and Faunce 1972).

To take the latter issue first, Riskin and Faunce (1972) indicated that family research involves abstract theoretical concepts (such as double-bind, pseudo-mutuality, and marital schism and marital skew), while, at the same time, a number of relatively simple phenomena (for example, 'Who speaks to whom?'), which can easily be measured, are in operation. The connection between these abstract concepts and the readily operationalizable phenomena is, however, lacking. Further-

---

1 The outline of the historical development within communication oriented research on psychopathology is traced here only until 1972 when our present research project was launched. It is sad to report, however, that the general conclusions concerning the theoretical and methodological state of affairs presented here are still valid (see Blakar 1978a).

more, the superordinate concepts have been found to be unclear. For example, Schuham (1967) pointed out that there seem to be different sets of criteria about what the double-bind situation in fact really entails; and Mishler and Waxler (1968, p. 274) demonstrated the problems that arise in efforts to operationalize the double-bind phenonomenon. (These authors encountered the same kind of problems with the concept of 'pseudo-mutuality'.)

This criticism does not necessarily imply that double-bind situations or pseudo-mutuality phenomena do not exist. But it underlines the fact that *if* the proposed theories are to be confirmed (or disproved) through thorough empirical studies and replications, the core concepts have to be made more explicit. In this text, I wish to stress the facts that, in spite of the extensive number of empirical studies, there are few or no replications, and that the majority of researchers apply their own ad hoc concepts (see Riskin and Faunce 1972). In order to penetrate the jungle of concepts and in order to establish a solid empirical foundation for an understanding of psychopathology conceptualized within patterns of family communication, a more standardized use of concepts is necessary together with systematic replications of studies. A thought-provoking example which illustrates this point is Ringuette and Kennedy's (1966) replication of Weakland and Fry's (1962) case analysis of incongruent communication and double-binds in letters by mothers addressed to their schizophrenic children. In Ringuette and Kennedy's replication, the scorers did not even attain an acceptable interscorer reliability with respect to what was to be scored as a double-bind. (For a more general discussion of the double-bind theory see Blakar 1975e, 1978a.)

Haley (1972) ascribed the lack of progress more directly to a lack of adequate methods. This is clearly reflected in the following quote (Haley 1972, p. 35):

'. . . if we judge the exploratory research done to date by severe methodological criteria, one can only conclude that the evidence for a difference between the normal family and a family containing a patient is no more than indicative. This does not mean that schizo-phrenia is not produced by a type of family, nor does it mean that a family with a schizophrenic is grossly different from the average family. It means *that sufficient reliable evidence of a difference has yet to be provided. The methodology for providing that evidence is still being devised.*' (My italics)

I agree with Haley's (1972) and Riskin and Faunce's (1972) observations; I hesitate, however, to characterize either of these factors as *the cause of the lack of progress.* On the contrary, I think that these aspects are merely reflections of a more fundamental deficiency, namely, that the concept of communication used in family oriented research is usually vague and undefined (see Blakar 1974a; Solvberg and Blakar 1975). I have suggested in an earlier paper (Blakar 1974a) that in the keen attempt at redefining schizophrenia in terms of communication in the family it was almost forgotten to define communication.

In other words, there has been a tendency to 'explain' one mystery (schizophrenia) by another mystery (communication, or more adequately, deviant or pathological communication). When reviewing the literature on this subject, one is struck by the amount of knowledge available about schizophrenia, while that on communication, normal as well as deviant, is rather limited. In much of this literature one finds that concepts such as 'communication', 'interaction', 'cooperation', and so on, are used *without* being defined and are, hence, presented without clear conceptual or operational meanings and boundaries.

This state of affairs is reflected in the following quote (Riskin and Faunce 1972, p. 371):

'Many terms in today's research are often used in a formulalike ritualistic or ambiguous manner, and this tends to interfere with, or substitute for, clear thinking. For example, the word 'systems' at times does seriously represent a point of view that guides one's thinking and research strategy. At other times it seems to be used as a cliche, almost as a badge of high status, in a way similar to the use of the concept 'dynamics' in psychoanalytic case presentations. 'Process' is another 'in' term which is at times used by researchers who are actually dealing with outcome scores. *An instance of ambiguous usage is 'communication'*, which sometimes seems to be synonymous with 'behavior' and at other times appears to refer specifically to verbal messages. And 'interaction' is used in exceedingly variable ways. One wonders, if these expressions were stricken from the vocabulary, would hard thinking be encouraged, or would other terms immediately fill the vacuum?' (My italics)

I subscribe to this general criticism and will later elaborate my own critical stance concerning the usage of the concept of communication in particular:

1 The attempts that have been made towards presenting definitions of 'communication' are much too general and extensive.

2 In most studies, operationalizations of 'communication' entail oversimplifications which means that essential aspects of communication are not considered.

The co-occurrence of points 1 and 2 in much of the research adds to my criticism. As regards the issue of too extensive definitions (the 'definitions' are usually left implicit), these can be classified as two types: First and foremost, communication is often presented as almost synonymous with *behaviour*. Watzlawick et al. (1967, p. 22) provided a classic and in many respects 'authoritative' example when they claimed: '. . . all behaviour, not only speech, is communication – even the communicational clues in an impersonal context – affects behaviour'. Secondly, communication is often vaguely characterized as '*the flow of information*'. This type of a definition is usually only indirectly reflected in the scoring of categories such as 'information exchange' (Ferreira and Winter 1968a, b), 'information giving' (Goldstein et al. 1968) or 'informing' (McPherson 1970). The underlying concept of communication, however, appears to be as extensive as the definition put forward by Athanassiades (1974, p. 195): 'Verbal and non-verbal communication, i.e., *the flow of information, impressions, and understandings from one individual to others.*' (My italics)

Given this situation, one can ask *why* a concept of communication is at all needed, and in particular, *why* it is such an essential concept, when *all* behaviour is communication? In such a case, it seems, one would rather need a more specified concept of behaviour. Similarly, one can ask these questions of those who define communications as 'the flow of information'.

Ideally, definitions should prove useful in revealing and specifying the subject matter. Vague and extensive definitions of the above type only serve to disguise fundamental distinctions. That this is actually so, can already be realized when the above definitions of communication are compared with the following quote from Rommetveit (1968, p. 41): 'The communicative medium is related to the message it conveys only via an intentional act of encoding'. Without pointing out a particular stance with respect to Rommetveit's general theoretical position, it can be realized immediately that a number of crucial issues, which are neglected in the above definitions, are exposed. To be of any use, a definition of communication must make explicit issues such as: Does it make sense to speak about communication which is 'not-intended' or 'non-intended'? Are there any fundamental differences between 'receiving messages' and 'getting information'? (For a more detailed exposition of the crucial issues which definitions of communication should explicitly incorporate see Blakar 1978a).

My second criticism is that the operationalizations of communication in most studies in the field involve oversimplification. Here are some of the dimensions which have been frequently researched:

Who speaks?
Who speaks to whom?
How long (much) does each of the participants speak?
Number of interruptions?
Who interrupts?
Who is interrupted?
How long and/or how complex are the sentences which are used?

I do not wish to say that these aspects of communication are of no interest. However, the *interpretation* of each one of these observations depends on one's theory of communication (which may involve vague, or none at all, definitions). For example, an interruption may reflect a power struggle, but it may also reflect perfect mutual understanding between participants ('I have already understood/anticipated what you are going to say'). Nothing much, therefore, can be learnt by an atheoretical counting of interruptions. Similarly, incomplete sentences may reflect lack of verbal or communication competence, but it may also reflect perfect mutual understanding (ellipsis) where elaborated sentences would not be needed and could even create an impression of alienation. These examples illustrate, first, that the operationalizations of communication frequently involve oversimplification, and, secondly, that a more explicit and elaborate theory of communication is needed so that observations may be interpreted adequately.

At this point I wish to indicate that I am not criticizing the lack of progress and succcess in the study of communication *per se*, as the development of an adequate theory of human communication represents a complex and difficult task. At present there is no fully elaborated theory of communication available, which could be applied to the study of psychopathology. My criticism, therefore, refers to the predominant tendency to *pretend* that problems are solved by means of vague and too extensive definitions. Furthermore, there is a strong tendency to employ the existing concepts *as if* they were unproblematic and everyone would know and agree about what, for example, 'normal communication' is or implies. Even the best and 'authoritative' expositions of the idea of communication in relation to schizophrenia (and psychopathology in general) strike one as vague and implicit as regards the use of the concept of communication for analytic purposes. When a thorough exploration of the theme 'psychopathology and communication' is sought, I suggest that it is necessary to operate with a far more stringent and explicit use of the concept of 'communication'. In developing adequate methods and intermediate concepts in this field, one cannot rely exclusively on limited forms of knowledge of, and insights into, schizophrenia and psychopathology, but one has also to take into account, and to capitalize on, a *general* theory of communication (see Blakar 1975b, 1978a, d).

As was mentioned above, the evidence for differences in the communication in families with and without psycho-pathological members is presently only indicative. However, Haley (1972, p. 35) pointed out: 'When faced with a task on which they must co-operate, abnormal family members seem to communicate their preferences less successfully, require more activity and take longer to get the task done'. In other words, the communication in families containing members with psychopathological symptoms seems to be less efficient than that in control families. But quantitative measures (for example, time used) of families' efficiency in communication are, of course, of no or little interest in themselves and give no answer as to *why* families containing, for example, a schizo-phrenic member are less efficient. In order to answer, or shed some light on, the question of *why*, the qualitative aspects of communication, which make for its efficiency or inefficiency, have to be identified and examined. An analysis of such qualitative aspects, however, presupposes a more thorough understanding of the concept of communication than is pres-ently available. With a few exceptions (for example, Ruesch and Bateson's 1951 early programmatic statements) the con-cept of communication applied in family and interaction oriented studies of psychopathology has remained vague and implicit (see Blakar 1976, 1978a, 1978b; Solvberg and Blakar 1975). On the other hand, an enormous body of theoretical and empirical work bearing upon general communication theory has been accumulated in disciplines such as psycho-logy, anthropology and linguistics. But alas, as Riskin and Faunce (1972, p. 369) pointed out: 'interdisciplinary isolation is striking' in the field of interaction oriented studies on psychopathology. In the light of the above mentioned concep-tual and methodological problems in the field, the interdisci-plinary isolation seems to be paradoxical as well as tragic. In our work, we tried to overcome this isolation by taking our point of departure from a general social-cognitive theory of language and communication (as developed by Rommetveit 1968, 1972a, 1974; Blakar 1970, 1975c; Blakar and Rommetveit 1975; Rommetveit and Blakar 1978).

To conclude the aims of the paper can be summarized as follows: First, I believe that the communication perspective is fruitful in the study of psychopathology in general and of schizophrenia in particular, but that this field of research has suffered from the use of an implicit and vague concept of communication. Secondly, starting from general communication theory, I propose a method (a standardized communication conflict situation) which has been developed some time ago (Blakar 1972, 1973a) and which is directed towards the identification of some prerequisites of communication. Thirdly, it will be shown, using our research (Solvberg and Blakar 1975) that this method is sensitive to differences in the communication of parental couples with and without a schizophrenic child. A variety of new questions emerged from our first exploratory study, and a series of follow-up studies were conducted (Blakar 1975a, 1975b, 1978a). The integrated research programme within which our studies were and are conducted, and the theoretical and methodological rationales for each of the types of studies conducted make up the substantial body of the paper. Finally, I will briefly comment upon some of the findings and the conclusions achieved in our research.

2   The Method and Its Theoretical Background

Our communication-oriented project on psychopathology represents an integrated part of an alternative approach to human communication in general (Rommetveit 1968, 1972a, 1974; Blakar 1970, 1975c, 1978a; Rommetveit and Blakar 1978). We enquired theoretically and empirically into issues concerning prerequisites for intersubjectivity, for example, how something is made known under varying conditions, the structure of messages, and so on; during this work critical attitudes towards the dominant traditions within the study of language and communication have emerged (Rommetveit 1972b, 1974; Blakar 1973b, 1978e). In particular, we became critical about the predominant tendencies to neglect the communication perspective implicit in all language use and to study language and language processing *in vacuo*, independent of the relevant (social) contexts. Over a series of theoretical and empirical analyses of language processing, where language was studied in use and embedded in social contexts and where an explicit communication perspective was taken, an alternative conceptual framework for the study of language and human communication emerged (Rommetveit and Blakar 1978). Only a brief outline of this general approach to human communication is given here. However, I hope that in the later presentation of our communication–oriented research on psychopathology the underlying general theory of communication will be clearly reflected.

In order to solve the problems of traditional approaches to psychopathology within the communication perspective mentioned previously, we need to consider the definition of communication on which our methods and conceptual framework depend. In defining communication, the main problem is to capture the essential aspects of this common and universal human activity, while *at the same time* 'communication' is distinguished from processes and activities carrying basic resemblances with communication. The most essential characteristic of communication is that something is being made known to somebody. It follows from this that an act of communication is *social* and *directional* (from a sender to a receiver). A crucial characteristic distinguishing communication from the general flow of information is that the sender has an intention to make something known to the (particular) receiver. (The intentionality in acts of communication is reflected, for example, in the equifinality of different means). When communication is defined as a (sender's) intentional act to make something (the message) known to others (the receiver), then the behavioural as well as the informational aspects of the definitions discussed in the introduction become integrated *at the same time* as we manage to distinguish communication from behaviour and information processing in general. A comprehensive exposition of a theory of communication along these lines has been provided by Rommetveit (1974).

From the above definition methods for studying, and concepts for analysing, processes of communication can be derived (Blakar 1973a, 1978a). In this perspective, a whole series of enquiries and corresponding strategies for research to gain insight into the riddles of human communication readily offer themselves. It would be no point trying to list them all here.[2] I will only comment on the basic enquiry question underlying, and in many respects integrating, our research: What are the prequisites for (successful) communication, i.e., under what conditions will somebody succeed (to a reasonable degree) to make something known to somebody else? To (clinically oriented) psychologists the counter-part of this enquiry question may be even more intriguing: Which of the preconditions have *not* been satisfied when communication fails? An important aim of research, with obvious theoretical as well as practical implications, is, hence, an identification and systematic description of the various prerequisites for (successful) communication. Such a research programme needs to encompass individual and situational as well as social variables (Blakar 1974b, 1977).

In an effort to identify and describe some of these prerequisites for communication, we developed a particular experimental method (Blakar 1972, 1973a). The method was directly derived from our general theory of communication, and it was further inspired by various studies of communication breakdowns, especially those typical for children (for

2 The extensive interplay between these superordinate programmatic statements and empirical research is considered in Rommetveit and Blakar (1978).

example, Piagetian studies on egocentrism), and also by analyses of everyday misunderstandings and how they occur (for example, Ichheiser 1970; Garfinkel 1972).

The general idea of the method was very simple, but in practice it proved very difficult to realize. This was to try to create a communication situation where one of the preconditions for (successful) communication was *not* satisfied. If one were able to create such a situation, one would be able to study, at least, the impact of that particular variable on communication, the potential 'missing' requirements or preconditions to which the subjects would attribute the resultant communication difficulties, and what the subjects actually do in order to try to 'improve' their communication when it goes astray.

It can be hypothesised that the most basic precondition for successful communication, in order to take place at all, is that the participants have established '*a shared social reality*', a common 'here-and-now' within which the exchange of messages can take place (Rommetveit 1974; Blakar 1978a). An ideal experimental situation would thus be one where two (or more) participants communicate with each other *under the belief* that they are 'in the same situation' (i.e., have a common definition of the situation's 'here-and-now'), but where they are in fact in different situations. In other words, we tried to create a situation where each participant speaks and understands what is said on the basis of his own particular interpretation of the situation and *falsely believes* that the other speaks and understands on the basis of that same interpretation as well (as in everyday quarrels and misunderstandings).

The problems that we encountered in developing an experimental situation that 'worked', i.e., a situation where the subjects would communicate for a reasonable period of time without suspecting anything awry, cannot be reported here (see Blakar 1972, 1973a, 1978a). The final design, however, was simple and seemed quite natural. Two persons, A and B, are each given a map of a relatively complicated network of roads and streets in a town centre. On A's map two routes are marked with arrows, one short and straightforward (the practice route), and another longer and more complicated (the experimental route). On B's map no route is marked. A's task is then to explain to B the two routes, first the simple one, then the longer and more complicated one. B will then, with the help of A's explanations, try to find the way through town to the predetermined end-point. B may ask questions, for example, ask A to repeat the explanations, or to explain in other ways, and so on. The experimental manipulation is simply that the two maps are not identical. An extra street is added on B's map. So, no matter how adequately A explains, no matter how carefully B carries out his instructions, B is bound to go wrong. The difference between the two maps has implication only for the complicated route, however; the practice route is straightforward for both.

The practice route was included for three reasons: to get the subjects used to the situation, to strengthen their confidence in the maps, and to obtain a sample of their communication in the same kind of situation, but unaffected by our experimental manipulation (a 'before-after' design). The two participants sit at opposite ends of a table, with two low screens shielding their maps from each other. The screens are low enough for them to see each other and allow natural eye-contact (Moscowici 1967; Argyle 1969). Everything said is tape-recorded, and for certain analyses the tape is subsequently transcribed.[3]

3 In presenting the standardized communication situation I have been strictly descriptive. The following excerpt from an analysis of this particular cooperation situation (Blakar and Pedersen 1978, p. 4) clearly demonstrates how core social variables such as *control* and *self-confidence* are involved:

'. . . the subjects participate two-and-two in a rather common type of interaction situation. One subject is going to explain something to the other, and the latter is going to carry out the task according to the explanations and directives given by the first. The communication situation is structured so that one subject is given some information which the other one needs. In other words: The two subjects are ascribed to the roles of an *explainer* and a *follower*. Furthermore, the standardized interaction situation consists of two apparently similar, but in reality highly different communication tasks, in that whereas

A study where students served as subjects convinced us that the experimental manipulation was successful (Blakar 1972, 1973a). The most interesting findings in this first study were:
1. It took an average of 18 minutes from the start on the experimental route *before* any doubt concerning the credibility of the maps was expressed. During this time the subjects communicated under the false assumption that they were sharing the *same* situation (the same 'here').
2. Moreover, the situation proved successful in demonstrating how the subjects 'diagnosed' their communication difficulties, and what kinds of 'tools' they had at their disposal in order to remedy and improve their communication. The experimental situation seemed to make great demands on the subjects' powers of flexibility and ability to modify their communication patterns, and also on their capacity to decenter and see things from the other's perspective.

These findings in particular led to the idea that the method could possibly be used to illuminate communication deficiencies in families with schizophrenic members. They also go together well with certain aspects of recent research, as Haley (1972, p. 35) has indicated:

If we accept the findings of the research reported here and assuming it is sound, evidence is accumulating to support the idea that a family with a patient member is different from an 'average' family. As individuals, the family members do not appear different according to the usual character and personality criteria. Similarly, evidence is slight that family structure, when conceived in terms of role assignment or dominance, is different in normal and abnormal families. On process measurements there is some indication of difference:

---

the first one is simple and straightforward the other one is more complicated and a communication conflict is induced.
While the roles as explainer and follower involve different types and degrees of *control*, the subjects' reactions to situational variants – simple versus conflict communication situation - may reflect their *self-confidence* and *self-esteem*. In order to resolve the communication conflict induced in the more complicated situation, the subject has to demonstrate confidence in himself/herself (as well as in the other).'

Abnormal families appear to have more conflict, to have different coalition patterns, and to show more inflexibility in repeating patterns and behavior. *The most sound findings would seem to be in the outcome area: When faced with a task on which they must cooperate, abnormal family members seem to communicate their preferences less successfully, require more activity and take longer to get the task done.* (My italics)

Our standardized communication conflict situation was designed precisely for the purpose of making possible more detailed analyses and descriptions in 'the outcome area'. Here communication difficulties were bound to emerge. Concepts such as attribution (how and to which cause the induced communication difficulties are attributed), the ability to decenter and take the perspective of the other, the capacity to endorse, maintain and modify interactional contracts, and so on, became consequently of central significance in the analysis. Our method thus enabled us to draw upon theorists within general psychology such as Heider (1958), Mead (1934), Piaget (1926), Rommetveit (1972, 1974) and others in the description of deviant patterns of communication in abnormal families.[4]

4 For a presentation of the more general theoretical rationale for the clinical application of this method see Blakar 1974a, 1975c, 1978a, b. Here it should be emphasized that, while we in our varied analyses of this particular communication conflict situation (Blakar 1972, 1973a, 1974a, 1978a, c; Blakar and Pedersen 1978; Moberget and Reer 1975; Endresen 1977) remained *within* the framework of social-cognitive theory of communication, intriguing approaches have been suggested within quite different theoretical frameworks. The most interesting ones are those formulated by Haley (1975), Andersson and Pilblad (1977) and Holte (1978). Haley (1975) pointed out that the communication conflict induced should be characterised as a double-bind situation. In Andersson and Pilblad's (1977) analysis the interaction situation is modelled according to the framework of the stucturalist-functionalist small group theory. Holte (1978) argued that the patterns of communication revealed in the conflict situation may be most aptly understood in terms of what he calls 'ethical preconditions' for communication. Furthermore, the standardized communication situation has been applied for different purposes within various theoretical frameworks without reanalysing or reinterpreting the communication conflict situation as such. For example, within the symbolic interactionist approach the method has been used to expose coding

3 An Exploratory Experimental Study

In the first exploratory study (Solvberg and Blakar 1975) we chose, both for theoretical and practical reasons, to concentrate on the parent dyad. Obviously, this is the core dyad in the milieu into which the child is born and within which he later matures into a healthy or pathological person. Moreover, we did not want to include the patient himself in this very first study in which the method itself was to be tried out.

Since the communication task given to each couple was in principle unsolvable, we had to decide beforehand the criteria for terminating the experiment:[5]

1   The task would be considered finished successfully as soon as the error was correctly localized and identified.

2   The task would also be considered resolved when the route was correctly reconstructed to the location of the error and when one or both of the subjects insisted that the maps were not identical and, hence, that it was pointless to go on. In this context, it must be mentioned that the experimenter was instructed to neglect all suggestions that something might be wrong and give the impression, for as long as possible, that everything was as it should be (Blakar 1973a, p. 418).

3   If no solution according to criteria one or two was reached within forty minutes, the communication task would be brought to an end. The subjects would then be shown the discrepancy between the maps and told that the task was actually unsolvable. The forty-minute limit was based on findings of earlier experiments (Blakar 1973a) and pre-tests.

4   Finally, it was decided that if the task should upset the

---

processes (Braten 1974, 1978); within attribution theory to analyse person versus situation attributions of people knowing or not knowing each other (McKillip 1975); and to analyse the general process of understanding and misunderstanding (Brisendal 1976).

5   Additional research has forced us to refine these termination criteria in the light of a more explicit theory concerning the solution of communication conflicts (Moberget and Reer 1975; Endresen 1977; Blakar 1978a).

couple too much, the experimenter would stop and reveal the true nature of the experiment.[5]

In order to simplify comparisons between the various couples, the distribution of the two different maps among the spouses had to be standardized. To counteract culturally determined male dominance, we gave the map with the routes drawn into the wives so that the husbands had to follow the directives and explanations of their wives.

THE SAMPLE AND THE ADMINISTRATION OF THE EXPERIMENTAL PROCEDURE

A very important issue in this exploratory study was to establish two comparable groups, one consisting of parents *with* schizophrenic offspring (Group S) and one matched control group *without* (Group N). During this exploratory research we chose to limit ourselves to small but strictly controlled and matched groups.

We concentrated on establishing Group S first. We decided to accept the definition of schizophrenia generally held in Norwegian psychiatry, namely, that provided by Kraepelin. Our point of departure was that the reference person in Group S had been diagnosed as being a schizophrenic at a psychiatric institution.[7] The use of the diagnostic category entailed that all reference persons would be over 15 years of age. We put the upper age limit at 30, and within this range we sought the youngest possible reference persons to ensure that they had not been separated from their families for too long.

Establishing Group S was a long and laborious process (Solvberg 1973; Solvberg and Blakar 1975). Having established Group S, much effort was put into assembling a match-

---

5 In all the studies in which this method has been applied, it was never necessary to use this criterion.

7 For a detailed discussion of problems encountered in communication oriented research when applying the traditional nosological categories in selecting subjects see Blakar 1978d; Blakar and Nafstad 1978.

ing Group N. Variables such as age, number of years of marriage, education, employment, social group, annual income, domicile, living conditions, number of children and their sex and age, were all matched satisfyingly (for details of the matching see Solvberg 1973, p. 62–67). Group N represented a 'normal group' in the sense that it included ordinary couples *without* problems that had led themselves or their children into contact with treatment or penal institutions. Nothing else is implied by 'normality' in this study.

HYPOTHESES

Since the primary purpose of this exploratory study was methodological, our hypotheses bearing upon the differences between Group S and Group N couples were not very refined. They were, to some extent, based on reviews of the literature. Our hypotheses were:

1   Couples from Group S will communicate less efficiently than those from Group N *if* the cooperation situation is vague and complicated, requiring critical evaluation and change in patterns of communication. In other words, the Group S couples will have *more problems* and will require *more time* in solving the experimental route where the communication conflict is induced.

2   Couples from Group S will manage as well as couples from Group N *if* the cooperation situation is plain and simple in the sense that no readjustment is required from their usual pattern of communication or cooperation. In other words, no difference in time spent on the simple task (the practice route) is expected.

3   Qualitative differences in the communication between Group S and Group N couples will be revealed, and such differences are expected regardless of whether the communication situation is simple or complex. In addition, it is expected that such qualitative differences observed in communication in the simple and straight-forward situation will shed

some light on *why* Group S communication fails when the communication situation is more demanding.

RESULTS

All couples became involved in the task. The experimenter had no particular problems getting them to grasp the instructions and start on the practice route, although some of the couples put some pressure on the experimenter to structure the situation more explicitly.

Let us start by examining some quantitative measures related to efficiency in solving the communication task. None of the couples seemed to experience serious problems with the practice route. The actual time spent, however, ranging from 2 minutes 2 seconds to 9 minutes 56 seconds, indicates that the task and communication situation were not equally easy for all of them. If we compare the two experimental groups, we find that Group S used 4 minutes 50 seconds in mean (ranging from 2 minutes 9 seconds to 9 minutes 56 seconds), while Group N used 4 minutes 57 seconds in mean (ranging from 2 minutes 2 seconds to 8 minutes 52 seconds). Actually, this is very close to the student dyads, with a mean of 4 minutes 27 seconds on the practice route (Blakar 1973a). Until then, all the student dyads we had run had solved the induced communication conflict according to criteria one or two above, and *within* the forty-minute limit. However, only six of the ten parent couples managed to solve the communication conflict according to criteria one or two. Four of the ten couples went on for more than forty minutes, and were consequently stopped and shown the discrepancy between the maps. In dealing with the experimental route, therefore, the ten couples formed two sub-groups: six solvers and four non-solvers, and the crucial question is how the Group S and the Group N couples were distributed over these sub-groups. While all five Group N couples solved the induced communication conflict, only one of the Group S couples managed to do so. All the four non-solvers were thus Group S couples.[8]

As regards the practice route, where no conflict was induced and hence no critical evaluation and readjustment of communication strategy was required, Group S parents performed as well as Group N parents, and actually similarly to the younger and more highly educated student dyads. However, *when a discrepancy with respect to premises* was induced, most Group S parents failed.

The primary aim of the Solvberg and Blakar (1975) study was methodological, and our findings suggested that the method used would be worth the investment of more effort in further elaboration and refinement. A more qualitatively oriented analysis was also carried out at this stage of the research. Three types of analysis were conducted in order to identify further differences and similarities in patterns of communication between the two groups of couples:

1   The tapes were blind-scored by a communication-oriented student trained in clinical psychology.

2   A detailed analysis (on utterance level) of the organization of the communication process was carried out.

3   The emotional climate was assessed on a set of five-point scales.

For two reasons these analyses are presented here: First, the findings, although based on preliminary analyses, revealed in fact qualitative differences in patterns of communication. Secondly, they provided convincing support for my initial argument that there is a strong need for theoretically grounded methods for analysing patterns of communication. On the basis of this exploratory study we introduced the framework of a social-cognitive psychology (Rommetveit 1968; 1972; Blakar 1970) in order to develop systematic procedures for describing the communication process *in terms of* degrees of egocentrism and decentration, patterns of attributions of com-

---

8 As a curiosity only, I mention that we learned afterwards that the one Group S couple that had managed to solve the communication conflict was the only one of the five that had been given some family therapy in connection with the treatment of their hospitalized daughter.

munication difficulties, proposed and endorsed contracts, and
so on.

1 *The clinical analysis of communication:* In order to obtain
some clinical 'validation' of the differences revealed by the
time measures and to achieve a more global and qualitative
description of the communication patterns, a student trained
in clinical psychology was given the ten recordings with the
following instruction:

These tapes record what took place when ten parent couples were
presented with a standardized cooperation task. Five couples are
parents of a person diagnosed as schizophrenic. The other five
couples have offspring with no obvious form of psychopathology.
You may listen to each of the ten tapes as many times as you wish,
and then give a short description of each couple and what takes place
between them. Then decide which of the recordings you believe to
be of the schizophrenic's parents and which not.

On the basis of her *clinical evaluation,* she correctly identified
four couples whom she felt certain to belong to Group S. In
the communication of the other six she found no particular
characteristics which, according to her clinical knowledge,
would lead her to classify them as belonging to Group S.
When forced to guess about the last Group S couple, she was
wrong, but she stressed that she was in severe doubt. For what
this finding may be worth, it suggests that potential pathological characteristics of communication *are highlighted in this
situation* to such an extent that they can be identified fairly
easily by a clinical psychologist. In comparison, the extensive
notes on how each couple appeared to the experimenter *outside*
the experimental setting revealed no systematic differences
between Group S and Group N couples. They all appeared to
him (also trained in clinical psychology) to be normal, well-
adjusted, middle-age couples (Solvberg 1973).

A closer examination of the scorer's descriptions of the
communication patterns shows that the Group S couples (as

compared to the Group N couples) were characterized by more rigidity (in explanation strategy, in role distribution, and so on), by less ability and/or willingness to listen to, and take into account, what the other said, by a more imprecise and diffuse use of language (imprecise definitions, concepts, and so on) and by more 'pleasing' and/or pseudo-agreement in situations in which the erroneous maps had produced interaction problems.

2 *An utterance analysis of communication:* The categorization system, which was developed to analyse the organization (on utterance level) of communication, represented a preliminary attempt *to bridge the gap* between the communication-oriented studies of schizophrenia and a more general theory of language and communication. Our categorization system as applied in this study was immature and very laborious, and the more promising aspects of it were and are developed further and refined in follow-up studies. Therefore, the system is not presented in detail here, but will only be outlined to the extent that some of the most interesting of the preliminary findings can be discussed.

Each utterance was classified with respect to some formal and some content aspects. For practical as well as theoretical reasons the practice route was chosen. For practical considerations, as the couples spent much less time with the practice route and as such an analysis is extremely time-consuming. For theoretical reasons, as, if any qualitative differences were found on the practice route, where the two types of couples had been equally efficient and where they had not been influenced by our experimental manipulation, these qualitative differences would, perhaps, indicate *why* the Group S couples failed when the communication conflict was induced.

Our detailed analysis of the utterances used in dealing with the practice route revealed various differences between the two groups, of which only the three most significant will be mentioned here:

a   Every utterance was classified as being either *active* (in the sense that it was initiated by the person himself) or *reactive* (in the sense that it represented a reaction to something the other had said or done). When we examined the distribution of active utterances within each couple, we noted that the Group S wives tended to produce a larger proportion of these than the Group N wives. Four of the five Group S wives had more active utterances than their respective husbands, whereas three of the five Group N husbands had more than their respective wives. This tendency toward 'marital skew' in the schizophrenic family (Lidz 1963) becomes even clearer when all 'questions' and 'comments' are excluded from the active utterances, so that 'directives' only are considered ('go there and there', 'do so and so', and so on). In all five Group S couples, the wife gave many more such active directives (on the average, almost twice as many as the husbands), whereas in the Group N couples the distribution between the spouses was much more equal (in three couples the husband gave more, and in two the wife gave more such active directives).

b   The active utterances were classified as 'directives', 'questions', and 'comments'. Comments were further classified as being either *task-relevant* (comments that could be of help in solving the task) and *task-irrelevant* (comments that were judged to be entirely irrelevant from the point of view of solving the communication task). First, at group level, the Group N couples produced more comments (almost twice as many) as the Group S couples, but there was some overlap. However, when the distribution of task-relevant and task-irrelevant comments within each couple was inspected, it was found that a much larger proportion of the comments in the Group S couples were task-irrelevant (a mean of 57 per cent of the comments were irrelevant) as compared to the Group N couples (in mean 19 per cent of the comments were irrelevant). And, with respect to the total number of relevant comments, there were, on the average, three times as many in the Group N as in the Group S couples.

This finding is of particular theoretical interest in that relevant comments may reflect a capacity and willingness on behalf of the spouses *to decenter* (for example, one describes to the other what the map looks like where he or she is) and thereby re-establish a shared here-and-now within which meaningful communication can take place.

c   Furthermore, for every active utterance elicited by either member of the couple, the reaction of the other was classified as being *adequate* (confirmation, disconfirmation, relevant answer or question, and so on) or *inadequate* (in particular, ignoring and no response). In Group S a larger proportion (an average of 36 per cent) of the active utterances were ignored by the other as compared to Group N (an average of 21 per cent). In addition there was almost no overlap between the two groups with the exception of one Group S couple where very few active utterances were ignored by the other spouse. This couple obviously involved pseudo-mutuality, as described by Wynne et al. (1958).

3 *The emotional climate:* The emotional climate was assessed on five-point scales (from 'very much' to 'very little') of the following type: 'To what extent is the interaction character-ized by warmth (openness, confidence, helplessness, intima-cy, mutual respect, and so on)?' All ten couples were scored by two psychology students. This scoring procedure did not reveal any differences between the two groups. An analysis of variance (2 groups × 2 raters) did not show any significant differences than would be expected by chance. The reasons for this may be many, apart from the obvious one that there may really be no differences. (An obvious counter argument against this hypothesis is the fact that in the above analysis a student of clinical psychology easily picked out four of the five Group S couples). Other reasons for the insignificant findings could have been: Our two student raters were not sufficiently well trained to detect more subtle differences, and on many variables the interscorer reliability was low. (However, sepa-rate analyses for each of the two raters did not produce any

significant group differences either); furthermore, on many of the variables all 10 couples scored either very high or very low, so that no differences could possibly be demonstrated.[9] As regards this particular analysis, the evidence seems to be inconclusive.

4 The Emergence of New Questions

Our results were in line with earlier findings (see, for example, Haley's 1972 summary), while many intriguing new questions also emerged. These were:

1 Do Group S couples use a more egocentric and less decentrated form of communication? In other words, are Group S spouses less able and/or willing to take the perspective of, and speak on the premises of, the other? For instance, utterances such as '. . . and then you go up *there*', '. . . and from *here* you take a right', when 'here' and 'there' could, obviously, not be known to the other, were frequently observed in communication of the Group S couples.

2 Are Group S couples less able and/or willing to endorse (and adhere to) contracts that regulate and monitor the various aspects of their communication (for example, role distribution, perspective, strategy of explanation)? Only a few contractual proposals were found (regarding, for example, categorization and explanation strategy). Furthermore, many cases were observed in which implicitly or explicitly endorsed contracts were broken or ignored.

3 Do Group S couples show less ability and/or willingness to attribute (adequately or inadequately) their communication difficulties to any potential causes? The Group S couples could apparently return to the starting point again and again without any (overt, explicit) attempt to attribute their communication difficulties to anything.

9 As regards the standardized communication conflict situation as such, it was promising that all ten couples scored high on: 'To what extent is their interaction characterized by involvement.'

These were some of the most significant questions that emerged from our first exploratory study. All these questions are formulated *within a conceptual framework* dissimilar to that usually employed in the study of schizophrenia. The formulations are inspired by the theoretical work of people such as Heider, Mead, Piaget, Rommetveit, and others, as outlined above. More systematic research has to be carried out in order to settle these questions. But the mere stating of these questions represents a contribution towards describing (and hence in part explaining) schizophrenia using the framework of a general social-cognitive theory of language and communication.

5   Theoretical and Methodological Constraints of the Solvberg and Blakar (1975) Study

Retrospectively, our first exploratory study may be seen as a lucky shot. However, this should not be understood to mean that the project was based on, and that the findings were achieved by, mere chance. The method was derived so directly from a general psychological theory of language and communication, and the experimental manipulation interferes with such fundamental preconditions for communication (Blakar 1973a, 1975a, 1975c, 1978a), that *if* it is the case that the family as the immediate environment of the schizophrenic involves abnormal patterns of communication, then it would certainly become apparent in this particular situation. As an incentive for future research it was our good fortune that the method proved to be even more sensitive in revealing these abnormalities in communication patterns than we hoped at the onset of our work.

Our first study must be seen as a point of departure for further research rather than as having provided sufficient answers to the issues considered above. I will, therefore, first identify the theoretical and methodological shortcomings of the study, and then describe our follow-up studies which appeared to be logically and methodologically necessary to achieve satisfactory conclusions.

A satisfactory solution to the problem complex of schizophrenia, I think, necessarily involves the integration of knowledge gathered in different disciplines where the subject matter is studied from different perspectives (for example, psychology, genetics, pharmacology and anthropology). In the following analysis, however, I restrict myself to the various continuations of our initial project which were conceptualised *within* the psychological framework of our communication theory. An integration of this approach with other perspectives is a task of the future.[10]

Our theoretical and methodological considerations were also determined by the fact that we did not wish to change the communication conflict situation itself. Given the promising results which were achieved in our first study this seemed to be a reasonable choice (Blakar 1978a).

The analysis of theoretical and methodological shortcomings of our initial study revealed six different issues which required and require further research work before, eventually, it will be possible to draw any definite conclusions (Blakar 1975b, 1978a). These were:

1   *Replications and expansions of the samples:* First and foremost, it was found desirable to increase the size of the two samples. Even though the matching between Groups S and N with regard to the relevant background variables was almost perfect, groups of 5 and 5 couples seemed too small. But merely to increase the size of the sample *without* improving the conceptual framework and developing more adequate methods of analysis was not regarded as sufficient.

2   *Different demand characteristics:* From a purely methodological point of view we asked whether the differences found

10 Elsewhere I have argued (Blakar 1978d) in which ways the communication perspective constitutes a supplementary, but vital, perspective in an integrated understanding of psychopathology.

between Group S and Group N reflected the fact that the two groups of couples were actually exposed to fundamentally different social situations. With respect to the subjects' expectations, the Group S couples *knew* that they were made objects of research *because* one of their children was schizophrenic. The Group N couples obviously participated in the experiment on different premises. Haley (1972), among others, criticised research in this field for not taking these basic methodological considerations into account (i.e., the different 'demand characteristics' inherent in the experimental situation).

More urgent than increasing sample size, therefore, was the need to 'test' the parents of children with diagnoses *other* than schizophrenia in this particular communication conflict situation. In selecting alternative diagnostic categories as additional control groups, decisions must be based on considerations about how general this particular source of methodological error is assumed to be: a. If it is assumed that our findings do not pertain exclusively to the familial communication of the schizophrenic, but are characteristic of the communication pattern in the family of *all* (seriously) ill patients, then it would follow that one should start by studying the communication of parents of patients with a (serious) illness where there is little or no theoretical reason to assume that there should be any connection between the familial communication patterns and the pathological development of the offspring.[11] Illnesses such as congenital heart disease and cancer should then constitute appropriate controls. b. If, on the other hand, it is assumed that the findings do not pertain to the familial communication of all who are seriously ill, but only to those with some kind of psychopathology, then obviously other forms of psychopathology than schizophrenia would be relevant as control groups.

11 It should be underlined that within our present approach, nothing definite can be said about causality (Blakar 1974a, 1975a, 1978a, 1978d; Wikran, Faleide and Blakar 1978).

3 *Parent-child interaction:* Even though our present design does not address the issue of causality directly it would be very interesting to investigate the communication between the parents and the child (schizophrenic vs. control) in this particular communication conflict situation. In order to obtain a more exhaustive understanding of the connection between the development and maintenance of schizophrenia and the familial communication, it will be essential to see *if* (and *how*) the peculiarities of the parental communication pattern, which we have exposed, affects their interaction with the child. As in the study of parental communication, this design involving the parent-child constellation will necessarily require control groups in addition to Group N families.

4 *General variables in communication:* In my critical analyses of research into communication and psychopathology (Blakar 1975a, 1978a, 1978d) I pointed out that many of the theoretical and methodological weaknesses can be explained by the lack of contact with *general theory.* The fact that our research approach was explicitly derived from a general communication theory (Blakar 1972, 1973a) constituted an obvious improvement, but, nevertheless, there is an obligation to explain our findings concerning schizophrenia (and psychopathology) further in terms of general theory, and to relate these to general social, personality and developmental variables.

a Anthropological and sociological studies have explored the ways in which people from different cultural and social (class) backgrounds employ different patterns of communication and language use (Hall 1959; Labov et al. 1968; Bernstein 1971). Further, it is known that the occurrence and distribution of various forms of psychopathology varies in different cultures and classes. In other words, communication characteristics which prove to be specific to, and 'normal' in certain subcultures (for example, a social class) could easily be interpreted as deviant characteristics in the familial communication of the schizophrenic. Hence it is desirable to obtain knowledge about how general social variables such as socio-economic status, urban as opposed to rural background, and so on, are reflected in the patterns of communication in this communication conflict situation.

b   In spite of the fact that the concept of personality, for many reasons, is both problematic and controversial (Mischel 1968, 1973), there is, nevertheless, no doubt that the kinds of variables which, traditionally, have been described as 'personality traits' will be reflected in different ways in patterns of communication. General variables such as anxiety, aggression, degree of confidence (in oneself and others) or rigidity as opposed to flexibility will obviously affect the communication process. To assess the implications of the (deviant) communication patterns found in the family of the schizophrenic, it will, therefore, be of vital importance to know *how* the communication patterns of rigid (or other relevant variables) persons deviate from the communication patterns of more flexible persons *within* the so-called normal range. In addition, in order to indicate whether the communication patterns of rigid (or flexible) persons have common characteristics with the patterns found in the familial environment of the schizophrenic, this type of study needed also to entail a conceptual clarification of variables, such as aggression, which have been used to characterize individual and social phenomena (Blakar 1974b, 1977).

c   Many of the concepts employed in our descriptions of familial communication patterns of the schizophrenic obviously involve developmental aspects and are based on developmental theory. For example, the communication of the Group S couples was characterized as egocentric, as lacking the capacity to decenter and take the other's perspective. In the literature (Piaget 1926; Glucksberg et al. 1966; Ovreeide 1970; Strono 1978) the capacity to decenter is described as developing from the child's nearly total egocentrism to the adult's (periodical?) decentration. Knowledge about the communication patterns in conflict situations demonstrated by children at various stages of development, i.e., with different capacities to decenter, would illuminate the 'deviations' found in the communication patterns in the family of the schizophrenic.

5   *Methods of analysis:* Our exploratory study revealed that we, as other research in this field, are practically without systematic methods for analysing and describing *the qualitative aspects* of the communication exposed in the communication conflict situation. A blind scorer, basing his predictions on clinical judgement only, correctly identified four of the five Group S couples by listening to the tape recordings from the communication conflict situation. This indicated that our conceptual apparatus was not yet sufficiently explicit and detailed. Although we *did* have some relevant concepts (such as egocentrism), we lacked corresponding adequate methods (with the exception of descriptive case reports) by means of which systematic scoring (of, for example, egocentrism and decentration in the communication process) could be conducted.

6   *The conceptual framework:* The outcome of our exploratory study constituted a great challenge·towards further development of our theoretical framework and conceptual apparatus to enable us to capture and understand the various patterns of communication which were so vividly exposed in the communication conflict situation. Actually, it was the need for further explication and clarification of communication theory in general which orginally led to the development of the communication conflict situation (Blakar 1972, 1973a). Problems of theory building have thus continuously remained within the project (Blakar 1978a).

6   The Realization of the Communication Oriented Research Programme: A Progress Report

In the previous section, I discussed our project on the basis of ideal type theoretical and methodological considerations. But a thorough and systematic investigation of each of these issues would have demanded more resources than we had and have at our disposal. I will briefly mention the most important factors which made it possible to realize at least parts of the

research programme outlined above: First, a number of students became interested in writing their degree theses in
connection with our project. This constituted a great potential
of interest and work, and the strong involvement of the
students produced good results. The main disadvantage,
however, was that each thesis has to represent an autonomous
piece of work. It was, therefore, impossible to direct the
research only in accordance with strict theoretical and
methodological criteria, and, instead, each study had to be
adapted to each student's special interests. Hence, attempts at
integrating the finding *post festum* became more difficult than it
otherwise would have been. This paper may be read as an
example of such an attempt (see also Blakar 1975a, 1978a, c;
Blakar and Pedersen 1978). Secondly, without cooperation
and assistance from the relevant institutions it would have
been impossible to come in contact with relevant research
subjects and their families. I will now present a summary
presentation of our studies so far, that is, June 1978.

1   *Replications and expansions of the samples:* Paulsen (1977)
carried out a replication of our initial study (Solvberg and
Blakar 1975). This study was, however, not just a replication
of the original study, but, by moving the study from Oslo
(urban) to a rural district, social cultural and ecological variables were systematically varied. By combining the original
study and the replication, we obtained a 2x2x2 design which
enabled us to describe *under what* conditions the communication patterns of families containing schizophrenic members
deviated, and in which manner they deviated (Blakar, Paulsen
and Solvberg 1978). The crucial point is that not only were
two types of couples (parents with and without a schizophrenic offspring) with different social cultural backgrounds
(towns versus country) involved in the study, but also that the
couples communicated in two different cooperation situations
(one simple and straightforward vs. one in which a conflict
was induced). With regard to efficiency of communication,
the significant differences between parents with and without a

schizophrenic offspring were reproduced. In addition, considerable differences in communication efficiency between rural and urban couples were found. This suggests that one should generally be cautious in generalizing particular findings and that methods and models have to be adapted in accordance with social cultural variations of styles and patterns of communication.[12]

Rund (1976, 1978) went a step further and tried to specify more clearly the connection between the parent's pattern of communication and the specific deviance in thought processes displayed by the schizophrenic patient. This was achieved by testing thought deviances of schizophrenics by means of traditional tests and by investigating the communication pattern of the parents in using our standardized communication conflict situation. Finally, through a blind scoring procedure it was predicted which patient belonged to which parental couple. The, in part, negative results (failure to predict) in this study illustrated the weaknesses of theories that have been developed in this subject area (Ronbeck 1977; Glennsjo 1977).

2 *Different demand characteristics:* As regards the important methodological issue of situational demand characteristics, several independent and substantially interesting studies have been conducted. Alve and Hultberg (1974) studied the communication of parents of 'borderline' patients. Wikran (1974) studied the pattern of communication of parents with children who suffer from asthma as compared to parents whose children had congenital heart diseases. Rotbaek (1976) studied the communication of parents of children who suffered from enuresis. Finally, Faetten and Ostvold (1975) studied the communication patterns in couples where not an offspring, but one of the spouses, was diagnosed.

From a theoretical and methodological point of view, the most interesting finding here is that the parents of borderline patients demonstrated patterns of communication that dif-

12 Presently, Valdemarsdottir is replicating Solvberg and Blakar's (1975) study at Iceland.

fered from *both* the Group S *and* the Group N couples (Alve and Hultberg 1974; Hultberg, Alve and Blakar 1978). Furthermore, parents of children with congenital heart disease, as was expected, demonstrated communication patterns similar to that of Group N (Wikran 1974; Wikran, Faleide and Blakar 1978a, 1978b). Without inspecting the results here in any more detail, it is possible to conclude that the differences found in our initial study (Solvberg and Blakar 1975) between the communication patterns of Group S and Group N parental couples *cannot* reasonably be explained by different expectations (demand characteristics) towards the experimental situation. If one were to reject this conclusion, one would then have to explain *why* the parents of borderline patients should display expectations towards the experiment which are systematically *different from* the expectations of the parents of those with a diagnosis of schizophrenia.

3   *Parent-child interaction:* As regards the issue of parent-child communication, three independent studies have been conducted so far. In these studies mother and father *together* were asked to explain the two routes to their daughter or son. Jacobsen and Pettersen (1974) analysed the patterns of communication between the parents and their schizophrenic or 'normal' daughter. Differences in communication between Group S and Group N families were revealed just as clearly in this three-person setting as in our initial study which involved the parents alone (Mossige, Pettersen and Blakar 1976).

It could be argued, in the context of this research, that differences in communication arise from differences in situational demand characteristics for the two groups of families. Haarstad's (1976) investigation of parent-daughter communication in families in which the daughter was diagnosed as suffering from anorexia nervosa settled this issue, however, in that families of this kind revealed communication patterns definitely different from *both* Group S *and* Group N families. Hence, it can be concluded, as above, that the differences in communication patterns *cannot* be explained by differences in expectations towards the experimental situation alone.

Finally, Glennsjo (1977) compared the patterns of communication in families containing a schizophrenic son with those containing a schizophrenic daughter. This particular study thus represents a critical empirical test of the theory developed by Lidz et al. (1957). Glennsjo's study revealed great differences as to how families containing a schizophrenic member structured the communication process, but there were *no* systematic differences between families containing a male (son) and families containing a female (daughter) diagnosed as schizophrenic. These findings are contrary to the predictions which can be derived from the theory presented by Lidz et al. (1957).

4 *General variables in communication:* As has been pointed out in the introduction, clinically oriented research in psychopathology and communication has not been properly integrated with more generally oriented communication research. It follows from the general research programme outlined above that it is desirable to conduct more clinically oriented studies of familial communication and psychopathology *as an integral part* of a more general study of the process of communication, as it is only *within* the framework of a general communication theory that it is possible to contribute fruitfully to the understanding of psychopathology from a communication perspective. Concentrating exclusively on the investigation of patterns of communication in families *with* and *without* psychopathological members obviously involves the risk of labelling as 'deviant' or 'pathological' patterns of communication which would be *within* the 'normal range' if one took care to systematically explore the variation of 'normal' patterns of communication depending on background variables.

The studies conducted so far (Lagerlov and Stokstad 1974; Dahle 1977; Blakar and Pedersen 1978; Strono 1978) have demonstrated the impact of *general variables* (such as sex, social background, age or anxiety) on the communication process in our communication conflict situation.

To investigate how personality variables are reflected in the process of communication, Lagerlov and Stokstad (1974) analysed the communication of persons with varying *levels of anxiety*. They compared the patterns of communication among students with high vs. low levels of anxiety (as measured by Taylor's Manifest Anxiety Scale).

It should be emphasized that we are not dealing here with extreme or 'pathological' anxiety, but with levels of anxiety found amongst normal students. As regards the simple and straightforward communication situation (the practice route), there was no difference in efficiency of communication between the two groups. As regards the communication conflict situation, however, there was a marked difference in that, while all low level anxiety dyads solved the induced conflict, more than half of the high level anxiety dyads failed.

With respect to social (anthropological) variables, Dahle (1977) has analysed the patterns of communication of couples with different social backgrounds (urban vs. rural, and working class vs. middle class). She demonstrated that variations in style and efficiency in communication within the range of 'normal' couples, i.e., those couples who do not have an offspring with some kind of psychiatric problem, is considerable, and covary systematically with social background. Again, the interaction with the *types* of communication situation should be noted, in that, while no differences in communication efficiency were found in the simple and straightforward situation (the practice route), clear differences emerged in the conflict situation.[13] These two and other studies presently under preparation make valuable contributions to an understanding of social control and communication in general (Blakar 1978a, d).

13 Further, Blakar and Pedersen (1978) demonstrated the pervasive influences of sex upon verbal communication; the four combinations of male or female explainer and follower yielded very different patterns of communication. According to common sense 'knowledge' about sex and communication, male female dyads constituted the most efficient and female male the most inefficient ones. However, this was true for the simple situation only. The pattern was totally *reversed* in the conflict situation in that the male female dyads were the most inefficient in solving the induced communication conflict.

Finally, Strono (1978) has analysed the process of communication using our communication conflict situation for the purposes of developmental psychology. She investigated the communication of children of various ages (6–16 years) and found, as was expected, an, with age, increasing capacity to decenter and to take the perspective of the other (Piaget 1926; Mead 1934); that is, the communication became more adequate and efficient, the more age increased. The categorization system initially developed by Strono for the identification and description of the various manifestations of egocentrism in the process of communication has now been developed into a geneal framework within which the patterns of communication of different categories of families (for example, families containing a schizophrenic member) can be assessed.

While the studies discussed above are not aimed at investigations of how general social, developmental, and personality variables are reflected in the process of communication (Blakar 1978c), a number of important insights into the relationships between patterns of familial communication and psychopathology in specific social contexts have been gained.

First, only through this type of study (especially that of Dahle (1977)) can we explore the *normal* variations. *Without* thorough knowledge of normal variations in patterns of communication according to social class, cultural, and ecological background variables, one will be unable to assess and describe properly deviant or pathological communication. Studies of this kind are particularly important because the underlying (often implicit) model of 'normal communication' from which pathological communication *deviates*, is seriously questioned and investigated. We have elsewhere (Blakar, Paulsen and Solvberg 1978) argued that a *particular experimenter ethnocentrism* has been displayed by students of psychopathology and familial communication, in that the 'norm' for 'adequate communication' has been implicitly defined as the communication of *the normal middle class family living in cities.*

Secondly, knowledge about how general variables (such as level of anxiety or age) affect the process of communication may contribute to the identification of *what* (if anything) is failing in the communication of families containing members with psychiatric problems. Conclusions concerning causality cannot be drawn from such covariation studies, but systematic comparisons of the communication of people with, for example, a high level of anxiety with the patterns of communication in families containing, for example, a schizophrenic member could give valuable clues for future research.

5   *Methods of analysis:* The fact that we succeeded in developing a standardized communication situation which proved *sensitive* with respect to revealing the patterns of communication in different types of families is important.[14] However, as regards the general research programme outlined previously, this constitutes only a first, albeit critical, step. One next step is the development of methods which will enable systematic analyses of *qualitative characteristics* pertaining to the communication of the different types of families or parental couples.

As with the development of the standardized communication situation, methods of analysis are needed which are *explicitly* grounded in, and derived from, general communication theory. It should be underlined that in this field of psychopathology and familial communication this is not an obvious demand, as many studies apply linguistically inspired, but, within a perspective of general communication theory, highly questionable units or categories such as 'number of words per sentence' or 'ratio of nouns to verbs'. In particular, when it comes to a *qualitative analysis* of communication in families with and without psychopathological members, most researchers seem to work without using designs

14 In this paper, families are classified according to the diagnoses attributed to one particular member of the family. The relations between the diagnosis of the individual family member and the family as a social system, however, are complex and problematic (Blakar 1978d; Blakar and Nafstad 1978).

grounded in general communication theory. Overwhelmed by the richness of, and the variation in, the material, they resort to mere clinical-casuistic descriptions, freely employing everyday language and *ad hoc* terms (Riskin and Faunce 1972; Blakar 1976).

Besides the lack of use of adequate communication theory, I have already pointed out that interdisciplinary isolation is striking in the field of communication and psychopathology. But if one turns, for example, to social-cognitive psychology, a large number of relevant and theoretically grounded concepts become available. For illustrative purposes, a few examples will be given: A basic precondition for successful communication is the participants' ability *to take the perspective* of the other (Mead, 1934), and *egocentrism* (lack of *decentration*) (Piaget, 1926) may strongly hinder the flow of communication. Related to this is Rommetveit's (1968) notion that 'encoding involves *anticipatory decoding*'. Another essential prerequisite for successful communication is that the participants have to endorse *contracts* (contracts concerning categorization, topic, perspective, and so on) against which the act of communication is being monitored (Rommetveit 1972, 1974; Blakar 1972, 1978a). When communication runs into trouble, it is essential, in order to re-establish successful communication, that the difficulties are adequately *attributed* by the participants (Heider 1958). It is immediately apparent that these concepts originating from social-cognitive psychology are of *direct* relevance in the analysis of patterns of familial communication.

To investigate the above mentioned concepts we have developed methods of analysis and scoring procedures which help to assess the theoretically relevant qualitative aspects of the process of communication. These methods of analysis will now be considered.

Alve and Hultberg (1974) took as their point of departure the concept of *attribution* and developed a procedure which helps to describe the process of communication in terms of the couples' patterns of attribution of communication difficulties.

(*Who* attributes *how* to *what*, and *how* does the other spouse *react* to the attribution). Haarstad (1976) adapted the method for an application in a more complex (three-person) parent-child interaction. Systematic differences in the various categories of families' or couples' patterns of attribution in the communication conflict situation were revealed (Hultberg, Alve and Blakar 1976).

Already in our first exploratory study (Solvberg and Blakar 1975) the concept of egocentrism (vs. decentration) proved useful in capturing qualitative differences in the patterns of communication of parental couples with and without a schizophrenic offspring. Since then much work has been invested in developing systematic scoring procedures for assessing the degree of, and the development of, egocentrism and decentration as displayed by the various types of participants in the communication conflict situation (Jacobsen and Pettersen 1974; Kristiansen 1976; Mossige, Pettersen and Blakar 1976; Kristiansen, Faleide and Blakar 1977; Strono 1978). In his analysis, on the level of utterances, Kristiansen (1976) managed to assess the *degree of*, and the *development over time* during the process of communication of, egocentrism as well as the *types of reaction* to the egocentric utterances. By this method of analysis, systematic qualitative differences in the patterns of communication of various types of parental couples (parents of children with psychosomatic illnesses compared with three control groups, i.e., parents of children with congenital heart disease and parents of schizophrenic and borderline patients) were revealed (Kristiansen, Faleide and Blakar 1977).

Paulsen (1977), in his study of parental couples (urban vs. rural) with and without a schizophrenic offspring, developed a scoring procedure for assessing the couples' ability to cope adequately with free and bound information (Rommetveit 1974; Blakar and Rommetveit 1975; Blakar 1978a). He found that, across the social background variation, the Group S couples tacitly took for granted more frequently and to a larger extent (as free information) critical information which could not yet possibly be known to the other spouse.

The contractual aspect is characteristic of the process of communication (Rommetveit 1974, 1978; Blakar 1972, 1975c, 1978a). Having identified the various types of contracts (contracts concerning topic, perspective, roles, categorization, and so on) which were used by participants to monitor the process of communication in the communication conflict situation and the process by which contracts are endorsed (Blakar 1972, 1973a), Moberget and Reer (1975) developed a systematic procedure for classifying and describing the endorsement of contracts. From a theoretical point of view, the concept of contract was proposed to characterize the dynamic aspects of communication. In the empirical studies of familial communication, the analysis of contracts has enabled us to describe in detail *the control relations* reflected in the monitoring of the process of communication. By means of this contractual analysis Oisjofoss (1976) revealed distinctively different patterns of control in married couples depending on social background variables (urban vs. rural, middle class vs. working class). Furthermore, he found a high correlation between *flexibility* in patterns of control and efficiency in communication (whether they solved the induced communication conflict or not). Glennsjo (1977) adapted the scoring procedure for application in a more complex (three-person) parent-child interaction.

From a methodological point of view the greatest advantage of the communication situation design is that we can study the communication process in two apparently similar, but actually highly different situations. The one is simple and straightforward (the practice route), while in the other a conflict is experimentally induced.[15] In principle, this methodological advantage may be exploited in a great number of ways to gain insight into the process of communication (Blakar 1978a). So far, however, we have mainly used various

15 The fact that in a study, where 24 student dyads participated, a rank order correlation of ·19 was found between efficiency (time used) of communication in the two situations shows that we managed to establish two apparently similar, yet *in reality* highly different, communication situations (Blakar and Pedersen 1978).

prediction or blind scoring procedures. The general approach may be described thus: The scorer is only allowed to listen to the recording of the simple and straightforward situation (the practice route). On the basis of his analysis of the pattern of communication in the simple situation, he is asked to *predict*, and give the reasons for his predictions, *how* these particular participants (a family or couple or dyad) will manage to cope with the induced communication conflict. In this manner we can, to a certain extent, put our insights and the different methods of analysis to a *test*.

A brief discussion of a study by Teigre (1976) will serve as an illustrative example. He assessed the degree of confidence 30 married couples had (in oneself and in the other) during the simple situation, and on the basis of the type and degree of mutual confidence, he predicted the outcome of the communication conflict situation. Similar prediction procedures can, in principle, be used in conjunction with all the qualitative methods of analysis discussed above. So far, however, predictions about the conflict situation, based on performances in the simple situation, have only been conducted in the case of contractual analysis (Moberget and Reer 1975).

When discussing our forms of analysis I restricted myself to single concepts (for example, contract, attribution of communication difficulties, confidence, egocentrism vs. decentration and free and bound information). Obviously, these concepts are interconnected; they are all derived from the same theoretical framework (Blakar 1978a). The existence of such interrelations may be illustrated thus: The egocentrism of one of the family members may result in him tacitly taking for granted (as free information) something which could not possibly be known by the others. This may result in communication difficulties, either directly or indirectly. In order to re-establish commonality, the communication difficulty experienced has to be identified (attribution of communication difficulties). As a consequence of the (adequate or inadequate) attribution of communication difficulties, the underlying contracts are frequently modified or new contracts are endorsed to prevent further tangles of the same kind (Blakar 1978a).

In order to keep track of these integrative aspects, the systematic and detailed analyses on, for example, egocentrism vs. decentration have to be continually *supplemented* by more free case studies in which all relevant concepts are exploited in the description of the patterns of communication of the various types of families and couples. In our project this approach was realized in a series of studies (Wikran 1974; Faetten and Ostvold 1975; Rotbaek 1976; Dahle 1977; Blakar 1976). In our present studies, much effort is invested in simplifying and standardizing the various scoring procedures.

6   *The conceptual framework:* The analytical distinction between my discussion of our methods and the development of our conceptual framework does *not*, of course, reflect a division of labour. Theoretical clarification is a *necessary* prerequisite for the development of adequate methods of analysis, while the development of methods propels theoretical clarification. The various methodological developments described have all contributed to theoretical clarification. As a transition to the discussion of conceptual problems, I will, therefore, consider an issue which was originally encountered as an irritating methodological problem in the analysis of the process of communication, but which proved to involve intriguing basic theoretical issues: *When* is a communication conflict solved? The trivial problem of analysis, which originally compelled us to undertake the enterprise of analysing these issues in general, was the fact that we soon ran into trouble in applying our set of criteria for *distinguishing* between those who managed and those who did not manage to solve the induced communication conflict (Blakar 1978a; Mossige, Pettersen and Blakar 1976; Wikran, Faleide and Blakar 1978a; Hultberg, Alve and Blakar 1978). This problem will not be discussed in any detail here; only a brief illustration of its nature will be given.

First, in some cases only one of the participants would

realize that the maps were not identical, while the other(s) were greatly surprised when this was later uncovered by a direct comparison of the two maps. This type of solution, which we have classified as an *individual* solution, is very different from cases where all of them (both) are firmly convinced of the existence of the error (a *social* solution). If the experimenter *too* readily accepted an individual solution, we would lose the chance to study how the member with insight into the deception convinces or fails to convince, the other(s). This situation could be very revealing as regards factors such as power and control.

Furthermore, there were various combinations of the degrees to which participants indicated insight into the deception to the experimenter, and that they were convinced about it. On the one extreme, we have the couples or families where one (or all) members indicated that they were convinced that something was wrong, and, consequently, that there was no reason to continue, but *without* having identified and localized the error on the maps. On the other extreme, we have the couples or families who achieved a certain insight into the deceptive maps (the degree of insight varied from vague doubt to full understanding), but who were unsure of their own judgement and therefore hesitated to reveal their suspicions to the experimenter. The latter involves a distinct contrast to those who, on the basis of vague and diffuse suspicions only, put the experimenter under a heavy social pressure to admit that something is wrong.[16] The phase when the participants advance and work their way from vague and diffuse suspicions towards a full understanding of the deception and thus solve the communication conflict in which they have been involved (or fail to do so), may be very revealing as regards their patterns of communication. In order not to lose critical information about the process of communication, the termination criteria were reconsidered in that it was decided that the

16 For example, the solvers among the parents of borderline patients demonstrated a strategy distinctively different from the Group N solvers in that they, on the basis of vague and diffuse suspicions, put the experimenter under heavy pressure to admit 'the manipulation' (Hultberg, Alve and Blakar 1978).

experimenter should 'press' the couples or families as much as possible toward criterion 1 (task finished when error identified), and not accept solutions according to criterion 2 (task resolved when subjects indicated that it was pointless to go on). Furthermore, the experimenter should hesitate to accept individual solutions and try whether the couple or family can reach a joint solution.

Not only among the solvers (those who manage to have the experimental session terminated according to the criteria within the 40 minutes limit) have different patterns of behaviour been identified; also the non–solvers (those who continue for more than 40 minutes) revealed distinctively different patterns. The most important distinction within this latter type is between those who one or more times *explicitly* question the credibility of the maps, but without achieving any conclusion or identification of the error, and those who *never* explicitly question the credibility of the maps. In this context it must be mentioned that the analysis of attribution of communication difficulties is particularly revealing with respect to *how* various participants may oscillate between attributing the communication difficulties to the situation (the maps), to themselves or to the other participant(s) (Hultberg, Alve and Blakar 1978).

An important issue to be indicated here is how the analysis of these problems entailed an explication of a general theory concerning *social conflicts and their solution*. In order to develop adequate criteria for terminating the experimental session and to accept the induced communication conflict as being unsolved, an explicit model or theory of conflict solution has to be outlined (Endresen 1977; Blakar 1978a).[17] The above mentioned aspects (social vs. individual solution, cognitive insight vs. social pressure, and so on) represent essential problems for a theory or model of social conflict solution. Such a model is desirable as it is possible to derive a set of theoretically

17 Interestingly, many couples or families containing psychopathological members *transform* the induced conflict (induced in terms of lacking common premises) *into* a conflict involving conflicting personal interests (for example, *who* of us is right, *who* of us is stupid).

grounded criteria. Here it may just be noted that the set of criteria orginally used were based, primarily, on intuitions (Solvberg and Blakar 1975).

7   *Conclusion*

As regards the questions posed in the introduction, a preliminary conclusion on the basis of our research carried out so far would involve three points:

First and foremost, the conceptual as well as the empirical basis of the best-known and most influential theories within this field of research seems to be fragile and speculative. To the extent that we have managed to test these theories empirically, the results have mainly been negative, and theoretical analysis has revealed considerable conceptual vagueness.

Secondly, on the basis of the series of studies conducted within our research programme, the finding in our first study (Solvberg and Blakar 1975) seem to be theoretically as well as empirically sound.

Yet, thirdly, the most honest conclusion, at the present stage, is that almost every study conducted within our research programme has posed as many new questions and issues as it has brought to rest. Hence, communication oriented research on psychopathology involves a very intriguing challenge. However, the studies conducted so far have convinced us that a systematic investigation of the patterns of familial communication represents at least *one* promising way to gain insight into the complex processes that lead an individual into the development of psychopathological behaviour.

References

S. Alve and H. Hultberg, 1974, 'Communication Deficiencies in Parental Couples with "Borderline" Offspring', unpublished final degree thesis, Oslo University ★

★ Original in Norwegian.

R. Andersson and B. Pilblad, 1977, 'Interaction in Parental Dyads, A Methodological Contribution', unpublished final degree thesis, Oslo University *

M. Argyle, 1969, *Social Interaction*, London: Methuen

J. C. Athanassiades, 1974, 'An Investigation of Some Communication Patterns of Female Subordinates in Hierarchical Organizations', *Human Relations*, Vol. 27, pp. 195–209

G. Bateson, 1960, 'Minimal Requirements for a Theory of Schizophrenia', *Archives of General Psychiatry*, Vol. 2, pp. 477–491

G. Bateson, D. D. Jackson, J. Haley and J. H. Weakland, 1956, 'Toward a Theory of Schizophrenia', *Behavioral Science*, Vol. 1, pp. 251–264

G. Bateson, D. D. Jackson, J. Haley and J. H. Weakland, 1963, 'A Note on the Double-Bind – 1962', *Family Process*, Vol. 2, pp. 154–161

B. Bernstein, 1971, *Class, Codes and Control*, Vol. 1, London: Routledge & Kegan Paul

R. M. Blakar, 1970, 'Context Effects in Verbal Communication', unpublished final degree thesis, Oslo University *

R. M. Blakar, 1972, 'An Experimental Method for Inquiring into Communication, Theoretical Background, Development and Some Problems', published working paper, Institute of Psychology, Oslo University *

R. M. Blakar, 1973a, 'An Experimental Method for Inquiring into Communication', *European Journal of Social Psychology*, Vol. 3, pp. 415–425

R. M. Blakar, 1973b, *Language as a Means of Social Power*, Oslo: Pax *

R. M. Blakar, 1974a, 'Schizophrenia and communication, A Preliminary Presentation of an Experimental Approach', *Nordisk Psykiatrisk Tidsskrift*, Vol. 28, pp. 239–248 *

R. M. Blakar, 1974b, 'Distinguishing Social and Individual Psychology,' *Scandinavian Journal of Psychology*, Vol. 15, pp. 241–243

R. M. Blakar, 1974c, 'Why an Explicit Communication Perspective has to be Adopted in the Study of Language', *Tidsskrift for Samfunnsforskning*, Vol. 15, pp. 169–176 *

R. M. Blakar, 1974d, 'Language and the Oppression of Women, A Complex Problem', *Ventil*, Vol. 4, No. 4, pp. 3–10 *

R. M. Blakar, 1975a, 'Psychopathology and Communication, A Report about a Series of Experimental Studies', published working paper, Institute of Psychology, Oslo University*

R. M. Blakar, 1975b, 'Psychopathology and Communication,

Further Elaborations of Our Experimental Approach', *Tidsskrift for Norsk Psykologforening*, Vol. 12, No. 8, pp. 16–25 ★

R. M. Blakar, 1975c, 'Human Communication – An Ever Changing Contract Embedded in Social Contexts', published working paper, Institute of Psychology, Oslo University

R. M. Blakar, 1975d, 'How the Sex Roles are Represented, Reflected and Conserved in the Norwegian Language', *Acta Sociologica*, Vol. 18, pp. 162–173

R. M. Blakar, 1975e, 'Double-Bind Theories, A Critical Assessment', *Tidsskrift for Norsk Psykologforening*, Vol. 12, No. 12, pp. 13–26 ★

R. M. Blakar, 1976, 'Psychopathology and Communication, A Critical Assessment of the Field of Research', *Tidsskrift for Norsk Psykologforening*, Vol. 13, No. 6, pp. 3–18 ★

R. M. Blakar, 1977, 'Ruminations about Conceptual and Methodological Problems in Disentangling Social and Individual Psychology', *Tidsskrift for Norsk Psykologforening*, Vol. 14, No. 5, pp. 2–11

R. M. Blakar, 1978a, *Contact and Conflict*, Oslo: Pax ★

R. M. Blakar, 1978b, 'Psychopathology and Communication, A Critical Assessment of the Research Area', in: L. Hem and H. Holter (Eds.), *Social Psychology*, Oslo: Universitetsforlaget ★

R. M. Blakar, 1978c, 'Language and the Oppression of Women, Sociolinguistics and the Zeitgeist', in: I. Kleiven (Ed.), *Language and Society*, Oslo: Pax ★

R. M. Blakar, 1978d, 'Family, Communication and Psychopathology, Some General Theoretical and Methodological Problems', published working paper, Institute of Psychology, Oslo University ★

R. M. Blakar, 1978e, 'Language as a Means of Social Power', in: R. Rommetveit and R. M. Blakar (Eds.), *Studies of Language, Thought and Verbal Communication*, London: Academic Press (published 1979)

R. M. Blakar and H. E. Nafstad, 1978, 'The Family as the Frame for the Study of Development, Theoretical and Methodological Problems', published working paper, Institute of Psychology, Oslo University ★

R. M. Blakar, O. G. Paulsen and H. A. Solvberg, 1978, 'Schizophrenia and Communication Efficiency, A Modified Replication Taking Ecological Variation into Consideration', *Acta Psychiatrica Scandinavica* (in press)

R. M. Blakar and T. B. Pedersen, 1978, 'Control and Self-Confidence as Reflected in Sex-Bound Patterns in Communication, An Experimental Approach', in: S. McConnell-Ginet, N. Furman and R. Barker (Eds.), *Language in Women's Lives*, Ithaca: Cornell University Press (published 1979)

R. M. Blakar and R. Rommetveit, 1975, 'Utterances in vacuo and in Contexts, An Experimental and Theoretical Exploration of Some Interrelationships Between What is Seen or Imagined', *International Journal of Psycholinguistics*, No. 4, pp. 5–32

C. G. Brisendal, 1976, 'On Misunderstanding, A Communication Theoretical Analysis', unpublished final degree thesis, Oslo University *

S. Braten, 1974, 'Coding Simulation Circuits During Symbolic Interaction', Congress Proceedings of the Association Internationale de Cybernetique, Namur, Belgium, pp. 327–336

S. Braten, 1978, 'Competing Modes of Cognition and Communication in Simulated and Self-Reflective Systems', paper presented at the Third Richmond Conference on Decision Making in Complex Systems

M. Dahle, 1977, 'Social Background and Verbal Communication', unpublished final degree thesis, Oslo University *

A. Endresen, 1977, 'A Model for the Solution of Communication Conflicts', unpublished final degree thesis, Oslo University *

A. Faetten and M. Ostvold, 'Hysteria and Communication', unpublished final degree thesis, Oslo University *

A. J. Ferreira and W. D. Winter, 1968a, 'Decision-Making in Normal and Abnormal Two-Child Families', *Family Proceedings*, Vol. 7, pp. 17–36

A. J. Ferreira and W. D. Winter, 1968b, 'Information Exchange and Silence in Normal and Abnormal Families', *Family Proceedings*, Vol. 7, pp. 251–276

H. Garfinkel, 1972, 'Studies of the Routine Grounds of Everyday Activities', in: I. D. Sudnow (Ed.), *Studies in Social Interaction*, New York: The Free Press

K. B. Glennsjo, 1977, 'Marital Schism and Marital Skew – A Communication Theoretical Investigation', unpublished final degree thesis, Oslo University *

S. Glucksberg, R. M. Kraus and R. Weissberg, 1966, 'Referential Communication in Nursery School, Method and Some Preliminary Findings', *Journal of Experimental Child Psychology*, Vol. 3, pp. 333–342

M. J. Goldstein, E. Gould, A. Alkire, E. H. Rodnick and L. L. Judd, 1968, 'A Method for Studying Social Influence and Coping Patterns within Families of Disturbed Adolescents', *Journal of Nervous and Mental Disorders*, vol. 147, pp. 233–251

B. E. Haarstad, 1976, 'Anorexia Nervosa, An Experimental Study of Familial Communication', unpublished final degree thesis, Oslo University *

J. Haley, 1972, 'Critical Overview of Present Status of Family Interaction Research', in: I. L. Framo (Ed.), *A Dialogue Between Family Researchers and Family Therapists*, New York, Springer Publishing Co.

J. Haley, 1975, Personal Communication to the Author

E. T. Hall, 1959, *The Silent Language*, Greenwich, Conn.: Fawett Publications

G. Handel (Ed.), 1967, *The Psychosocial Interior of the Family*, Chicago: Aldine

F. Heider, 1958, *The Psychology of Interpersonal Relations*, New York: Wiley

A. Holte, 1978, 'Communicational Prerequisites for Emotional Development,' published working paper, Institute of Psychology, Oslo University *

M. Hultberg, S. Alve and R. M. Blakar, 1978, 'Patterns of Attribution of Communicative Difficulties in Couples Having a "Schizophrenic", a "Borderline" or a "Normal" Offspring', *Informasjonsbulletin fra 'Psykopatologi og kommunikasjonsprosjektet'*, No. 6, Institute of Psychology, Oslo University

G. Ichheiser, 1970, *Appearances and Realities, Misunderstandings in Human Relations*, San Francisco: Jossey-Bass

S. M. Jacobson and R. B. Pettersen, 1974, 'Communication and Cooperation in Families with Schizophrenic Members', unpublished final degree thesis, Oslo University *

T. S. Kristiansen, 1976, 'Patterns of Communication of Parents Having Children with Psychsomatic Problems', unpublished final degree thesis, Oslo University *

T. S. Kristiansen, A. Faleide and R. M. Blakar, 1977, 'Patterns of Communication of Parents with Children with Psychosomatic Problems, An Experimental Investigation', *Tidskrift for Norsk Psykologforening*, Vol. 14, No. 12, pp. 2–24 *

W. Labov, P. Cohen, C. Robins and J. Lewis, 1968, 'A Study of the Non-Standard English of Negro and Puertorican Speakers in New York City, Final Report', *U.S. Office of Education Coopera-*

tive Research Project No. 3288, Columbia University

T. Lagerlov and S. J. Stokstad, 1974, 'Anxiety and Communication', unpublished final degree thesis, Oslo University *

T. Lidz, 1963, *The Family and Human Adaption*, New York: International University Press

T. Lidz, A. Cornelison, O. Terry and S. Fleck, 1957, 'The Intrafamilial Environment of the Schizophrenic Patient: Marital Schism and Marital Skew', *American Journal of Psychiatry*, Vol. 114, pp. 241–248

J. McKillip, 1975, Personal Communication to the Author

S. McPerson, 1970, 'Communication of Intents Among Parents and Their Disturbed Adolescent Children', *Journal of Abnormal Psychology*, Vol. 76, pp. 98–105

G. H. Mead, 1934, *Mind, Self and Society*, Chicago: University of Chicago Press

E. G. Mishler and N. E. Waxler, 1965, 'Family Interaction Processes and Schizophrenia, A Review of Current Theories', *Merrill-Palmer Quarterly of Behavior and Development*, Vol. 11, pp. 269–315

E. G. Mishler and N. E. Waxler, 1968, *Interaction in Families, An Experimental Study of Family Processes and Schizophrenia*, New York: Wiley

W. Mischel, 1968, *Personality and Assessment*, New York: Wiley

W. Mischel, 1973, 'On the Empirical Dilemmas of Psychodynamic Approaches: Issues and Alternatives', *Journal of Abnormal Psychology*, vol. 82, pp. 335–344

O. Moberget and O. Reer, 1975, 'Communication and Psychopathology, A Methodological and Conceptual Contribution', unpublished final degree thesis, Oslo University *

S. Moscovici, 1967, 'Communication Processing and the Properties of Language', in: L. Berkowitz (Ed.), *Advances in Experimental Social Psychology*, Vol. 3, New York: Acadaemic Press

S. Mossige, R. B. Pettersen and R. M. Blakar, 1976, 'Egocentrism versus Decentration and Communication Efficiency in Families *with* and *without* a Schizophrenic Member', *Informationsbulletin fra 'Psykopatologi og Kommunikasjonsprosjektet'*, No. 4, Institute of Psychology, Oslo University

O. Oisjofoss, 1976, 'Power and Control in the Communication of Married Couples,' unpublished final degree thesis, Oslo University *

H. Ovreeide, 1970, 'Verbal Communication among Peers,' unpublished final degree thesis, Oslo University ★

O. G. Paulsen, 1977, 'Schizophrenia and Communication, A Replication', unpublished final degree thesis, Oslo University ★

J. Piaget, 1926, *The Language and Thought of the Child*, New York: Harcourt-Brace

E. L. Ringuette and T. Kennedy, 1966, 'An Experimental Study of the Double-Bind Hypothesis', *Journal of Abnormal Psychology*, Vol. 71, pp. 136–141

J. Riskin and E. E. Faunce, 1972, 'An Evaluative Review of Family Interaction Research', *Family Process*, Vol. 11, pp. 365–455

R. Rommetveit, 1968, *Words, Meanings and Messages*, New York: Academic Press

R. Rommetveit, 1972a, *Language, Thought and Communication*, Oslo: Universitetsvorlaget ★

R. Rommetveit, 1972b, 'Deep Structure of Sentences versus Message Structure, Some Critical Remarks to Current Paradigms and Suggestions for an Alternative Approach', *Norwegian Journal of Linguistics*, Vol. 26, pp. 3–22

R. Rommetveit, 1974, *On Message Structure*, London: Wiley

R. Rommetveit, 1978, 'On Common Codes and Dynamic Residuals in Human Communication,' in: R. Rommetveit and R. M. Blakar (Eds.), *Studies of Language, Thought and Verbal Communication*, London: Academic Press (published 1979)

R. Rommetveit and R. M. Blakar (Eds.), 1978, *Studies of Language, Thought and Verbal Communication*, London: Academic Press (published 1979)

K. L. S. Rotbaek, 1976, 'Enuresis, An Experimental Study of Familial Communication', unpublished final degree thesis, Oslo University ★

J. Ruesch and G. Bateson, 1951, *Communication: The Social Matrix of Psychiatry*, New York: Norton

B. R. Rund, 1978, 'The Schizophrenic's Disturbances of Thought and the Communication of Parents, An Explorative Study', *Nordisk Psykologi*, Vol. 30, pp. 238–254

K. Ronbeck, 1977, 'Familial communication and Schizophrenia, A Critical Assessment of the Field of Research', unpublished final degree thesis, Oslo University ★

A. I. Schuham, 1967, 'The Double-Bind Hypothesis a Decade Later', *Psychological Bulletin*, vol. 68, pp. 409–416

I. Strono, 1968, 'Egocentrism and Communication,' unpublished final degree thesis, Oslo University ★

H. A. Solvberg, 1973, 'Communication and Cooperation in Couples with a Schizophrenic Offspring', unpublished final degree thesis, Oslo University ★

H. A. Solvberg and R. M. Blakar, 1975, 'Communication Efficiency in Couples *with* and *without* a Schizophrenic Offspring', *Family Process*, Vol. 14, pp. 515–534

H. O. Teigre, 1976, 'Confidence (in Self and Other) as a Prerequisite for Communication', unpublished final degree thesis, Oslo University ★

P. Watzlawick, J. H. Beavin and D. D. Jackson, 1967, *Pragmatics of Human Communication*, New York: Norton

J. H. Weakland and W. Fry, 1962, 'Letters of Mothers of Schizophrenics', *American Journal of Orthopsychiatry*, Vol. 32, pp. 604–623

R. J. Wikran, 1974, 'Communication and Cooperation in Couples with an Asthmatic Child', unpublished final degree thesis, Oslo University

R. J. Wikran, A. Faleide and R. M. Blakar, 1978a, 'Communication in the Family of the Asthmatic Child, An Experimental Approach', *Acta Psyciatrica Scandinavica*, Vol. 57, pp. 11–26

R. Wikran, A. Faleide and R. M. Blakar, 1978b, 'Patterns of Communication in Parental Couples with an Asthmatic Child, An Experimental Approach', in: A. Faleide (Ed.), *Children with Asthma*, Oslo: Universitetsforlaget (published 1979) ★

L. Wynne, I. Rykoff, J. Day and S. Hirsch, 1958, 'Pseudo-Mutuality in the Family Relations of Schizophrenics', *Psychiatry*, Vol. 21, pp. 205–220

Developments in the Syntax of Action

DAVID D. CLARKE *Oxford University*

---

1 *The Problem*

It is quite clear that we are in urgent need of a better under-standing of the nature and sources of human action. This is partly because of the obvious irony of living in a scientific age which has taught us so much about the natural environment and so little about ourselves and partly because so many contemporary problems seem to spring from the misunder-standing and mismanagement of human affairs. What is not so clear is the form the understanding should take, and the means by which it is to be achieved. Here, there are a number of alternatives to be considered, some of which are set out below, with comments on their relative merit.

The object of research in this field is to explain the working of certain systems of thought and activity, and to produce resources for practical action. By explanation I mean the discovery of the underlying mechanism or generative process by which observed events are called into being. Since the process is not directly accessible, this usually amounts to the proposal of imaginary mechanisms and then a demonstration, part rational and part empirical, that they could reproduce the facts as we observe them (Harré 1976). This is not unfamiliar as a form of argument in the other sciences and allows us to be certain that some of our models are false when facts arise which they could not explain, although we can never be sure that a model is true. According to this view of science, theories fall into two classes: those which have already been falsified and those which have not yet been falsified. None has ever been, nor ever could be, verified.

A resource for practical action, in this context, is a body of knowledge which informs some remedial or inventive practice, such as medical science guiding the actions of a physical, or mechanics assisting an engineer in the design of sound and workable structures.

In such a body of knowledge two explanatory concepts play a central part: causation and structure. One might almost say that all of science is devoted to two kinds of questions: one, typical of much of physics, asks after the causes of events; the other, typical of much chemistry, asks after the structure of things. Psychology in setting out to study human action has for the most part modelled itself on the predominantly causal disciplines and overlooked the precedents of the predominantly structural ones such as chemistry, anatomy and linguistics. It is our concern in this collection of readings, among other issues, to redress the balance and look at human activities in such a way as to illuminate their *structure*.

In doing this, three kinds of objects have to be considered. The smallest which I will call simply *parts* are like the atoms in chemistry, the organs in anatomy or the morphemes in linguistics. Next comes the *wholes*: molecules, bodies and sentences respectively. The largest object of analysis concerns the *domain* which may be that of stable substances, or an animal species or a language. What the structural sciences aim to do is to capture the combination of *parts* into *wholes* which are characteristic of that *domain* to the exclusion of those combinations which could only occur outside the *domain*. In this way the domain as a whole comes to be characterized by a set of structural principles or rules.

An attractive feature of a structural approach, found particularly in modern linguistics, is the use of generative models.

The domain, in this case a language, is captured not merely by a passive description of organizational features but by an active model, a generative grammar consisting of rules which, after the fashion of a formal theorem-proving system, can derive all sentences from a simple axiom S. This in its turn requires a linguistic theory to have a certain coherence which is often lacking in psychological theories. The rules of a grammar are not independent constraints on linguistic form, but interlocking elements in a kind of abstract simulation which specifies exactly the nature of its own use, dictating from moment-to-moment which rules may be invoked next and with what effect.

By turning attention from the study of languages to the study of grammars, Chomsky (1957, 1965) brought an essential feature of the advanced sciences into linguistics. While most sciences distinguish between processes and the products or observations to which the processes give rise, it is only the advanced sciences like physics which use products as indicators to investigate process; leaving the primitive sciences like behaviourist psychology to invoke process only as an explanation of product. As Chomsky (1963) put it: 'As a general designation for psychology, "behavioral science" is about as apt as "meter-reading science" would be for physics . . .' The psychologist cannot afford to ignore product/process distinctions, nor to treat processes only as the explanans of products, thereby giving the latter a priority they hardly deserve.

So far then we have seen there are good precedents, if not good reasons, for wanting to look at human action according to its structure, in order to get at the processes by which it is regulated, bearing in mind that regulatory process may well imply a causal chain of brain states as in the psychologist's attempt at a performance model of language, or a formal generator, as in the linguist's theory of competence. In the former case we take a structural interest in the product and a causal interest in the process, while in the latter case both product and process are seen in purely formal terms.

In such an analytic scheme there is typically a generalized

process, such as the grammar, which represents all product *wholes* in the *domain,* while a particular path through the generative network represents and assigns a structural description to an individual instance of a *whole* within that *domain.*

The emphasis on generative aspects in a structural subject allows us to synthesize as well as analyse the domain in question. As Bronowski (1973) points out, the impact of scientific thinking on everyday life has come about not so much as a result of man's abilities to reduce complex phenomena to their constituent parts, as of the power to reconstitute the parts into more appealing arrangements. This is the essence of most technology, and the strength of the native speaker's *creative* grasp of the nature of his language.

In sketching out this provisional blue-print for the kind of psychology we envisage, another distinction needs to be mentioned. In its original form it arose as the vexed question of the relationship between *mind* and *brain.* In the present era of ubiquitous computer jargon we might talk of human *software* and *hardware* to mean much the same thing. The point is this. An explanation of human action may be rendered in (at least) two forms, one having to do with the succession of electro-chemical events in the brain which controls motor activity, and the other having to do with the circumstances, reasons, thoughts, attitudes and values which appear to the actor as the source of his actions and which constitute the bulk of lay analysis of behaviour. The kind of explanation which the student of action structures seeks is rather more like the latter than the former but with additional requirements imposed. The supposed mental states which guide behaviour are to be defined in a sufficiently general yet precise way, that they take on the character of a generative model or simulation of the person or people concerned. This means that the mental model should be able to predict for any set of circumstances a choice of action which is *at least* a member of the behavioural domain to be modelled, and preferably the same course which the subject selects. The empirical validity and predictive use-fulness of the model are not the only things at issue, however. Its own formal properties are also interesting, and we should not overlook the possibility that many of the behaviour patterns which we now investigate empirically may be deduced from premises about human nature which none of us would dispute (Smedslund 1978). We would then be able to investigate in theory the properties of activity systems which do not occur in practice. Although that sounds fanciful it is important for a really profound analysis, since we can only get beyond the superficially observable features of any phenomenon when we have a way of reasoning about hypothetical processes, and the observable properties which they would give rise to if they were to exist. It is also important for practical applications, since analysis and resynthesis in the social world, or the selection of policies with regard to their effects, will only succeed when we have the theoretical means of knowing how each scenario would turn out before we create it in the real world.

The crux of the matter is to find some way of interpreting various courses of events which has the explanatory and predictive power of a theory in natural science, without losing sight of the human qualities and values which are involved. What is more, we must preserve the structural integrity of the phenomenon and not dismember it into myriad disconnected parts. Such an analysis of the social world, all too common in the contemporary literature, is as unhelpful as an exploded diagram of a machine one is expected to operate, or the early attempts at biochemistry in which the delicate architecture of molecules was destroyed, and only the proportions of the basic ingredients reported. The biochemists have mended their ways, and discovered techniques for representing the intact molecule in all its stereo-chemical beauty. It is time that we learned to follow suit. In the remainder of this paper I will discuss various ways in which we might achieve a similar understanding of the structure of action.

2   Experiments

The prevailing approach to psychological enquiry, and the

one I shall consider first, is the laboratory experiment. This way of conducting psychological research has been much criticized in recent years, particularly as it is applied to human social behaviour (e.g. Harré and Secord 1972). The general criticisms do not need much rehearsal here, but the difficulties of laboratory work, which are specially troublesome for the analyst of behavioural structure, should be mentioned.

The first difficulty is that experiments are not the right instruments for the job. Our aim is to analyse structure whereas experiments are concerned primarily with testing hypotheses of causation, by manipulating what is taken to be the cause and observing what is taken to be the effect, in order to establish a contingent relation.

Theoretical poverty is partly to blame for the poor outcome of many experiments, since no procedure for testing theories can have much to work on, in an area in which theoretical work itself is so much despised.

Nor are experimental methods an essential hallmark of science, as is so often supposed, since many successful sciences such as astronomy manage well without them. On realizing that some sciences are experimental and others not, we may be tempted to ask what the difference is. Part of the answer must surely be that laboratory environments are relatively small and short-lived, so if the phenomenon in question is large or long-lived, the laboratory is not the place to study it. It is not surprising then, that oceanography, meteorology and geology are not based on laboratory experiments, when chemistry, physiology and particle physics are. Nor is it surprising that a subject which sets out to study human activity in vitro should spend so much of its effort on the perception of tone bursts, and the measurement of reaction times, and so little on the nature of careers, biographies, families, wars, policies and other configurations of human activity which are arguably just as interesting. Even if we decided that human affairs were in principle small-scale phenomena, suitable for the laboratory, we should still find other criteria hard to satisfy. We should need the causal factors to be manipulable, which many trivial influences on human action are, but if major determinants of human behaviour could be so readily and arbitrarily controlled for the sake of seeing what happens, we should find ourselves in great ethical difficulty. There might also be something rather paradoxical about factors which are interesting because they rule us, but which can be so casually changed as a means of investigation.

Similarly the effects have to be observable, which is not always the case, and the relationship between the cause and effect have to be identifiable. That is no great problem for a simple system with very little memory, like a crude black-box problem. An input pulse gives rise to an output pulse and the correspondence between them is clear. If on the other hand there are many interacting causal factors which have delayed effects, it can be impossible to disentangle their contributions to the final outcome. If anyone doubts that sweeping generalization, there is a simple exercise which makes it much more compelling. One takes a small computer (by which I mean one which an individual user can monopolize for a while) whose program and language are unfamiliar. One now has a very simple psychological experiment, far simpler than any real psychological problem would be, in which a perfectly determinate and reproducible interaction between man and machine should in time expose all causal relations between input and output, that is to say the program. Anyone who can do this for a non-trivial program in less than a thousand lifetimes is well qualified to disbelieve my generalization.

As in the above example, any psychological experiment requires an interaction between the investigator, who must be able both to manipulate and observe, and the system. However many interesting activity systems are effectively closed. They will either reject a causal input from an investigator or be changed by it to a different kind of system from the one to be studied. Consider, for instance, the examination of sequential structure in conversation, a topical interest in philosophy, sociology, psychology and linguistics, and one which is addressed for the most part by non-experimental means. A conversing dyad is in many respects a closed system. To investigate the effects of one remark on another, one would either have to wait for the right occasion to arise spontaneously, which is not strictly an experiment, or arrange by participating or employing a confederate, that the causal remark be inserted according to some pre-arrangement, but that is to make it non-contingent on the preceding conversation, and to fracture just that cycle of mutual contingency which one is at pains to study.

The dependence of experiments upon the notion of causation is not only ill-suited to the structural enquiry set out here, but perhaps also inappropriate for human action in general. The idea of a causal universe has a long history and has grown up as an explanatory device for the natural world. The world of human behaviour, however, has its own explanatory mode with an equally long history which should not be usurped too lightly. The idea that action is causally determined is an assumption which may be untrue or at least unhelpful, especially if it leads us to overlook the crucial role of meaning and interpretation in human affairs. It is not so much the physical properties of our environment which influence our reactions, as the significance they hold for us. A ringing bell will evoke a reaction which depends not on the sound quality it produces but on what its significance is thought to be. The fact that people take to the fire-escape when the fire bell rings and wander into dinner when the dinner bell rings, would seem very curious to someone trying to interpret the pattern of sound waves as a 'cause' in the way that one set of sound waves may shatter a glass while another does not.

It is interesting to note that only one social science uses laboratory experiments to investigate the issues which many disciplines hold as common ground. Either experimental social psychology is marching out of step, or all the other social sciences are.

Experiments in the laboratory also tend to be fragmentary and atomistic, and to disregard many factors. It is common to hear an experimenter say that many factors remain to be examined in future research, but at least a few have been examined in the work so far. If the research were done in an applied setting where important decisions rested on the outcome it would be no consolation at all to claim that some aspects of the problem had been tackled although the majority escaped attention. The experimental method is singularly ill-suited to the production of a comprehensive and coherent picture of particular patterns of events or cases.

Context often has to be ignored in the design of experiments or deliberately 'controlled' out of existence while the actors' complexity, individual and cultural differences, and multiplier effects have to be undervalued.

Some of the 'variables' which are to be investigated are not variables at all, but parameters of the persons concerned (such as sex or race) and much of the logic of experimentation is invalidated when two groups of people with different para-meters are treated as if they were a 'variable' (Harré and Secord 1972).

Laboratory situations are notoriously artificial. Their artifi-ciality may not only be great but immeasurable since the laboratory situation would only be indicated if an analysis of real cases showed similar results, thereby making the laborat-ory procedure unnecessary. Such a use of surrogate examples seems only to be justified in cases such as a computer simula-tion which can reproduce by explicitly known means, data patterns in the real world whose origin is unknown.

Before leaving the subject of the laboratory experiment it is worth pointing out that the criticisms above do not necessarily invalidate laboratories or experiments, provided they are not combined. Field experiments can avoid many of the problems posed by their laboratory counterparts, while laboratories used for the analysis of samples and recordings from the real world have a value, even in the macro-sciences like geology. One such use of laboratories for sample analysis will be considered next.

3   Statistical Ethology

The next line of recourse for the production of a behavioural syntax or some similar global map of the possible forms that sequences of action can take, is systematic recording and sequence analysis as used by the animal ethologists (e.g. Dawkins 1976). This approach has the advantage of dealing with real behaviour as opposed to a laboratory surrogate, and giving a single coherent view of behavioural structure. However it is not without its drawbacks. It is inductive rather than generative, and can at best only provide a summary statement about a given corpus of data. Insofar as it resembles the process of reconstructing a map of some unknown terrain from descriptions of individual journeys (the observed sequences) it relies on a certain orderliness in the hypothetical terrain to be mapped. For instance in a real landscape where journeys are possible from point A to B to C and from point D to B to E, it is necessarily possible to make journey ABE and journey DBC (Clarke 1978). A landscape is a first order structure in which the places which can be reached next from a given point are independent of the past history of the journey. Using a graph theoretical representation in which points represent places (or behavioural events) and arcs or arrows the possible transitions it is possible to do justice to a road map but not a grammar (Chomsky 1957) or a system of behaviour sequences (Clarke 1975). More light will be shed on the adequacy of different representations when we come to the section on mathematical models.

Since the method is essentially a summary of data and no more, it falls short of the ideals of scientific theory construction and evaluation, and tends to deal mostly in concrete, small-scale, non-symbolic behaviour.

The methodology was devised for animal studies and it works well for that purpose. When transferred to humans, however, it can become very artificial and inefficient. The 'objective' stance of the analysis means that most of the information we would normally use in making sense of action, such as its conventional meaning, is discarded. Furthermore the statistical procedures which extract summary sequences and paths from a mass of data are only sensitive to frequency of occurrence as a criterion for treating

one chain of events as more important than another. Again the
animal studies work well; fixed action patterns do recur and
are novel to the analyst when discovered. For commonplace
human actions, on the other hand, the only behaviour chains
which are frequent enough to emerge from such a method are
usually obvious and familiar in the extreme.

The method does not do justice to the creativity of behaviour, and, unlike a grammar, is unable to predict from the
analysis of certain examples, what the remaining possibilities
should look like. There is no test of adequacy for such a
description of sequences, no set of well-formed cases which it
is required to reproduce. There is just a generalized commentary on the patterns which emerged from a particular sample
of data. Chomsky (1965, p. 18) put the disadvantage of this
kind of work succinctly when he said: 'Like most facts of
interest and importance, this (*the speaker's competence*) is neither
presented for direct observation nor extractable from data by
inductive procedures of any known sort.' (My italics)

4   *Generative Models*

If we took the linguistic analogy more seriously and tried to
produce a literal syntax of action we should proceed as follows. Working at first from native actors' intuitions of a
familiar behavioural structure we should propose a set of
formal generative rules. A grammar is said to have no discovery procedure, only an evaluation procedure. The rules would
then be tested for their adequacy, that is their capacity to
produce all well-formed *wholes* in the *domain*, and possibly
provide other information correctly about each one as well.
This is in a sense a reversal of the ethologist's procedure since it
produces strings from rules not rules from strings. It is not as
some people have assumed a flight from empiricism and a
rejection of data, it is simply the adoption of a classical
hypothetico-deductive approach in which tentative theories
are tested according to the truth of their theorems, rather than

the naive empiricism of an inductive methodology which can only harvest and classify data. This kind of study does produce generative models of a domain which are holistic and coherent, and enable us to simulate novel cases and to model future scenarios. It also goes a long way towards combining the richness of the native actors' knowledge of behavioural structure with the rigour of a formal model. However, this approach too is beset with drawbacks, two of which are crucial. Unlike a grammar for a natural language, a syntax of action has to deal with the ordering of a set of *parts* which is indefinitely large and possibly infinite. There are no direct counterparts of the morpheme set which can be used as the vocabulary in which *wholes* are to be created and described. Speech act or action taxonomies (Austin 1962; Searle 1969, 1975) are a help but in themselves are insufficient as a set of descriptions for activity *parts*. Consequently the rules which specify how *parts* may combine into *wholes* cannot be written until there is a descriptive language for *parts* which is concrete enough to be governed by a formal generative system (or a computer simulation) while at the same time being rich and human enough that a string of such descriptions will provide a satisfactory representation of the activity sequence under study. One possibility for such a notation uses speech act terms as main descriptions, with a series of sub-parameters which have values peculiar to that class. For example:

THREAT, A, B, x, y, z

could be used to represent A's threat to B that x will befall him unless he carries out requirements y within (time) limits z. The advantage of such a notation is that later acts can refer explicitly to earlier ones as in

COMPLY, B, y

where 'y' is a previous speech act such as

DEMAND, A, x.

The notation can be used recursively as in

QUESTION, B, A, (THREAT, A, B, x, y, z)

and

EXPLAIN, A, B, (THREAT, A, B, x, y, z)

where the whole of one speech act descriptor is used as a variable within another, meaning *B questions A about A's threat to B of x unless y in limit z* and *A explains to B his threat of x unless y within z*, respectively.

The notation would also allow context dependent rules of equivalence to be formulated such as

EXPLAIN, A, B,   QUESTION, B, A,

(THREAT, A, B, x, y, z)   (THREAT, x, y, z)

≡ANSWER, A, B (QUESTION, B, A (THREAT, A, B, x, y, z))

This would allow the system to 'know' and use the principle of context-dependent interpretation that *If A explains a threat to B, which B has asked him about, B's question may be read as answered.*

The other and less tractable issue has to do with the format of the generative rules themselves. If the behavioural syntax is even as complex as a standard syntax we might expect models having the power of finite state, push-down stack and linear bounded automata respectively, to fail essential criteria of adequacy if only by a diminishing margin. (These are increasingly complex automata formats, which nonetheless turn out to be inadequate as generators of natural language, Chomsky 1963.) A full blown generative/transformational grammar, however, like any reformatted Turing machine fails as a behavioural model by being non-interactive and determinate. Human social behaviour is apparently indeterminate (at least with respect to observable factors) and by definition interactive. In addition, the behavioural categories in the model require peculiar definitions. They fit uneasily into the conventions of set theory where a membership function can only take values of 0 or 1, meaning an element is outside or inside a set. When fuzzy definitions are added to the specification of a biogrammar (Westman 1978) the membership function can range over the interval 0 to 1, but by then the formalization begins to look too exotic for mere mortals, and the suspicion creeps in that there are more straightforward ways of understanding the structure of action than this.

5   A Possible Solution

What then is a 'straightforward' approach like? Are there any reliable alternatives which will serve as more than straw men to set up and knock down? One possibility seems at present to hold out the most promise, and the remainder of this paper will be devoted to it.

Consider a change in direction in social psychology away from the usual course of trying to reconcile science and human affairs by taking the elements of logic, mathematics and scientific methodology and imposing them upon the world of human action, as exemplified in the three approaches described above. Now imagine in its place the reverse programme in which the point of departure becomes the (scientifically) pre-theoretical view of human action embodied in art, law, drama, commerce, common sense and so on. The problem is now to harness these insights to the scientific enterprise, to collect, codify, check and extend them. This seems to make for more sense from the standpoint not only of the man on the Clapham omnibus who regards behavioural science as an unnecessary and expensive restatement of common sense, but also of the historian of science, who must surely agree that all the fundamental sciences like physics, chemistry and, if I may include it, geometry grew from the popular view then informing people's dealings with natural forces, substances and shapes. It was only from that point of departure that they were able to correct and extend their thinking into the modern sciences as we know them. No successful science (with the exception of the secondary subjects like bio-chemistry, or astrophysics which are quite another case anyway in having other sciences rather than direct experience of a phenomenon as their point of departure) could prosper by setting aside all accepted wisdom about the phenomenon in hand, and proceed *de novo* from an arbitrary starting point borrowed from a separate and quite unsuitable discipline. The aim then is to try to make our understanding of man more scientific, making explicit what was previously implicit, rather than trying to apply the apparatus of science to human affairs.

How then is this to be undertaken? Again, in the matter of methodology, it is to the pre-theoretical view that we must turn for guidance. Everyday lay activities give many psychological examples of the ways people have devised for coming to understand one another, for making sense of the enigmatic, for testing hypotheses, classifying cases and settling differences. These all have a conceptual infrastructure which can be elaborated into a sophisticated scientific methodology. Much of this is in the spirit of the 'new paradigm psychology' (Harré and Secord 1972). In this approach, it is the everyday concepts suggested by confrontation with real episodes of temporally structured behaviour which must guide further analyses, and the selection of more deeply penetrating techniques. Similarly, in setting the goals for analysis, there is more light to be shed on the understanding we are trying to achieve by the ordinary notion of 'understanding another person' than ever there is to be gained from the concept of scientific explanation in the purely mechanistic sense.

The first step, then, in the preferred approach to the analysis of behaviour sequences, would be to gather a number of instances of the type to be studied, together with as much background information as possible on the participants, the setting, the beliefs and expectations of those present and so on. The events themselves could be recorded on audio or video-tape, and the background information collected by extensively cross-checked interviews (see Harré and Secord 1972 on the 'negotiation of accounts'). In this there is clearly much to be gained by comparisons with medical case history taking and legal and other professional practices.

The next step is to attempt an analysis of *each case in turn,* sticking at first as closely as possible to the benefits and concepts supplied by the actors. A case-by-case analysis, although unusual, has the benefit of yielding general as opposed to aggregate propositions. General propositions are generalizations about a set of things which are true of all its members, while aggregate propositions (such as averages) may well be untrue for all members of the set and are clearly less valuable. In this case, general propositions come about because each sequence is analysed individually and statements are made which are true of it when taken alone. Later a summary may be made across sequences of the properties to be found in many or all of them. In other words, analysis is done in each case and the results aggregated, whereas in the weaker case of the aggregate proposition, aggregation typically precedes analysis. *Structure preserving* generalizations can only be made from valid analysis of specific instances.

On the other hand, it might be argued that nothing can be said of one case in isolation, and that would probably be so if we were confined to the use of *internal analysis,* that is, comparison and generalization within the case materials under explicit analysis at the time. However, using *external analysis,* that is, referring features of the case to other sources in background knowledge, tentative results may be reached which can then be cross-validated by internal analysis after a number of cases are complete. That may sound circular, but this is how many instance-by-instance analyses, including those of sentential syntax, are able to get started.

The procedure so far, though necessary, is far from sufficient. The attributions made of actors and events on the basis of lay pre-theoretical intuitions must be turned into a workable model with some predictive capability. Here it is crucial that a process of synthesis and reintegration occurs as an analysis resulting merely in an unordered list of parts is unhelpful. Ideally, some kind of model of the generative process needs to be constructed which can express the interrelation of all the elements in the analysis and their effects on behaviour. This could take a concrete realization, such as a computer simulation, or an abstract one, such as a generative grammar of action. Ultimately, we must know how the system fits together, not just how it resolves into parts.

Since the model, dealing in actors' beliefs, values, wishes and so on, must make behavioural predictions it must embody a psychologic whereby propositions about such mental states may be made to entail other propositions about behaviour. This, in itself, is a major undertaking and, it must be realized, a formal rather than an empirical one. A major reason for the paucity of much psychological theorizing is the lack of a system of argumentation which could connect postulates about profound mental states with any observable signs. This would also give us a number of new tools for thought about human activity systems which are all too scarce at present.

Such a model, which might be called a humanistic biogrammar, would have two further advantages. It would provide nonterminal reference, that is to say a product/process system, which unlike a sentence grammar, has observable and recognizable nonterminal elements or processing stages. It would not be a 'blind' simulation which could use any form of algebra with no particular 'meaning' so long as the output matched behaviour, but rather a model of human action couched in comprehensible terms of human mental processes as we take them to be. It would also 'use the same language' as experts in other fields of social science, for whom thoughts and reasons are not alien concepts, making it much easier to interface between disciplines.

Next, the model has to be put through its paces, and tested for its adequacy. The first task is to reproduce from the model the particular sequences of events that went into its construction. Later, it will have to match the real system in the production of word sequences given novel circumstances as input. All of which is like the requirements made of a generative grammar (Chomsky 1965), a production system model of problem solving (Newell and Simon 1972) and social system simulation (Forester 1972) or a session of economic or strategic modelling. A further requirement for the model may be that it arrives not only at a similar output to the real system, but that it does so by dangerous means. This is usually taken to mean that in the case of production it assigns an appropriate structural description to the string of events.

It is important not to forget Weizenbaum's (1976) critique of modelling which maintains that people are not just information processing systems and that there is a great deal more to understanding human action and experience than simply building mechanical analogues with similar activity patterns. However, the use of experiential elements as the processing stages in the model may go some way towards overcoming this problem.

In what sense then could such a model predict the output of real systems? Does it offer the possibility of scientific behavioural forecasting, and would that be a good thing? Let us consider the working of the model in a single case. A sequence of events is under way and the outcome is to be predicted by the model. (This is the mode of operation in which an incomplete scenario is to be completed, although complete scenarios can also be analysed.) We can all think, given a story so far, of a number of well-formed, sensible, coherent futures which could follow from it, and ignore other combinations of events lacking in structural integrity. The difficulty would be in deciding between the possible futures in order to make a definite prediction. Let us call the set of plausible alternatives the *possibility space* or *possibility tree,* and the path which the system finally chooses the *real vector.* The model could be asked to predict the possibility tree or the real vector, although the former is easier and more directly determined by the organizing principles of action. This is rather like saying that a sentence grammar can produce the family of well-formed sentences but not predict what a person will say at a given time. If the first requirement is to generate the possibility tree from the given circumstances, tbe real vector can be generated later by refinements to the model or standard decision analysis (Moore and Thomas 1976). Thus the biogrammar would perform the all important problem-structuring stage which formal decision analysis lacks. It may be useful to some degree to look upon the actions as constrained rather than generated by circumstances; a matter of choice rather than necessity.

This connection with decision analysis brings us to the practical applications of the method, from which we began. It is becoming increasingly important and difficult to understand and manage human affairs. Particularly when some crisis or conflict looms we need better ways of understanding what is likely to happen and how all the parties to the situation see their options. Very often the need is for better methods, not better data, since in many real problems the 'facts of the matter' are available in abundance. The difficulty is to integrate them into any usable picture. The point of the humanistic or 'soft' biogrammar method set out above is largely to provide a kind of psychological sensitive operational research method which would assist the decision maker in two ways. Firstly, by articulating the *possibility tree* for the problem situation, from the (often different) perspectives of different participants, and secondly, over the course of a number of case studies, to codify the mechanics of certain recurring types of problem situation. The ultimate aim is to put him as much in touch with the workings and dynamics of conflict, say, as the physician is with the physiology and pathology of the human body.

For this the models must be able to distinguish accurately between well-formed and ill-formed vectors, and to *reproduce* the characteristics of the real system. Most social psychological analyses fail in these respects. They include over-generalizations which would apply as well to many ill-formed strings as to the well-formed ones, rather like a grammar which simply says *A sentence is any set of words in any order*. Of course it encompasses all the sentences of the real language, but as it also encompasses all conceivable varieties of nonsense as well it can hardly be counted as a useful characterization of the working of the syntactic system. Unfortunately, such over-generalization is all too common in accounts of social behaviour. A summary is given which, although true of all recognizable forms of social interchange, is rendered useless as a scientific description by being equally true of the most insanely surreal scenarios one can devise. Furthermore, many analyses end up with a list of components and forces whose systemic properties cannot be recovered. We have all had enough of the helpful child who can take anything to bits but is not too hot at putting it back together and getting it working again. All too often a study of the mechanics of interaction lists the individual components, signals and cues used, but fails to capture their interplay in such a way that the theory can reproduce whole and realistic descriptions of social episodes, which is, after all, the interesting and difficult part. Such an analysis fails in the way that a theory of language would fail if it only listed as component parts the various word and phrase types, and make no attempt to capture the design principles that differentiate a message from a browse through the dictionary.

This method is unlike much of the current work in decision making and problem solving in that it does not pose exercises with known characteristics to people in order to study *problem solvers*. It is quite the reverse. It is a method for using the expertise that problem solvers already have for building up a corpus of knowledge about the mechanics of the problem systems themselves. It is primarily a study of a phenomenon in the world and only secondarily a study of the layman's knowledge of that phenomenon.

In dealing in this rather mentalistic way with problem

situations, the method allows for a disaggregation into individual viewpoints and objections, rather than a single monolithic expression of one perspective.

Finally a word about rules. If the guiding principles of the models are to be regarded as some kind of behaviour generating rules, then it must be clear that they go beyond the rules we acknowledge in everyday life. These are not just superficial modifiers of behaviour to which a person may conform, they are the expression in abstract of what that person is, and they must embody all facets of his nature, without recourse to an additional homunculus to make sense of, and follow them.

In this kind of work a theory is evaluated according to its ability to stimulate reality. An adequate rule model of man would reproduce human behaviour without human assistance, just as an adequate grammar would produce language. To envisage, as a model of human conduct, a set of rules which requires human interpretation is wholly unsatisfactory from this point of view. In many respects the rules in a behavioural model are more like the equations of natural science than the rules of a game, except that they deal in discrete events rather than continuous variables, and relations other than equality. For example, consider the differences between the equation

$$y = mx + c$$

in which continuous variables are related by equality; the linguistic rule

$$S \longrightarrow NP + VP$$

in which discrete, but abstract, and unfamiliar states are related by the transformation '$\longrightarrow$'; and the game rule

Pawns may only be advanced one rank
per turn, except on their first move

which is stated as a permissible relation between circumstance and action, in the terms which may be familiar to the actor himself.

6   *Conclusion*

The key theme throughout has been that of technique tempered with judgement. We will not achieve a workable psychology by calculation alone, nor will we make a useful contribution as a helping profession if we continue to place mechanical aids to reasoning like statistics above the acquisition of professional acumen. For that we shall need to take seriously the accumulated wisdom of centuries on the subject of human nature, to confront problems which perplex real people beyond the ivory tower, and to be prepared to mix the new science and the old humanity with a fair blend of humanity. Then we may just proceed beyond mere explanation, and approach a state of understanding.

References

J. L. Austin, 1962, *How to Do Things with Words*, Oxford: Clarendon Press

J. Bronowski, 1963, *The Ascent of Man*, London: British Broadcasting Corporation

N. Chomsky, 1957, *Syntactic Structures*, The Hague: Mouton

N. Chomsky, 1963, 'Formal Properties of Grammars', in: R. D. Luce, R. R. Bush and E. Galanter (Eds.), *Handbook of Mathematical Psychology*, Vol. 2, London: Wiley

N. Chomsky, 1965, *Aspects of the Theory of Syntax*, The Hague: Mouton

D. D. Clarke, 1975, 'The Structural Analysis of Verbal Interaction', unpublished D.Phil. thesis, Oxford University

D. D. Clarke, 1978, 'The Structuralist Analysis of Communication, An Example of Problem-Centred Methodology', in: M. Brenner, P. Marsh and M. Brenner (Eds.), *The Social Contexts of Method*, London: Croom Helm

R. Dawkins, 1976, 'Hierarchical Organisation: A Candidate Principle for Ethology', in: P. P. G. Bateson and R. A. Hinde (Eds.), *Growing Points in Ethology*, London: Cambridge University Press

J. W. Forrester, 1972, 'Understanding the Counterintuitive Behaviour of Social Systems', in: J. Beishon and G. Peters (Eds.), *Systems Behaviour*, London: Open University Press

R. Harré and P. F. Secord, 1972, *The Explanation of Social Behaviour,* Oxford: Blackwell

R. Harré, 1976, 'The Constructive Role of Models,' in: L. Collins (Ed.), *The Use of Models in the Social Sciences,* London: Tavistock

P. G. Moore and H. Thomas, 1976, *The Anatomy of Decisions,* Harmondsworth: Penguin

A. Newell and H. A. Simon, 1972, *Human Problem Solving,* Englewood Cliffs, NJ: Prentice-Hall

J. Searle, 1969, *Speech Acts,* London: Cambridge University Press

J. Searle, 1975, 'A Taxonomy of Illocutionary Acts', in: K. Gunderson (Ed.), *Language, Mind and Knowledge, Minnesota Studies in the Philosophy of Science,* Vol. 7, University of Minnesota Press

J. Smedslund, 1978, 'Bandura's Theory of Self Efficacy: A Set of Common Sense Theorems', *Scandinavian Journal of Psychology,* Vol. 19, pp. 1–14

J. Weizenbaum, 1976, *Computer Power and Human Reason,* San Francisco: Freeman

R. S. Westman, 1977, 'Environmental Languages and the Functional Bases of Animal Behaviour', in: B. Hazlett (Ed.), *Quantitative Methods in Animal Behaviour,* New York: Academic Press

Social Being and Social Change

ROM HARRÉ   *Oxford University*

I am going to concern myself with the problem of how to contrive social change. By formulating what I would take to be an adequate theory of social change can we find ways to induce social changes by using social psychological knowledge? It seems to me that the vast improvement in methods of social psychological research of recent years suggests we ought now to consider the answer to this question seriously. Marx says somewhere that it is no good proposing a method for altering the social world unless you know how the social world alters naturally in the pre-scientific phase. I am sure that is quite correct, and what follows is in accordance with the spirit of that observation.

1   *Social Forms: Some Basic Principles*

The issue of the nature of social change can hardly be sensibly addressed without careful analysis of social forms, that which might change. One must also look at the principles involved in the maintenance of these forms, since they will act to slow down or frustrate the tendency to change.

A basic postulate of my treatment involves the distinction between the practical order and the expressive order of society. Indeed, this distinction goes far to exhaust the possibilities of social interaction. They are not only analytically distinct orders, but they must also be supposed to be existentially distinct, though they interact in complex ways.

The practical order is the system of the production and change of material things, including changes in the human body as an object of work, by work and the social organization needed to achieve any given mode of production. The practical order is realized in an economy, in the rules of cooking, in the medical practice and so on of a society.

To understand change we must make a fundamental distinction between the practical and the expressive orders of society. The practical order is built around work and the production of the means of life. As Marx demonstrated, it is a social order. The expressive order is made of two closely related systems: the system of the means (symbolic, stylistic, etc.) for self-presentation according to the favoured stereotypes of a local culture, and the system of hazards in passing or failing when we enhance or lose reputation. There are rituals and conventions by which we mark success and failure in these hazards, in the course of which a public reputation or 'character' is built up. We could speak of the whole progress as a moral career. The expressive order is realized in the conventional markings of respect and contempt shown in day-to-day dealings between people. I believe that while the practical order is reproduced in the overt institutions of society, the expressive order is reproduced covertly. The social customs of childhood are repeated generation by generation in the autonomous precursor world of childhood. This appears in the social life of children between the ages of about five and twelve, and is largely independent of adult influences. This 'world' has been only occasionally entered by an adult observer. We shall have occasion to return to a more detailed discussion of its structure and its role in the processes of social change in a later section.

We must also take account of the distinction traditionally drawn between micro and macro properties of societies by which we distinguish systems of human relations according to orders of magnitude. I prefer to distinguish the properties of face-to-face interactions, from those of institutions, and both from gross structural properties of large collectives. The distinction between practical and expressive orders in society can be made at both the lower levels. It is uncertain whether the distinction has any meaning at all on the level of the hypothetical but empirically unknowable macro properties of societies.

What is the relation between the practical and the expressive orders? I believe that is is most accurately represented by a principle I shall call Veblen's Law:

In general for most societies at most times the expressive order dominates and determines the practical order (see Veblen 1957).

It is important to notice that this law is stated in a qualified form, since I do not wish to deny that there have been occasional periods in certain societies when the dominance passed to the practical. I believe that the early to mid-nineteenth century in Britain was just such a period. But in most of human history the dominance of the expressive over the practical can be seen both psychologically in the preoccupations of the majority of the folk and socially in the degree to which the productive system is devoted to producing those goods which have a symbolic role in the genesis, maintenance and display of aspects of the expressive order. That order usually develops independently, since it develops prior to its realization in the practical order of material change wrought in the world by active intervention in natural processes. The distinction can even be seen in the way the choice of dishes to serve at a meal is dominated by the social relations drawn from the expressive order, relations that need to be marked, changed or confirmed. This has been amply demonstrated by Mary Douglas (1972).

Looked at from the point of view of individuals it is evident that most people will sacrifice practical advantage for expressive satisfaction; witness the loss of matches by star tennis players who sacrifice the possibility of winning to the satisfaction of the illustration of feeling, temperament and character. The dominance of the expressive over the practical shows very clearly in contemporary industrial relations, where not only is practical advantage routinely sacrificed to expressive satisfactions, but even such a matter as unemployment seems to be experienced as a matter of the loss of dignity and worth, since it no longer has any effect on biological survival.

These empirical observations lead one to make a sharp break with one of the central theses of Marx's analysis of the social order (and consequently with his conception of the dynamics of social change). In contrast to Veblen, Marx seems to have thought that through the system of production the practical order is either the dominant order or determines which is the dominant order in this or that society. This idea seems to be factually false for many societies and for most times.

2   'Natural' Social Change

SOCIAL CHANGE IN GENERAL

After the searching criticisms of sociological method, particularly concerning the social construction of data by Douglas (1967) and others, it has become clear, among other issues, that no method is available for the empirical study of the properties of very large aggregates of people in interaction. It seems unlikely that in the foreseeable future any such studies could be made. If we cannot have direct knowledge of global properties, then it follows that we have no direct knowledge of any changes that may occur in those properties. At most, we can infer from the kind of evidence which is available, namely observable social behaviour and decipherable social interpretation and theorizing, that some change in the background of human social action has occurred. This suggests that

  i. we should regard statements about large scale

phenomena, particularly statements about alleged systems such as the economic organization of a culture, and about structures, such as the alleged structure of 'classes' as hypotheses which can be tested only indirectly by testing for the truth of their consequences.

ii. in the absence of any theory as to how such properties and processes and structures could affect day-to-day practices and the workings of man-sized institutions these features of social life, if indeed they exist at all, must be treated as an environment which acts as a selection condition for those social activities which we do manage for ourselves. This immediately suggests an evolutionary perspective to the understanding of social change, somewhat in the Darwinian style.

iii. But, as Bhaskar (1978) has argued, the macro properties of large social groups of men in interaction should be regarded, not as the properties of some mysterious supra-individual, but as the properties of a network of interpersonal relations. It follows that the properties of such networks are some function of the properties of the interpersonal relations. It does not follow from this observation that the networks can have no emergent properties. It is very likely that they do. Nevertheless there is likely to be some kind of causal influence running from changes in the properties of small scale interactions and man-sized institutions to the network. It also seems obvious, though I know of no serious empirical study of this matter, that some small scale changes will have no effect on the network. For instance, provided the external relations of nuclear families are conserved or stabilized, the macro structure could tolerate great internal changes in family organization.

The focus of empirical studies of change must then be on the changes in small scale interactions that can be studied by adequate empirical methods. Theoretically there are a limited range of categories of possible social change. Broadly speaking social interactions can be divided into the intrumental, coordinated activities bringing social and material products into existence, and the self presentational, where the outcome is a step up or down in public reputation and moral career. Leaving aside the material production and concentrating only on social activities which have social ends, the core of social episodes can be found in sequences of public actions in the course of which social acts are performed. Readers may like to be reminded that by 'acts' I mean events which have distinctive social meanings, such as insults, marriages, convictions, cementations of friendships, and so on, and by 'actions' the locally accepted conventionally associated ways by which acts such as the above are performed. We can now lay out the range of changes that could occur in small scale social interactions:

i.   A new convention might appear associating a different action with the same act. For instance, there has been a systematic change in the titles of respect used to perform acts of social deference and respect, while arguably the acts have remained stable.

ii.   Sometimes the same action is performed as heretofore, but it is now understood as the performance of a rather different act. For instance, a modern industrial strike can no longer be regarded as a protest against economic exploitation, but seems to be the performance of a self-presentational act publicly emphasizing workers' power and dignity.

iii.   A more complex kind of change can occur when a novel act/action structure appears, but the social microstructure that is generates seems to be much the same as that generated by the old act/action sequence which has been superseded. A contemporary example seems to be the spread of common law marriage, where the institution that is created is much like the old, but the ritual steps leading to its establishment are different.

Similar kinds of change can occur in presentational activities. Changes occur in the acceptable range of personas and characters admitted as legitimate and proper presentations in a society. These are often accompanied by changes in the stylistic and symbolic devices by which they are publicly displayed. So we find the same persona/character presented in different ways at different times. Sometimes different personas are presented with what seem to be traditional devices, while there may be changes in both.

And, of course, along with these changes go changes in the accounting resources and the conventions that govern the selection of material that can be brought forward for use in accounting occasions. A splendid example of this kind of change is the growth of the use of Freudian and pseudo Freudian concepts in accounting, the spread of which has been studied by Moscovici (1976).

THE SPECTRUM OF EVOLUTIONARY THEORIES

The picture I want to draw of natural social change (by 'natural' I mean before history and anthropology and social psychology become part of the social world) has to be understood by graphing the theory of social change on a general layout of all possible evolutionary theories. Evolutionary theories are distinguished by the fact that they analytically separate the mutation conditions which alter individuals generation by generation, and the selection conditions which destroy or impede some individuals preventing them reproducing while other individuals survive to pass on their characteristics. This is a familiar idea. It is not so well known that this analytic distinction constitutes a set of theories defined by the actual relation obtaining between mutation conditions and selection conditions, upon which depends the fate of mutations in given environments. A Darwinian theory can be defined as assuming no relation between mutation conditions and selection conditions. I shall call this an 'uncoupled theory'. At the other end of the spectrum is the Lamarckian form of theory which, though also an evolutionary theory, allows that the mutations are produced by the existing selection conditions. The little proto-giraffe struggling upwards to the leaves stretches its short neck and as it grows up with altered genomes, the next generation of little giraffes all grow up with slightly longer necks and so on. The selection conditions are causally interacting with the mutation conditions. We can call that a 'coupled theory' (see Toulmin 1972).

Some observations are called for on this spectrum of possible evolutionary theories. Clearly, the differences between these theories are empirical, and the world just might have been the kind of place where change took place through a coupled or Lamarckian process. It is also important to emphasize that, though in the Lamarckian theory there is a causal relation between selection conditions and mutations, there is no law of change. The theory is not historicist in cast. There are just a vast number of particular instantiations of the principle that adult activities to cope with existing environments produce changes in the genomes leading to the inheritance of acquired characteristics *whatever they are*. For instance, the proto-giraffes might have given up in despair and migrated.

Can this spectrum be applied to the understanding of social change? We have already noticed the implausibility of supposing a causal relation from the large scale properties of the social network which would determine new social forms in personal interaction or institutional organization. This suggests that an evolutionary style of theory would be worth considering, and it has the further virtue that it does not require the detailed specification of the selection environment, since it is only in its manifestations as the differential reproduction of the types of individuals that it must be considered. And so this too fits in with the unknowability of large scale social processes and properties. By adopting such a general framework for theorizing we are relieved of the necessity of introducing empty (Humean) causal relations between macro and micro levels of the social order, and of the consequential need to try to make specific attributions of global properties to large groups.

But there is a problem in making a direct graphing of theories of social change onto the evolutionary spectrum. Biological evolution, for which these theory-types were first devised, seems to be able to be understood with a simple duality between the selection environment, however internally complex it may be, and mutations at the level of individual organisms (lately seen as merely the carriers of 'selfish' genes). This simple duality will not do for social change, since it is obvious that there are a hierarchy of environments, each selectively potent to a specific level of mutant activity, but itself selected by a higher order environment. Thus individual mutant social practices may be selectively sanctioned by very small scale informal close groupings of people, their mutant practices selectively favoured or eliminated by institutions, and institutions by larger institutions, and finally those by the macroprocesses at whose properties we can only guess. For analytical purposes the continuity of scale can perhaps be broken by imposing an arbitrary division between individuals, small groups, institutions and societies, treating each as containing the selection conditions for the entity next below it in the hierarchy. This is a fiction, and must be immediately qualified, since clearly any level above a given level could act as a selection environment for mutant forms within the given level. And just as in biological evolution the environments are themselves subject to change through the life processes of the kinds of creatures they have originally selectively favoured, sometimes in such a way as to eliminate those very creatures, so social environments are similarly modified by the practices they favour, sometimes in such a way as to favour mutants. The history of capitalist forms of industrial enterprise seems to be such a sequence.

How can a mutation occur? In a section above I set out a scheme to locate possible social changes in a systematic format related to the ethogenic theory of social action. But I offered no theory at that point as to how such changes might occur. There seem to be two possible ways:

i.   Generation by generation social practices are never perfectly replicated. This may be for a variety of reasons which ought to be more closely studied than they have been so far.

ii.   Deliberate innovation may be attempted, either through 'official' policy and instruments (for example, attempts to change the way people spoke in the seventeenth century by government decree) or through unofficial but coordinated action (for example, Women's Lib) or through individual innovation (for example, fashion, the most striking instance being the 'miniskirt', whose exact history is known). Sometimes these changes 'stick', for instance, the change from riding on the left or aristocratic side to the right or democratic side instituted in the French Revolution. Sometimes they fail, as in the effort to eliminate personal moral careers from academic work in Mao's China, by forbidding such practices as putting one's name to a scientific paper.

I take it that in the pre-scientific social world change is occurring according to an evolutionary process close to the Darwinian limit, though not in a purely uncoupled way. That is, there is some knowledge as to how social practices and organizations might be modulated to deal with changing conditions. Let us imagine we are a Roman emperor trying to cope with a Parthian invasion. We might attempt to alter the constitution of the Roman legions, to train the soldiers in different ways, and to alter Roman military practice in order to cope with a new selection condition for Roman military ways. It seems that the Romans did indeed make just such changes.

VARIATIONS OF THE SELECTION PROCESS

Graphing social change onto the spectrum of possible evolutionary processes and the associated theories must be qualified by the possibility that the selection conditions are themselves changing, so that the successful spread of a practice through a society or the flourishing of an institution at a certain epoch may be as much explicable by change in the selection conditions as it is by mutation of the practice or the institution concerned. Unlike organic nature, human beings do repeat their social innovations time and time again, trying out again and again novelties that have failed to spread at previous trials. Communal living and attempts to gain social hegemony for manual workers are well documented examples.

Theoretically there could be four cases:

i.   Neither the selection environment nor the social practices and institutions change. I do not think there is any good evidence that these conditions of life have ever actually been realized.

ii.   The selection conditions are stable and survival is a function of differential properties of the mutants alone, with respect to those selection conditions. A good example of this can be found in the history of communes in the second half of the nineteenth century in the eastern United States. Systematic study suggests that the socio-economic conditions of the circumambient society, though obviously not absolutely unchanging were relatively stable, due partly to the relative ease with which innovators and dissidents were able to move westward leaving a relatively undisturbed social order behind them. And, though economic activity did not continue throughout this time always at the same level, it remained remarkably stable in form, and business cycles were of small amplitude and of short duration. But the survival and reproduction of communes was very differentiated. At the one extreme was the Oneida society still in existence today, though very much changed and, on the other, the many which disappeared within a single generation.

iii.   The selection conditions change but the successive mutants are similar. The survival of a mutant is a function of the differential properties of the selection conditions with respect to the properties of the mutants. An imperfect example of this condition can be found by comparing the efforts of women to promote new social practices between the sexes in the period of the suffragettes with the recent women's movement. Consultation of such documents as Henry James's *The Bostonians*, an acutely observed account of the radical ladies of Massachusetts in the late nineteenth century, suggests that a great deal of the innovative practices and much of the rhetoric has been repeated, indeed in the case of these movements in the United States it has been repeated very exactly. The ultimate fate of the innovations has been very different. Though in each era the vociferousness of the movement provoked a 'backlash', I think it is fair to say that in the period preceding the First World War no significant changes in the social and political position of women occurred. That had to await the mutant practices of the war years. And, though there has been of late a strongly felt return to traditional ways, the changes in the social practices ordering the microrelations between the sexes have been profound. I would contend that the evidence suggests that in this case it is the change in the selection conditions that have been the operative influences and not any change in the latest versions of the mutant practices.

iv.   Finally, there are the more complex and much more common cases where both the selection conditions and the mutants change. To describe these cases aright we need a commonplace philosophical distinction between a determinable and the determinates which fall under it. For instance, red is a determinate under the determinable colour. The cases I want to consider are different determinates under the same determinable. In the example of the determinable is a bid for power by the Trade Union Movement through the coal miners, and the determinates are the different forms the great Miners' Strikes took in 1926 and 1972. The selection conditions favouring or disfavouring the bid are the socio-economic conditions of Britain and the social psychological character of the contending factions. In 1926 coal was in common use as a fuel, but in a great many widely dispersed centres of consumption. The ruling oligarchy was of an authoritarian cast of mind, and the miners and the other manual workers were anxious to show in all their actions that they were peaceful and democratically inclined. But in 1972 the government was committed to some form of consensus politics on every issue, coal was used less widely but in a few enormous and crucial generating stations, while the miners were adamant in the psychological attitudes. Thus the selection conditions were very different. So too were the mutant practices themselves as determinates of the determinable. In 1926 the strike was physically located at the mines, the places of production, and was publicly promoted by an orator and demagogue in the person of Cook who both persuaded the miners that their victory was certain, to their detriment, and frightened the government into believing the revolution was just round the corner. In 1972 the strike was physically located at the places of consumption through the innovation of the 'flying picket'. It was managed, not by demagogues, but by people of a managerial style. Though they may have had their origins in the so-called 'working-class', they were of the same temper of mind and very similar social experience as their opponents. Putting together these brief descriptions we have the outlines of a selection/mutation account of why the strike of 1926 led to a long period of subjection for manual workers, and why in 1972 it led to a vast and consequential series of shifts in the centres of decision making in Britain.

GOFFMAN'S LAW

I have pointed out the need to insert a middle level of scale into the evolutionary theory between selection conditions considered as the overall or global environment and the mutant practices that can occur at the scale of individual action and face to face rituals. There are many associations of the modest scale of institutions, which can be cognitively encompassed by at least some of their members. Since they generally depend upon a theory shared by the members of that institution, indeed a cluster of theories, there is a mode of change found at associations of this scale that is found nowhere else. We have also noticed the fundamental distinction between the practical order of society in which coordinated action serves to carry out practical tasks, that is, tasks which are structured by interaction with the natural world, for instance, the construction of material things by working with raw materials, and the curing of diseases by the use of anatomical, physiological and other kinds of knowledge, and the expressive order which is concerned with those tasks which lead to the recognition by others of the social type and the social value of the actor undertaking the tasks. Goffman has pointed out that these tasks, though they seem immediately to benefit only one individual, are nevertheless the product of cooperative and coordinated activity among many people, the group he calls the 'team'. The expressive *order* consists of moral careers and the reputations generated in the course of such activities, and involves all kinds of matters from the style with which one ties one's tie to the content and manner of a funeral oration.

Examining real institutions such as schools, hospitals, and ministries soon makes it clear that most are subject to a certain law of development, one of the very few genuine laws of social change. It seems proper to call it Goffman's Law. It can be simply enunciated:

In fairly closed institutions the expressive order tends to become increasingly dominant over the practical order, with respect to motivations both public and private (Goffman 1968).

Along with this goes an important corollary, needed to understand the talk that occurs in institutions, since for the most part the members still talk as if the practical tasks were their main preoccupation when observation clearly discloses that they are not. The corollary is as follows:

The official theory of an institution subject to transformation from the practical to the expressive mode is represented in a rhetoric.

Thus, though it is abundantly clear that many mental hospitals are places for the confinement of tiresome or awkward people, there is a 'cure' rhetoric dominant in the speech of the staff. The inmates are not referred to as 'detainees' or 'prisoners' but as 'patients'. The staff are not called 'warders' but 'nurses', and so on. Even the disciplinary practices are called 'treatments'. A semi-fictional account of such an institution can be found in Kesey's *One Flew Over the Cuckoo's Nest*, closely confirming the observations of Goffman (1968) and Szasz (1961).

If an institution survives long enough and there are no outside pressures to force it to return to a literal rendering of the official rhetoric in practical action it may become wholly transformed. The City Guilds of London were wholly transformed from associations of tradesmen and craftsmen into something quite else. It is a long time since a fishmonger handled fish; yet in the rhetoric of these institutions is still full of the remains of the official theory of their being, appropriate to their first beginnings. One can detect the iron necessity of Goffman's Law at work in recent discussion about schools, in which the official theory is present in the talk of educationalists as a mere rhetoric.

3   Contrived Social Change

Bearing Marx's dictum in mind, we can now look at the possibilities of, and necessary conditions for, contriving social change, by some deliberate act of intervention in the conditions that generate social reality, exploiting the processes by which social change occurs, as it were, 'naturally'. But if we do undertake such intervention exploiting the knowledge we have acquired by studying social psychology, anthropology and history, we alter the very processes of change upon which our undertaking is based.

This superordinate change comes about through our increasing ability to couple mutation and selection conditions more effectively, while at the same time, since social psychology and sociology are not outside the social world coupling is anyway already taking place. There is some evidence that in recent years the drift into simplified 'models' of man has led to simplified forms of action, through a decline in confidence in historically given modes of action. Indeed, everything that social scientists do becomes in some measure part of the stock of knowledge, belief and, particularly, myth. And so the social world becomes more and more Lamarckian in character.

An example of the change in degree of coupling has occurred in the history of the design of cars. Some twenty-five years ago the first serious attempt to design a car to fit what was believed to be the wishes of the population of car purchasers, who make up the selection conditions for mutant car designs, led to the ill fated Ford Edsel. It was the product of a premature coupling between mutation and selection conditions, a mutant that failed. But as the skill of market researchers and those who interpret their findings in terms of design increases so the design of cars *for* a market becomes more and more effective. That the process has become more Lamarckian is witnessed by the huge success of the much later Ford venture, the Mustang.[1]

But the reconstruction of selection conditions to favour desirable mutant social practices has not been successful. Of course there are still optimistic proposals for government action by those, for example, who think by controlling the money supply one can alter the state of the nation. In evolutionary terms that assumes that one can alter social practices by altering the selection conditions associated with the economic system and to make people nicer to each other by favouring the spread of certain social practices. If this were to work the very process would pull us, the people, down in a Lamarckian direction. If, roughly speaking, this is the correct picture, the influence that we can exert will have to be carefully defined. Mutation conditions work on such social practices as how we address each other, how we marry each other, how we meet members of the opposite sex, how we treat children, how we treat people who work for, with and against us and so on. These are fairly small scale processes, social practices, as you might say, of a fairly micro order. The knowledge social

---

[1] A fictional version of the Mustang story, 'Wheels', recently made into a television serial, has some interesting sequences in which the designer tries to demonstrate a Lamarckian coupling between his design and the socio-psychological state of those who will buy cars.

psychologists profess ought to make us particularly good at revealing the inner structure of such practices. Supposing that all the research programmes mentioned in this book had been brought to a successful conclusion so that at least we know something about social practices, and even if we are unable to say anything about the socio-economic conditions which act as a selection condition of social practices, we could still contrive social change though we could not ensure success. If someone introduces a new way of organizing the relationships between parents to maintain the integrity of the family for the period required for bringing up children, that would be a new social practice.

4   The Contribution of Social Psychology

NEW RULES

If we conceive of legitimate social psychology as spread roughly between experimental studies (see Argyle 1969) on the one hand and ethogenic studies on the other (see Marsh, Rosser and Harré 1978) we could treat the whole range of work as if it was bringing to light in explicit propositional form the implicit rules of action. This characterization would be stretching the notion of rule well into the metaphorical range in the case of experimental studies. But though the delicate matter of mapping the metaphysical transformation of the concept of rule is of central importance in deciding on the ontological commitments of explanatory theories in social psychology, it is not important when one thinks of transforming knowledge from any part of that spectrum into the material basis of the construction of a new social practice. The point is nicely illustrated in Trower, Bryant and Argyle's (1978) studies of the automatic or habitual bases of interaction. It would seem extremely implausible to say that eye-contact, head nodding and so on are generated by rule-following *in rerum natura*, but when transformed into a social skills training programme the regularities experimentally observed are expressed as rules for the guidance of action; in short, they become a scenario or even a script in an explicitly dramaturgical transformation of real life. I take it that the general framework to which we all subscribe, however we may differ on details, is roughly something like this:[2] we have clear sight of people undertaking structured act/action performances and we believe that they are produced by something structured, be it intention or pre-generated for the occasion (for example, in the forms suggested by Kelly 1952) from what we can roughly call the rule system. Our analyses yield attributions of social knowledge to a social-cognitive matrix where one identifies situations, rules, arbiters and personas, and maps onto it the social knowledge one believes that particular people who can perform adequately must have. When we perform this operation we make what I take to be the implicit rule system into an *explicit* rule system. I think we all agree that whatever we may think about the ontology of rules something like them is implicit in our day-to-day activities. I take it to be the job of the social psychologist to make such implicit rule systems and the conditions for their operation explicit.

At the same time I believe it quite correct to remember that people all the time are accounting or ready to account for their actions. We can draw upon this material too. We have two routes then into this explicit rule system. Now we know in principle the ordinary social word is produced, it might be that there are parts of the productive apparatus which we can interfere with. Can we deliberately exploit its generative character to produce different sorts of act/action performances by introducing different kinds of rules? The process might go something like this: One might discover in analysing act/action performances that the social sex marking symbols used in banks and so on, namely 'Mrs.' and 'Miss' involve, or mark, a radical difference in treatment between people, for example, whether they can get bank loans, whether they can

---

[2] For convenience transforming everything into my terminology.

get mortgages and so on. One might discover that these two symbols have a very important implicit social loading. One might make that explicit by revealing such regularities in the form of the rules which are said metaphysically to govern the way people are treated. Then one might have the idea of deliberately and explicitly introducing the rule that all ladies are referred to by 'Ms.'. This would be a very simple example of the way in which one might construct an explicit rule system which will feed into the social world and might produce or facilitate certain mutant social practices, such as the granting of a mortgage to an unmarried woman.

NOVEL ACCOUNTING SYSTEMS

One important consequence of taking up the ethogenic aspect of social psychology has been the attention it forces us to pay to the techniques people use for accounting, for making their activities intelligible and warrantable, and to draw our attention to just how important a role these techniques play. A complete theory of the contrivance of change must involve not only changed practices at the act/action level, but also changed accounting systems. Now in the real social world novelties in accounting are continually appearing, derived from a wide variety of sources, and spreading at different rates through the social fabric, changing it by changing what sort of behaviour it makes possible to make intelligible and so to legitimate. Moscovici's study of *représentations sociales* has traced the spread of Freudian theory through French society. But he has not yet tackled the way in which making available even grossly transformed Freudian concepts has, as it surely must, made it possible to legitimate a great deal of otherwise unintelligible or unjustifiable behaviour. As the cartoonist in *The Times* very quickly spotted, the spread in explicitly formulated terms of the folk ethology that is used to legitimize football hooliganism is now available, thanks to Marsh, Rosser and Harré (1978), to all but the most dyslexic hooligan as an available accounting system. This kind of thing suggests that we ought to make a research effort to find out whether accounting resources are changed by *représentations sociales*, and if they are whether the availability of resources for accounting affects in any way the kind of behaviour that is routinely produced. Then we should give serious consideration to the possibility of the contrivance of social change using the knowledge we would have then acquired, supplementing the little we know, by deliberate supplementations to and sanctionings from accounting resources.

5 *Limitations*

Having sketched out in very schematic form the possibilities of transformation of the social world by the exploitation of social psychological knowledge one must turn to consider whether it is possible to lay down *a priori* any limitations to the possibility of putting these ideas to work.

The obvious point of application of explicit rule innovation is at the level of institutions, which can be plausibly argued to be actually rule-governed (particularly if they are bureaucratic as opposed to natural and informal). Furthermore it is clear how implicit theories of man and society are at work in social activities at the level of institutions, such as, for example, the system of criminal justice. Furthermore, most institutions can be cognitively encompassed by a single human individual and so are epistemologically unproblematic. However, it is also clear that there are severe limitations on the changes in social life that can be brought about by deliberate change of the rules governing institutions. For example the effort to alter the balance of social esteem between different kinds of workers in New Zealand society by altering the way the school system worked was frustrated by compensating shifts (internal migration) in the population, to 'capture' good schools. So the reform actually exacerbated social distinctions by bringing about a geographical separation of workers from different walks of life. This compensating change of course might have been frustrated by introducing a further set of rules determining where anyone might live by reference to their occupation, or by introducing 'bussing', and so on. Let us note this kind of difficulty as, at least in principle, a contingent limitation.

But more important are some limitations in principle. If we take the prime focus of the possibility of change as institutions, then we must bear in mind that they are poised between two other levels of social order which are intransigent. Institutional mutations must survive within an unknown and partly unknowable macro-social order whose properties and principles of change are not cognitively represented by anyone, even a sociologist. We have already noticed the necessity to hold this aspect of the social order apart as a Darwinian selection environment, at best the subject of theoretical speculation.

At the other end of the scale we have a perfectly knowable but immutable foundation to social activity, provided by two fixed microsocial orders.

i.   there   is   the   genetically   programmed,   the ethological/biological basis of life and interaction. A very simple example of some contemporary interest is the compensating changes that have to occur in marking of the biological differences between the sexes as various tertiary or socioconventional differences have been diffused, by changes in clothing and social habits. I shall return to the ethological component below.

ii.   The other immutable social foundation comes from the apprenticeship to specifically human modes of the establishment and maintenance of social order in the autonomous precursor world of childhood, in which all kinds of ritual and symbolic acts are generated, performative uses of words developed and practised, and elaborate devices for developing and marking social distinctions brought into play. This is the world of children's private games, of the ritual markings of friendship, of the control of property by verbal formulae, of nicknaming, of savage reprisals for violations of social norms and so on. It is the world illuminated by Opie and Opie (1959), and occasionally lit up by autobiographical works, such as *Cider With Rosie*. We know something about it now, but it remains stable (the Opies have established essential stabilities for four centuries) and we have no inkling of an idea of how it might be brought under the influence of deliberate social intervention in the interests of social change.

Within these constraints mutant social forms have to try to survive. But there is yet more trouble. It seems that the free construction of social forms, perhaps whole microsocieties within these constraints, is further limited by what I should like to call the possibility of lethal mutations, in this case the inclusion, within the design, of some proposed relationship which, given the psychological conditions of the members, is impossible to realize without powerful discipline imposed from above. The moment that discipline is removed the social structure dissolves. This happened at Oneida when the elders lost their power to the managers of the associated silver works. The sexual arrangements, which distributed the favours of the women and girls by reference to age and rank and not inclination, depended on that power. When it had gone the mating structure proved to be a lethal feature of the mutant community and accelerated the break up of the structure. A slow return to the usual nuclear family arrangement follows. But the point is not simple. If at some time t_1 there is a psychology p_1 it does not follow that psychology of t_2 would be the same as p_1. We may not suppose that there is a general psychology upon which we can call in attempting to avoid lethal mutations. There is a further, more subtle point. One assumes in thinking in 1978 about the construction of social practices that one might be able to adopt a new social practice to which we know operated in the Tobriand Islands in 1920. Assuming we know how to construct the rules for it, we might propose introducing this new social practice in 1979. But, of course, as Gergen (1973) has pointed out, it does not at all follow that it is going to be a possible social practice in 1978 for us. One must try to envisage the process of transformation from where we are now to where we might want to be. So if we are going to live according to a social psychology at t_3, in the future, we have to ask ourselves first of all whether there is a possible transition from psychology$_2$ to psychology$_3$. But at present we do not know, given any psychology, let us say one which has a certain distribution of a personality type, if it is possible to transform the social world and change social practices to introduce some other arbitrary set of personality types which would be expressively revealed in social practices. Gergen was perfectly right in raising this as a serious issue. We need to make a very careful historical study, to ask ourselves how are these transitions related to each other, what psychologies are possible, p_2 to p_n, given that we are at p_1. We do not know the answer.

Since social life is made up of innumerable act-sequences in the course of which social order is generated with the performance of culturally appropriate action-sequences we need to consider how far acts or the actions for performing them are drawn from a fixed repertoire. The obvious sort of fixedness would be if either or both were genetically programmed as subject to Darwinian selection, that is were elements in ethological routines. It could be that elements originally part of adaptive routines become detached though still programmed for (as behavioural vestiges, ethological *bricolage*, the debris of our adaptive history) and can be put to use in other routines whose overall structure is culturally determined and socially imposed.

Discussions of this issue in sociobiology have been confused by failure to distinguish elements and routines at the level of act, from elements and routines at the level of action. This makes it necessary to consider a complex tree of possibilities:

Acts as genetically   vs.   Acts as culturally
determined   determined

Actions realizing acts   Actions realizing acts
as genetically   as genetically

undetermined vs.   vs.   determined vs.
actions as culturally   actions as culturally
determined   determined

Yielding four categories:

	act	action	example
1	g.d.	g.d.	male bonding by ritual 'aggro'
2	g.d.	c.d.	triumphing by victory rolling a plane
3	c.d.	g.d.	betting by shaking hands
4	c.d.	c.d.	contracting by signing one's name

Given the relative rates of change genetically programmed and culturally determined routines, social change must take genetically programmed elements and routines as fixed points. Thus in our table we would expect category 1 to be stable, and subject to only minor historical variation; category 2 will see substitution of actions (for example, Achilles' behaviour at Troy); category 3 could vanish as a practice; category 4 might vanish, or if the act is relatively culturally stable there could be substitute actions (thumbprinting, for example). *All* these possibilities of change and stability exist at the micro-level of formal institutional and formal face-to-face coordinated action sequences.

6   *Pretesting*

As Peter Collett has pointed out (in a discussion) it is a dangerous thing to go about the social world trying out innovations, particularly given the relatively Darwinian state in which that world currently must remain. It is a dangerous thing to propose that all ladies should style themselves 'Ms.' because we have not much idea what the effects are going to be. The effects of educational reform in New Zealand stand as a warning to everyone. And we do not know what conditions are required for the transplantation of institutions into cultures whose socio-psychological basis is very different from those in which these institutions developed, for example, the difficulties in setting up parliamentary forms of government in Africa. There is one way I think of simulating real life that we have not yet really looked at deeply enough: theatre. I do not mean just scenario-game-playing but the real theatre that goes on out there in the real world in various forms. There is the traditional form of theatre in which a playwright utilizes his tacit knowledge of the social world to construct a script, and the actors and directors use their tacit knowledge to formulate a reality in accordance with it and construct a play. We as audience and critics can test that play for its simulation of reality. But there is always the problem that there are aesthetic criteria operating in the choice of acts and action, and related accounts in the way it develops. So it is by no means a perfect simulation, but it is not a bad one. Even more interesting is the experimental theatre. It is another way of testing for reality and psycho-social possibility because in the experimental theatre everybody *takes part*. The actors propose a new piece of social life. They may even be quite ethogenically inclined and deliberately construct new forms and try them out with the audience as participants. The audiences are drawn into the performance and begin to live a fragment of a new life. As Don Mixon (1971), and others, have found, not only the audience who are forced to participate but the actors also have a particular kind of feeling with relation to what is happening, which tests the plausibility, the reality, the emotional possibility of the forms of life with which one is experimenting.

References

M. Argyle, 1969, *Social Interaction*, London: Methuen

R. Bhaskar, 1978, 'On the Possibility of Social Scientific Knowledge and the Limits of Naturalism', *Journal for the Theory of Social Behaviour*, Vol. 8, pp. 1–28

J. Douglas, 1967, *The Social Meanings of Suicide*, Princeton, N.J.: Princeton University Press

M. Douglas, 1972, *Deciphering a Meal*, Daedalus, Winter

K. Gergen, 1973, 'Social Psychology as History', *Journal of Personality and Social Psychology*

E. Goffman, 1968, *Asylums*, Harmondsworth: Penguin

G. A. Kelly, 1952, *The Psychology of Personal Constructs*, New York: Norton

P. Marsh, E. Rosser and R. Harré, 1978, *The Rules of Disorder*, London: Routledge

D. Mixon, 1971, 'Behaviour Analysis Treating Subjects as Actors rather than Organisms', *Journal for the Theory of Social Behaviour*, Vol. 1, pp. 19–31

S. Moscovici, 1961, *La Psychoanalyse, Son Image et Son Public*, Paris: Presses Universitaire de France

T. Sasz, 1961, *The Myth of Mental Illness*, London: Secker and Warburg

S. Toulmin, 1972, *Human Understanding*, Oxford: The Clarendon Press

P. Trower, B. Bryant and M. Argyle, 1978, *Social Skills and Mental Health*, London: Methuen

T. Veblen, 1957, *The Theory of the Leisure Class*, New York: New American Library

Epilogue: A Conception of Situated Action

G. P. GINSBURG   *University of Nevada, Reno*

The writer of the epilogue for an edited volume has the distinct advantage of being stimulated by the other contributions to the volume, especially when they are as challenging to conventional approaches as are the present chapters. On the other hand, the epilogue author has the correlated burden of trying to summarize both the book and its individual chapters in a succinct, incisive fashion. This responsibility is lifted somewhat from my shoulders by Michael Brenner's excellent introductory chapter to the volume. In that chapter, Brenner articulates the focus of the book and identifies the substantive and methodological issues raised by each of the contributors. In turn, this frees me to offer a more substantive contribution than is frequently afforded by an epilogue chapter.

The major objective of this chapter is to extract certain important themes from the individual contributions and to weave them into a coherent model, one which reasonably might be called 'structural anlysis of situated action'. The pitfalls and shortcomings of that model, epistemological as well as methodological, will be noted along with its potential benefits. First, however, the book itself must be examined and placed in the context of contemporary trends in social psychology.

1   *The Book and Its Chapters*

As Brenner points out, this volume is concerned with the structural analysis of face-to-face interaction. However, the chapters invariably reflect theoretical and methodological views which diverge considerably from the conventional, positivistically grounded academic social psychology typical in the U.S., and common as well in Great Britain and on the Continent. To appreciate properly the book and its contribution, some attention must be given to recent criticisms of conventional social psychology.

In 1972, after several years of collaboration at Oxford and at the University of Nevada, Reno, Harré and Secord published *The Explanation of Social Behaviour*. Although the book contained many loose ends and received some justified criticism on those grounds, it also contained several very strong claims about what was wrong with social psychological research and how such research and theorizing should be conducted. Over time, the challenge of the book came to be taken seriously, and its basic paradigm – 'ethogenics' – has become a respectable label in the field, even appearing as a chapter in the important handbook series edited by Berkowitz, *Advances in Experimental Social Psychology* (Harré, 1977). The Israel and Tajfel volume, critically evaluating contemporary social psychology, also was published in 1972, but, as an edited volume, it did not offer as coherent a thesis as the Harré and Secord book. Nevertheless, its appearance and its acceptance serve as further indication of the intellectual reconsiderations of the time. This intense activity has continued, especially but not exclusively at Oxford; and its products – all necessarily intermediate, given the emergent nature of the activity – have been captured in a number of volumes and journal articles. Examples include Collett's (1977) interesting volume on social rules; the edited books by Brenner, Marsh and Brenner (1978) and Ginsburg (1979a) which emphasize the contextual grounding of our research activities and the research strategies which appear most compatible with the emerging theoretical perspectives;

the methodologically spotty but insightful research mono-
graph by Marsh, Rosser and Harré (1978) demonstrating the
rule-guided nature of violence on football terraces and in
classrooms; and a concise metaphysical challenge to Humean
causality and proposal of a natural powers conception as a
basis for scientific explanation (Harré and Madden 1975). The
Oxford social psychology group have been regular contributors to most of these volumes, including Argyle, Clarke
and Collett, as well as Harré. This activity is continuing and
other volumes, beside the present one, are sure to be published
in the next year or two.

Henri Tajfel's interest in the development of improved
paradigms for social psychology was further manifested in his
codirection, with Lloyd Strickland, of a 1974 conference on
that topic in Canada, later published in a volume edited by
Strickland, Aboud and Gergen (1976). Gergen, of course, has
been a major figure in the U.S. re-evaluation of social
psychological paradigms, especially since his challenging contention (1973) that social psychological knowledge and theory
cannot be transhistorical. Although he has tempered his original position somewhat, he also has tightened and extended its
arguments (Gergen, in press). Both in the U.S. and elsewhere,
a wider range of active social psychologists is being brought
into contact with these paradigmatic reconsiderations: The
Journal of Personality and Social Psychology devoted a special
section to the state of theory in the field (1978), the October
1979 *Newsletter* of the Society for the Advancement of Social
Psychology will focus on 'new developments' in social
psychological theory; the highly respected and selective
Society of Experimental Social Psychology presented a symposium on the topic during its annual meeting at Princeton in
November 1978; and the inaugural issue of the *Personality and
Social Psychology Review* will deal in part with emerging
theories.

Thus, social psychology is in a state of intense theoretical
activity, with immense potential for change in both its accepted modes of explanation and its conventional strategies of

research. This activity is taking place on a ground fertilized by the 'crisis' concerns of the late 1960's; but those concerns emanated largely from doubts about the wisdom and morality of the widespread use of deception as a research technique (see Ginsburg 1978 for a detailed review), while the current ferment is a creatively productive one which clearly is in the process of producing new theoretical and methodological perspectives for the field. Although the details vary considerably, many of the productively critical statements contain certain views in common: human action is situated, and to understand the action, one must understand the situation; persons are capable of monitoring their appearances as well as their instrumental activities, so that character management is an important feature of most human action; human action is meaningful, and the meanings of actions must be understood in order to understand the actions; human action develops and unfolds in real time, and has both a temporal and hierarchical structure; and persons are active agents, capable of acting as well as reacting, of planning as well as responding, and of continually negotiating the meanings of their actions (see Ginsburg 1979b and c for elaboration). The present volume is a product of this continuing advance and is designed not only to challenge conventional approaches but to propose advanced alternatives to them.

As noted, the book focuses largely on face-to-face interaction, or what is sometimes called 'microsociology'. The chapters deal with the contexts within which interactions occur, the presumptions underlying the fact of and the understanding of such interactions, what should be examined with regard to the interactions, and pitfalls which we must avoid in investigating interactional sequences. Furthermore, most of the chapters examine the *processes* of face-to-face interaction, and it is this which gives the volume its structural emphasis.

Four of the chapters constitute major conceptual statements which complement each other in an interesting fashion. These are the chapters by Harré, Argyle, Shotter and Rommetveit, and they will be considered in turn.

Harré's chapter is concerned with change in small scale interpersonal practices, including deliberate change based on the accumulation of social psychological knowledge. However, it is not the ostensive focus but the conceptual perspective which stands in complementary relationship to the other chapters. Specifically, Harré takes an evolutionary perspective concerning change and stability in social practices. He argues that the structures of large scale macrosystems are pragmatically immutable and serve as selection conditions, determining which social practices are likely to have a selective advantage. Similarly, biological and ethological factors operate as selection conditions, as do – according to Harré – the microsocial orders of the childhood world, which Harré views as a transhistorically stable precursor of the adult social world. It is important to note that these are selection conditions, not mutation conditions. That is, they are passive 'conditions under which . . .' rather than active 'conditions which cause . . .'. Harré does suggest that mutation conditions and selection conditions can be coupled, even though they are mutually independent in Darwinian theory, and that such coupling may be increased through accumulated social psychological knowledge. Also, if events or their effects persist long enough, they may function as both selection and mutation conditions. Changes in interpersonal practices, for example, can be brought about or be given the opportunity to succeed through the introduction of new rules or the development of new schemes of accounting.

There are many points in his chapter on which Harré can be taken to task. For example, the claim that childhood between ages five and twelve constitutes a precursor world which has been essentially stable for centuries and is little affected by the adult world, for which it serves as a body of selection conditions, is belied by more careful reviews. Both Ariès (1962) and Tuchman (1978) point out that during the Middle Ages, children were adults by age seven, albeit in miniature, and participated as members of the adult world. Ariès goes on to suggest that the adult world indeed influenced the content of the childhood world through incorporation and continuation by the latter of social forms which were or had been valuable among adults of the nobility and middle classes.

The claim that we have no theories which link macrostructures, such as an economic system, to the 'day-to-day . . . working of man-sized institutions' also is questionable. Just within the last few years, Oxford economists have theorized about the influence of government fiscal and monetary policies upon the daily buying habits of ordinary consumers and the investment activities of business and manufacturing firms. Theories of such linkages, although different in content, can be found in any economics text. We also have concrete illustrations of such linkages: The interpersonal and institutional relationships of the 19th century Japanese silk industry were revolutionized – in predictable manner – by the United States demand for large numbers of bolts of standard quality and pattern. A somewhat similar process of large scale technological and economic influences on institutional and interpersonal structures can be seen in the current threat to the Harris Isle tweed industry, where the loom size is smaller than the industrial standard, and the lack of mechanization is competitively disadvantageous.

The very heavy and unqualified reliance on accounts also poses a potential problem. The stated presumption that 'people all the time are accounting or ready to account for their actions' is difficult to accept, unless 'actions' are defined trivially and tautologically as activities for which one does or is able to account. Many actions, conducted within an act framework, are performed habitually, with little self-awareness (see Langer 1978). During the performance of such actions, people usually are not accounting for them, are not ready to account for them, and may not be aware that they are performing them. On the other hand, if challenged afterwards, people usually can construct a retrospective account. This poses a danger for the scientific use of the account, an issue of which Harré is aware and which he has addressed forthrightly elsewhere, but not in this chapter (see Harré and

Secord 1972; Harré 1977, 1978). In essence, accounts must not be used as a priority description or explanation of an action, but as negotiable statements which make the action intelligible and warrantable and thereby reveal the cultural rules and meanings extant within the setting.

Harré also disregards real problems of experimental design and reliability of data, and ignores large amounts of published material which bear on his arguments. However, I do not think the chapter should be criticized in detail as though it were a finished model put forward for serious consideration. Instead, it should be accepted as a provocative and somewhat audacious proposal, which is exactly what Kenneth Gergen (in press) claims is needed in science. In that spirit, Harré's examination of change in social practices within a framework of selection conditions is an important conceptual contribution, and considerable use will be made of it in the remainder of this epilogue.

Argyle's chapter on the analysis of social situations both complements that of Harré and extends it through a careful and detailed examination of situational properties. Those properties can be construed as consituting the selection conditions of moment-to-moment actions and the larger acts which they produce. The chapter is an advance over earlier writings by Argyle on this topic (1975, 1979) and reflects his continuing efforts to explore and systematize the initial contention that behaviour is a function of the situation. In his present chapter, Argyle implicitly assumes that all human action is situated, and argues that in order to understand and explain the situated actions of people, it is necessary to understand the situation within which the actions of interest occur. Furthermore, the situations must be understood in detailed and concrete terms, since global dimensions of situations do not differentiate among clearly different situations which call for clearly different actions.

Argyle conceives of situations as having several interdependent components, so that the situation is a system of interdependent parts. The components are the goals, repertoires of behavioural elements and sequences, rules, roles, concepts, skills and difficulties, and physical environment. The emphasis on interdependency among the components, as opposed to linear causality, is very important, because it links the analysis to a structural explanation, as will be seen later. Moreover, accepting as obvious the view that all human action is situated, it is *necessary* to understand the situation in order to understand the action. Argyle's specification of the components of situations is a large step in that direction. His chapter, somewhat in contrast to Harré's, is meant to be taken seriously in its details.

On those grounds, there are several ambiguities that must be addressed, the most important of which concern the location of the situational components. Even though Argyle quite explicitly, in the second paragraph of his chapter, identifies the components as 'features of situations', in the ensuing discussion they often are treated as desires, states, qualities and abilities of people. This ambiguity seriously undermines the force of Argyle's argument, since it removes the generative mechanisms from the situation and places them within the person. The concept of situation thereby is reduced either to a setting within which action takes place but which has no explanatory force regarding the action, or to a potential which has no force until it combines with a person to produce action, that is $B=f(P,S)$. Clearly, Argyle does not intend either of those.

Argyle's treatment of 'goal' illustrates the problem. The reasons and causes for action are located within the person in the form of needs and drives, and goals are the means provided by the situation for satisfying the needs and drives. Situations also may arouse needs and drives, as well as providing means for satisfying them. Therefore, exactly what constitutes the goals of a situation depends upon the needs and drives which a person brings to the situation or are aroused in him by it. In turn, the situation itself cannot be characterized independently of the participating persons' needs and drives. As noted, this is not what Argyle wishes to argue.

The solution to the dilemma is straightforward, I think, and is largely contained in Argyle's chapter. Situations provide the opportunity for specifiable accomplishments, and the description of a situation requires specification of the accomplishments which it affords. The range of afforded accomplishments is constrained by the roles and rules, the physical setting, and the other features of situations discussed by Argyle.

Intra-individual concepts, such as needs, drives, intentions and wants, are not necessary for situational characterization, although they may prove very useful in explaining why a particular person chose to enter or create a situation and why he succeeded or failed within it (see Bem and Funder 1978). Thus, goals are affordances which reside in the situation and are related in empirically determinable manners to the other components of the situation. They are not a function of personal states or traits of specific individuals, except as those individuals create, modulate or transform the situation, an issue which will be addressed shortly.

Similar problems arise with respect to concepts and skills. Are they features of people, or of situations? The resolution of the ambiguity is the same as that developed for goals: Given that situations exist only as people create and implement them, they are nevertheless emergent phenomena that can be discussed independently of specific people, and the components of situations reside in the situations, not in persons. A component such as 'skills' or 'required constructs' identifies that which participants in the situation must have or express for successful accomplishment of the situation.

Argyle's interesting treatment of sequences also raises some problems, especially regarding the universality of some two-step sequences and the bases for their presumed universality. Questions lead to answers and requests lead to action or refusal only if some sort of 'responsiveness' (Davis and Martin 1978; Davis and Berkowitz 1979) rule applies, in which the recipient is obligated to respond relevantly and with some probability greater than zero to the meaningful actions of the other. There are situations in which responsiveness is not the shared rule, as in some psychotherapeutic procedures. Also, such 'natural psychological tendencies' as response matching, reinforcement, and 'effects of friendly and hostile behaviour', do not always operate. For example, there are conditions under which reinforcing events or procedures do not reinforce or reinforce too much or too swiftly (Bolles 1972). In other words, the 'natural psychological tendencies' are themselves contingent, either on species-specific response proclivities or on pervasive cultural rules, so that the presumably universal sequences to which Argyle refers are likely to be contingent rather than universal.

A somewhat different issue is contained in Argyle's discussion of the physical environment. He unnecessarily commits himself to a linearly causal orientation, as reflected in his comment, 'The environment causes behaviour . . .'. In view of his conception of the situation as a system of temporally extensive interdependent components, including the physical environment, it would be more consistent to construe the physical environment as a set of material conditions under which action occurs and which the agent uses in his actions. The value of this rephrasing will become evident later, when causal and structural analyses are contrasted; but for the moment it can be noted that the rephrasing is more compatible with Harré's views about 'selection conditions', as well as being more consistent with the rest of Argyle's analysis of situations.

Three topics are given insufficient consideration, but they are treated in some detail in other chapters, thereby augmenting the complementarity referred to earlier. First, it is not clear how character presentation, style, evaluatively toned situated identity, and similar phenomena of impression management are handled by the model. There is no question that these involve features of the situation, as well as being aspects of the situated actions (see Alexander and Scriven 1978; also, see the third experiment reported by Bem and Funder 1978). It is conceivable that they can be handled by both goals and rules.

Second, is a situation, once construed, constant over various describers of it? Or does the perspective of the describer play an important role in the model of situational analysis? Some attention is given to this in Argyle's discussion of multiple goals and multiple persons, but only from the perspective of the outside observer. The issue of perspective is not addressed in the chapter; but it is faced directly in Collett's chapter. I think it will become clear that perspectives are important, that the 'observer' perspective is only one among several (but it is one and cannot be ignored), and that more than one situation may exist at the same time and place.

Finally, Argyle gives insufficient attention to the capacity of participants to create, modify and transform the situation, through individual action or negotiation. He is not aware of this capacity, as he reveals in his discussion of sequences and their episodic structure, but he gives it less attention than it deserves. On the other hand, the chapters by Shotter and Rommetveit deal with the matter extensively.

Thus, Argyle's detailed and careful model for the analysis of social situations provides us with a strong framework for understanding the actions of people. The model complements that of Harré, and in turn will be complemented by the arguments of Shotter and Rommetveit. Although Argyle slights the creation and modulation of a situation by its participants, most of that which is created by them can be described in terms of the features which he proposes.

Shotter's chapter is less straightforward than that of Argyle, and in some places it is decidedly abstruse. However, it presents such a basic challenge to conventional social psychological theory and research that it is well worth the effort to work through it. Shotter distinguishes actions – things one does – from things that happen to one. Actions are performed by active agents, whereas events happen to what Buss (1978) calls 'sufferers'. Intentional activities form a primitive class with respect to human action. The class includes intention, thought, and other 'mental activities', all of which point to something beyond themselves. That is, one thinks *about* something, or intends *to* act in some way. Furthermore, intentional activities are derived from or linked to something earlier. The acting person – the active agent – always exists in an extended moment of reality and has awareness of a fixed past, in the sense of events which already have occurred, and future potential. The present is a brief interval in which things are becoming, going on, being produced. This notion seems identical to William James' (1890) 'specious present', which Ayer (1974) links to a reasonable span of attention. The acting person *always* is in this brief interval of reality, a reality which is partly specified, and always specifiable further. Psychological theories, Shotter argues, must be framed around this fact; they must accommodate the perspective of the active agent.

A personal world can be ascribed to an acting person. It is the hierarchical organization of the person's experience, including the specious present, in which actions are nested within larger acts. Social worlds are joint products of interacting persons and depend upon the construction by the interactors of shared meanings. A person will not necessarily be accurate in accounting for his actions in a social world, because those actions depend for their production and intelligibility upon the somewhat unpredictable behaviour of another person – that is, as a joint product, actions in a social world constitute *joint* action. To understand an action requires understanding the personal and social worlds within which that action takes place *and makes sense*, since an action necessarily is a component of intentional personal and social worlds. It has no existence independently of them. Moreover, such worlds exist at the time – that is, during the specious present – and they reflect a past as well as imply a future. People create social worlds through their interactions with each other; those worlds are not fixed entities which exist and have influence independent of the realities created by the interacting persons. Action is a form-producing process, and people are rule makers (presumably in contrast to claims that people are rule followers).

Shotter argues strongly in favour of hermeneutic understanding, from the perspectives of the acting or interacting persons, as opposed to an explanatory mode based on causation in terms of external influences upon the persons. Psychology must capture phenomenal reality within its sytem of understanding and explanation.

As Shotter develops these arguments, it becomes clear that he is challenging the essential foundations of social psychological theory, as well as the practice of experimentally oriented research. Such concepts as active agency, actions, perspective of the actor in a continuously present reality, personal and social worlds, intentionality, hermeneutic understanding, shared meanings, and creation of social reality are either anathema or simply confusing to the vast majority of productive investigators in social and personality psychology. The adoption of Shotter's view would mean dramatic changes in the nature of social psychological theory and the conduct of research. But the nature of those changes, especially in research strategies, is unclear. For example, would the understandings which might be created through the adoption of Shotter's view be susceptible to rigorous empirical assessment and modification? I will return to the general issue of research strategies later in the chapter.

Several other features of Shotter's arguments require comment. His emphasis on action as a form producing process and on people as rule makers is laudable, but he under-emphasizes the fact that shared social worlds often exist in rudimentary form *a priori* with regard to any particular joint act. As Argyle points out, many situations are standard, and role–rule frameworks can be said to exist a priori once people enter upon those situations. Classrooms, family dining, sports, discos, even barroom pick-ups, are illustrations of relatively standardized situations. Therefore, there are many contextual constraints within which people operate, and the creative, negotiative function of persons in the production of social worlds is itself constrained and operates in conjunction with situational factors (see Backman 1979 for a development of this point).

Another problem concerns the stricture to understand the

personal and social worlds of persons such that their actions within those worlds make sense. One technique for making sense of a person's actions is to solicit accounts from him, and perhaps even to negotiate more satisfactory accounts. However, people often are unaware of the features of the physical (Gibson 1963, 1966) and social (Nisbett and Wilson 1977) worlds to which they are sensitive, and yet those social and physical features are the grounds within which they are acting. The intonation markers discussed by Kreckel (this volume), for example, are unlikely to be known by interactors to be influential events to which they are sensitive and which convey meaning. As noted earlier with respect to Harré's reliance on accounts, we must not ascribe to them a priority status regarding the accuracy or the completeness of an explanation of an action.

Nevertheless, these qualifications notwithstanding, Shotter's arguments are persuasive, and certain features will be reconsidered later. These include specification of perspectives, recognition of a continuously present reality which is partly specified but always specifiable further, and negotiative creation of social worlds and joint actions.

Rommetveit extends in great detail Shotter's concern with negotiation and joint action, and he further emphasizes the unavoidable facts of 'genuine ambiguity and multiple meanings' which inhere in any interaction. He does this through the development of temporarily shared social reality and its control by the interacting parties in their repeatedly exchanged roles of speaker and listener. The speaker generally can impose his private world on the listener, who by virtue of his participation in the dialogue is obligated to try to understand what the other person is talking about. This provides a basis for Rommetveit's later distinction between what is meant by what is said, and what is made known by what is said. Moreover, any act of human communication constitutes the creation and implementation of a temporarily shared social reality, and actual *and assumed* controls over what is being meant. The communicative act cannot be understood in terms of presumedly shared frameworks of unequivocal propositional knowledge about the world. The private worlds of people are contextually grounded and describable in terms of a range of presuppositions and potential perspectives. The construction of various degrees of shared social reality between people is made possible by their capacity to enter into revisable agreements ('drafts of contracts') about meanings in ordinary discourse and the range of perspectives to be taken in the discourse. Role-taking, in which one adopts a perspective of the other, is an essential capacity in Rommetveit's conception of communication, and takes place within what Rommetveit considers to be the primary contract of communication control.

Rommetveit's chapter reflects his long held view that the analysis of the communicative process is essential to an understanding of human action and experience, and that such an analysis cannot be founded on the assumption of an autonomous, linguistic text. Instead, communication must be seen as a social psychological process involving the creation and modulation of shared social realities, or 'intersubjectivities', based on role taking and incorporating the concept of meaning. In his chapter for this volume, Rommetveit has focused directly on the problems of determining not only the meaning of an act, but also what is meant, what is made known, and what is understood by its performance. He emphasizes both the negotiation and the reciprocal controls involved in the construction and maintenance of temporary states of intersubjectivity, and he does so in a more detailed and clear manner than I have seen to date. In my opinion, it is an excellent contribution to an emerging orientation in social psychology.

A number of points in the chapter deserve comment, however. First, in common with Harré and Shotter, Rommetveit relies exclusively on language as a basis for meanings and for their control and negotiation. This is unnecessarily and probably incorrectly restrictive, since it restricts the use of 'meaning' to theories about linguistic organisms, whereas there is strong likelihood that other species are capable of engaging in the negotiation of meanings. This seems to be the case even if reciprocal role taking is presumed necessary (for example, see Meddin 1979 and Gallup 1979 regarding higher primates). Obviously, language activities must receive focal attention in the analysis of human interaction; but meanings and their negotiation should not be defined exclusively in terms of language capacities and activities.

Second, and again in common with Shotter, Rommetveit stresses the actor's perspective and claims that the actor is informed about his 'real intentions' in a way that outsiders cannot be; the 'honest self-account thus has a unique status . . . (regarding) . . . the atribution of meanings to acts'. However, this relies on the concepts available to the actor, on his beliefs about why he does things, on his capacity to describe, and even on his idea of what he is doing. The actor may not even realize that he is aware of certain situational features or internal states, so there is always uncertainty about whether he can inform others about his awareness and reflection. Priority status should not be given to an actor's account; it is always susceptible to challenge and negotiation. This is as true with respect to accounts of the intentional actions performed by the actor as with accounts about the events which befell him, as implied by Rommetveit's own reference to the 'genuine ambiguity and multiple meanings' of human action.

It even is questionable whether the speaker 'cannot possibly misunderstand what he himself intends to make known'. If he expresses an intent silently to himself – an action in its own right – then he can match that action with its social manifestation and assess whether he had made known what he had intended. However, interaction often is rapid, and speakers may be guided unreflectively by the discourse conventions of their culture. In such a case, the speaker will not have an intent to make something known, although he still will be able to assess his action in case of a breakdown in the smooth flow of the interaction. For example, if the other person had just revealed something personal about himself, the speaker might follow convention and do the same, only to realize by the momentary embarrassment of the other that he had revealed too much or something of the wrong sort. He immediately would be able to explain, if called upon, that he had not intended to reveal that item, and his claim would be truthful – even though he had no specifically *substantive* intent prior to the embarrassing utterance. In other words, if the speaker does 'have an intent' to make a particular item known, then he will not misunderstand *that* intent; but he may err with respect to what he does not intend to make known (but reveals nonetheless) and with respect to whether he had a substantive intent to make a particular something known. Thus, the necessity for intent as a foundation for asymmetry in responsibility for what is meant by what is said should be reconsidered. The asymmetry is more directly handled through the role-taking concept and a response theory of meaning (Mead 1934), in which the speaker, through role taking, responds from perspective of the listener to what he is in the process of saying. If the listener's actions do not conform satisfactorily to the speaker's own covert responses to his utterances, a condition for correction or negotiation obtains. This is not meant to deny the existence of intent, but rather to remove the establishment and maintenance of intersubjectivity from its absolute reliance upon it.

Finally, does reciprocal role taking actually occur? The role-taking concept is central to symbolic interaction theory (see Mead 1934; MacPhail and Rexroat 1979), but there is relatively little rigorous evidence of its occurrence (although there is some, as MacPhail and Rexroat attest). In any event, Rommetveit might direct the attention of his students, or of those working with Blakar, to the empirical question of the occurrence of reciprocal role taking.

It is worth emphasizing certain features in the four chapters discussed so far. Harré's chapter emphasizes selection conditions, which we might view as a class of enabling conditions for the occurrence of social practices (see Harré and Secord 1972); Argyle proposes a conception of situations as systems of interdependent parts and as the location within which actions are generated; Shotter emphasizes perspectives and continually present reality, action and joint action, meaning, negotiation, continuity and intentionality; and Rommetveit stresses the establishment and maintenance of temporarily shared realities from individual private worlds and pluralities of meaning. Woven together and appropriately elaborated, these features will lead later to a model of situated action, analysed from a structural perspective.

Most of the other chapters in the book are more limited in scope or more sharply focused. Kreckel's chapter, for example, analyses communication conditions and patterns within the framework of her more general theory (Kreckel in press); but the present chapter is narrowly focused and empirically grounded. However, it makes an important contribution in its use of intonation patterns as markers for identification of meaning units in discourse. Her demonstration answers one of Collett's concerns regarding the difficulties inherent in any attempts to discover 'natural units' in sequences of interaction. Collett's review of the problems one faces in either generating or attempting to discover units of interaction is accurate but a bit depressing, in that it leaves one with little hope of resolving such impasses as whether to choose an etic or emic perspective. The answer to the latter, I think, lies in our development of a model which accommodates all pertinent, immediate-experience perspectives, including those of the investigator and his experimental subjects, both of which are etic perspectives. This is compatible with the arguments of Harré, Shotter and Rommetveit.

Allwood's chapter is highly programmatic and within a philosophical, linguistic tradition, patterned after other works on speech acts. Although the analysis of discourse in terms of felicity conditions is interesting, its payoff is unclear in the absence of evidence about the extent to which people actually make distinctions of the sorts proposed, and if they do, whether they use them as suggested. Also, too little attention was given to the interpersonal nature of communicative acts, and especially to the critical importance of shared frameworks.

Blakar's chapter, on the other hand, is empirically grounded, but its emphasis on schizophrenia seems slightly out of place in this book. Blakar's critical view of the communication models of schizogenesis is excellent; the only flaw is that the important issue of diagnosis of schizophrenia was not addressed. The communication model draws its major theoretical underpinnings from the work of Rommetveit and is set forth clearly. The incorporation of 'intentionality' into the definition of communication may be a problem in Blakar's model, as it may be in Rommetveit's. It is worth noting that Blakar and his colleagues use an experimental paradigm as the vehicle for application of their model. Although there is a possibility of experimenter-by-group confounding in the design, the investigations do demonstrate that a negotiative communication model and experimental research strategies are not inherently incompatible.

David Clarke's chapter is troublesome to me. It is tightly woven in its arguments, and the case it presents for generative models and their use is persuasive. However, it is programmatic, as Brenner notes, and therefore is limited in its advances beyond Clarke's other recent writings (see, for example, Clarke 1979). We will have to await the results of research currently under way at Oxford to assess his proposals. On the other hand, his earlier arguments, less tightly woven but of the same form as his chapter in this book, have led to interesting research by others. Specifically, Kent, Davis and Shapiro (1978) based their studies of construction and reconstruction of conversations on some of the techniques Clarke has developed for the analysis of structure. Again, it is worth noting that an experimental paradigm was used, despite Clarke's unqualified rejection of experiments as not being 'the right instrument for the job'.

In fact, Clarke's rejection of experimentation reflects what I consider to be a flaw in several of the chapters in this book, and more generally in the ethogenically oriented approaches themselves. They contain an almost faddish rejection of experimental designs and procedures. This is both unfortunate and unnecessary. It should be kept in mind that experiments,

when properly designed, provide protection through ran-
domization against unidentifiable and unknowable biases, and
allow for critical limitation of the range of conditions under
which the phenomena of interest can be observed. It is very
disturbing to see the logic and rationale of experimental
design, with its important advantages, being rejected out of
hand simply because a large number of social psychologists
have incorrectly claimed it to be the only procedure that
generates criterial data. As I have argued elsewhere (Ginsburg
1978, 1979c), we must avoid falling prey to the persuasive,
insightful investigator who knows his interpretation of a
phenomenon is correct, based on his single observation of a
single instance of it. Boring (1963, p. 251) properly ad-
monished us to mistrust our own capacity for forming un-
biased inferences and to insist on controls for protecting our
conclusions from our predilections.

On the other hand, the chapters by Argyle, Kreckel and
Blakar reflect the methodological stance which social psychology must maintain if it is to develop as a science. All three
reveal a continuing interplay between conceptual arguments
and empirical investigation, with the latter used at times to
advance the conceptions and at others to test them. This
interplay, combined with the healthy scepticism suggested
above, is especially important for conceptual orientations
which take an emic perspective and rely heavily on accounts.
The arguments by Harré, Shotter and Rommetveit would be
strengthened considerably if they would address the technical
issues concerning procedures by which the adequacy and
plausibility of accounts can be assessed and by which they can
be maximized.

Finally, none of the chapters addresses an important epistemological implication of structural studies, although Brenner touches upon it in his introduction. He cites the contention
by Duncan and Fiske (1977) that episodes of interaction should
be understood in terms of both the structure or form of the
interaction and the active persons operating within it. However, it is important to note that structural studies, in which

the structure and active processes of an episode are examined, involve analyses of that which already is completed, as opposed to the presumptive predictive orientation of conventional social psychological research. There is much to be said for the discovery and critical description of forms and processes which actually have occurred in natural settings of social action (see Harré and Secord 1972); but there are costs attendant upon it, such as increased difficulty in rejecting alternative interpretations, eliminating potential subject biases, and specifying the limits of generalization. Although these difficulties inhere in all research, they are augmented in structural studies. However, the benefits of structural orientation easily outweigh such costs, which in any case can be reduced by blending structural analyses with principles of experimental design, as I will suggest later.

2   The Major Themes

In this section, I shall reorganize major themes drawn from most of the preceding chapter into three classes, and examine each class in turn. The three classes are conditions under which human actions and interactions occur, the active agency of persons, and the features of the communicative action itself, especially meanings and units.

As discussed earlier, human action necessarily is situated; it occurs in a context. To understand the action, one must understand the context within which it is known or believed to occur; and to predict whether the action will occur again, one must understand the contexts with respect to which its future occurrence is being considered. Specification of the roles and rules of the situation, including the rules which guide character presentation, will help to make the action comprehensible, as will specification of the goals which the situation affords. At the very least, these are all selection conditions with respect to social practices displayed in the encounter, since they serve as conditions under which particular practices are selectively favoured. The same is true for the other features of situations proposed by Argyle – the physical features, the difficulties and requisite skills, the concepts, the behavioural elements and sequences. It is not necessary to construe them as having a causal or productive influence upon the behaviours, but only as constituting the temporally extensive, interdependent network of conditions which allow for certain performances and impede others. Even if a change in a situational feature is found to coincide with changed practices within that situation, as when certain rules of address between men and women are altered, it is not necessary to construe the situational change as causing the behavioural change. Instead, the set of conditions under which the actions occur has been altered – as when men no longer are aware of the marital status of women in a formal encounter because the women are introduced as 'Ms' (however that is pronounced). Harré's discussion of mutation conditions, I think, is applicable to enduring practices and their modifications; but the understanding of situated action is best undertaken by viewing situational features as selection conditions.

The preceding comments pertain to the understanding of an action that has occurred and to the prediction of occurrence of a specified action in the future. However, sometimes we are interested in what sorts of actions will occur in a particular situation. That is, our interest may be in the range of actions that would be reasonably likely in that focal situation. Again, specification of the situational features would be necessary – but it would not be sufficient. The set of actions which have a reasonable likelihood of being performed will depend on who enter the situation and how they construe it and modulate it. In other words, if situations are viewed in terms of the opportunities they afford for action, it is essential to keep in mind that different people, with different histories, capacities and susceptibilities, will discriminate different features and different possibilities in a given setting. Thus, predicting the actions likely to occur within a proposed situation will require specification of the situational features *and* of the types of people who may enter the situation. The typing of people for this purpose should be in terms relevant to the action opportunities afforded by the situational features, although Bem and his students have had notable success using a personality trait Q-sort procedure (see Bem and Funder 1979; Bem and Lord 1979).

In any case, the conceptualization of a situation as a set of interdependent selection conditions for human action reduces the temptation to construe the relationship of situations to actions as causal, and it allows for creation, modulation and transformation of situations by acting persons. In short, it is compatible with an active agency view. However, before turning to the theme of active agency, one other aspect of situations as sets of selection conditions is worth noting. Situations, as Argyle suggests in his discussion of episodes, do have beginnings and ends – they do have duration. Further-more, situations are contained within other temporally more extensive situations, so that a situation which constitutes a set of selection conditions for actions performed within it is itself operating within the framework of selection conditions which comprise the hierarchically superior situation within which it is nested. Human actions and their settings are necessarily nested, as Shotter points out in his discussion of time; but the nesting is never completely fixed. It can be revised by virtue of subsequent events or by reconstrual by the person.

The second major class of themes pertains to the active agency of persons. Although much has been said about active agency, in this book and elsewhere, I think an essential feature of it is the power to act intentionally – that is, to manipulate one's environment in order to achieve an end. Active agency seems inextricably tied to teleology (I do not mean 'tautology' or other inadequate arguments; see Woodfield 1976), in which an action is performed 'in order to . . .'. Stated in this manner, active agency is not restricted to our species. However, discus-sions of active agency often incorporate self-monitoring of character as well as instrumental performances within the conception, which restricts the notion to those species having the capacity for self concepts and self recognition. The evidence to date restricts the notion to people, chimpanzees (see Gallup 1979; Meddin 1979) and perhaps gorillas. Other highly social mammals, such as dogs, or especially cetaceans, may prove to have the capacity also. An additional restriction often is imposed upon the range of applicability of the active agency notion by basing its conceptual elaboration upon the linguistic powers of the agent. In that case, active agency would be restricted to most people, a few chimpanzees and one or two gorillas.

In my opinion, it is not necessary to restrict active agency to linguistic organisms, any more than meaning should be restricted to the actions of a linguistic organism. Nor is it necessary to require the capacity for self-recognition or the existence of a self-concept. The power to manipulate the environment in order to accomplish an end is sufficient for the attribution of agency, for it allows for some of the elements of Shotter's 'intentionality' class and the logical existence of a perspective. The latter is allowed because the end-seeking organism will discriminate and manipulate different features of the environment, depending upon what opportunities the environment affords relative to the organism's transitory states.

My purpose in these comments has been to reduce the dependence of the active agency conception upon language and to extend its applicability. However, the rest of my discussion of agency will be framed in the context of our species, presuming linguistic competence, self-recognition and self-concept.

Active agency *must* be taken into account in any attempt to understand human action, since people act intentionally and both choose and create the contexts of their actions. That is, people in part choose which situations to enter and which to avoid. Furthermore, once choosing to enter a particular situation, or finding himself in it, the person may modulate it or even drastically transform it by his actions. In other words, situations actually are produced or implemented by people and exist over some time interval. During that interval, situational features serve as selection conditions, as discussed above; but the actors in the situation also can act to alter the situational features and thereby alter the situation, even to the point of ending it – although even that is usually guided by the rule structure applicable to that type of situation (see Albert and Kessler 1976, 1978 regarding ending social encounters).

Another aspect of active agency concerns perspective, as noted above. The dominant perspective contained in conventional social psychological theories is that of the observer. Not only are the theories constructed from the viewpoint of a self-less observer, but the theories construe the objects of interest as observers of themselves. This is readily apparent in contemporary attribution theories and has received some recent criticism (see Buss 1978).

There are three social perspectives of which persons are capable, but two of them actually are variations of a single view. Specifically, a person can be an observer of another person; and he can be an observer of himself; and he can have the perspective of an active agent. In fact, a person can be presumed always to have an active agency perspective, although at the same time he may be observing and commenting upon someone's actions. The two observer perspectives actually involve not only observing the actions of a person, whether self or other, but developing or offering accounts about those actions as well. This reflective component of the observer perspective seriously distorts contemporary social psychological theories. Very few are framed in terms of the continually present reality of the active agent, which Shotter insists – I think correctly – is necessary. His own chapter reflects such a perspective, as does Rommetveit's, and de-Charms has attempted something along that line (Shea and deCharms 1976). Active agency, however, has limits that must be recognized. Many actions occur in a relatively automatic fashion, often as overlearned, habitual sequences (see Langer 1978). Actions also are constrained by the biological susceptibilities and states of the person, and by cultural and situational factors discussed earlier as selection conditions. Active agency exists but in biologically and socially constrained form.

The third class of themes deals with features of the communicative act itself, especially meanings and units. Actions have meanings, and for comprehensible interaction to occur, the meanings of actions must be shared by the interactors, although not necessarily totally. In fact, part of the content of interaction is the clarification, further elaboration and even creation of meanings of the actions being performed.

The process of interaction inherently involves the active creation of a temporary and usually only partially shared framework of social reality. Entry into an interaction carries with it certain requirements or obligations to establish and maintain that temporary framework of shared social reality, an establishment of an agreement about the 'here and now'. Within that framework, the performance of the signalling – or speaking – function carries with it more control over the meaning of the action being performed than does the receiving – or listening – function. Thus, the creation of the framework of shared social reality is an active process which may involve negotiation of meanings between the interactors. The shared framework, as a continuing intersection of meanings, is a product of joint action and cannot be explained or understood in terms of either person alone.

The negotiation of meanings at the outset of an interaction may involve different procedures and consequences from the corrective and elaborative negotiations that occur during the interactive episode. Moreover, meanings may be negotiated retroactively. In fact, given the nested and continually nesting nature of human actions, the meaning of any action is forever modifiable by the later inclusion of that nested action in a new, larger act.

It is clear that the negotiation and modulation of meaning is an essential theme in this book. But what is 'meaning'?

The question is not addressed directly, but several of the chapters provide conceptual leads. Shotter, for example, refers to the meaning of an action as partly specified and partly specifiable. This suggests that the meaning of an action has two components, both of which are implicational in nature. First, the meaning is given partly by the action *implications* of the action – that is, by the subsequent actions implied by it. This allows the performer of the action to modify it even as he produces it by covertly responding to it from the perspective of the recipient, a process stressed by Rommetveit (this volume) and developed at length by G. H. Mead (1934) under the rubric of role taking.

Second, an action also and necessarily constitutes the empirical manifestation of the implications of prior actions in the sequence. It is itself part of the implication structure of those prior actions. Therefore, the meaning of an action is its situated action implications *and* it as an implication of prior actions; the meaning is the action implications from the past and for the future. Of course, it must be kept in mind that the implications exist in the temporally and hierarchically nested structure discussed earlier, in which sequences of actions exist within an act which their successful performance is accomplishing, and that act may exist within a still more inclusive act which is being accomplished by its successful performance, and so on. The implicational definition of the meanings of actions is consistent with the notion of act/action structure. Furthermore, linguistic competence is not necessary for actions to have meaning; but if linguistic competence does exist and is operative in the interaction, then the range, subtlety and temporal extensity is vastly increased.

Rommetveit notes that meaning must be considered in terms of what is meant, what is made known, and what is understood by the utterance. These concerns direct our attention to three perspectives from which implications may have to be investigated: the actor, an outside and knowledgeable observer viewing the whole episode and the recipient, respectively.

Another aspect of this third class of themes concerns the units of action, specifically those which are meaningful. In order for any occurrence to convey meaning, the occurrence must be discriminable. It must have a structure in terms of which it can be responded to as a coherent entity in the continual flux and variations of one's immediate world. Furthermore, that structure must be of a form which the organisms of interest are capable of discriminating. In human action, for example, acoustic frequencies or light wavelengths that are beyond the range of human auditory or visual sensitivity would be uninformative, and the structures indicated by them would be undetectable. Similarly, movements or vocal sounds which have no meaning in a culture are unlikely to be discriminated by members of that culture, and people would not be sensitive to the appearance or disappearance of structures indicated by such phenomena. However, as long as the indicating stimuli are within the biological range of perceptual sensitivity of the members of the culture, people can learn to be sensitive to – or search the action environment for – such structures.

This argument derives directly from J. J. Gibson's (1963, 1966) distinction between sensation and sensitivity and his conception of perception as an active process of discriminating invariant patterns within a constantly changing world. From this point of view, the ability to articulate the existence of an invariant pattern or the grounds upon which it was discriminated is absolutely and demonstrably irrelevant to the fact of the discrimination. Meaningful units of action are to be discovered, but we should not require that the native users of those units be aware of them or of their effects. In contrast to Peter Collett's claim that the stream of behaviour is homogeneous in time and that segmentations are imposed upon it by an interpretive observer, segmentations and other structural features are not imposed but rather *detected* by us as we become differentially sensitive to them.

In short, it is important to discover meaningful units of action within whatever episode or class of episodes is of interest. However, it would be a mistake to require a reliance upon participants' abilities to articulate or make sense of the units. Instead, we simply should acknowledge that people display evidence through their actions as to the structural features to which they are perceptually sensitive in a flow of interaction. This will allow us to search for the units they used without having to rely exclusively on their awareness, knowledge and beliefs about those units. This also implies that there are natural, perceivable units of behaviour, even though there is no single, unique set of such units.

Kreckel offers an excellent example of such a unit in her chapter – the tone-unit, which she construes as the unit of particular meaning which the speaker wishes to convey. The speech contours of an utterance serve as markers of meaningful chunks, which can be used as a basis from which to explore the contents of the meanings and the understandings produced. Her tone-unit, which is similar to the 'phonemic clause' (Jaffe and Feldstein 1970, p. 22), is only one among many potentially perceivable structural features of action that have been used or proposed as meaningful units. Duncan and Fiske (1977) discuss several in their treatment of turn-taking signals and their more recent paper on strategy signals (Duncan, Brunner and Fiske 1979). Apple, Streeter and Krause (1979) link speech rate and pitch changes to subsequent attributions; and Brunner (1979) discusses smiles as back channels, which would serve as units by virtue of being discriminable and having implications for the tone and continuation of the episode. Bassili's (1976) demonstration of the importance of time and space contingencies in the interpretation of joint motions as intentional provides still another example, as does the demonstration by Condon and Sander (1974) of the infant's sensitivity to the rhythm of adult speech (but see the recent critique by McDowall 1978).

Many other examples could be given, but these suffice to demonstrate the existence of discriminable units of action which, themselves, have action implications. However, we do not know the degree of stability of those units or their substantive meanings across contexts, which Collett properly identifies as important issues.

In sum, I have extracted three classes of themes from the contributions to this volume. The themes pertain to the selection conditions under which actions occur, including the situation and its potentially modifiable component features, the active agency of persons, with special emphasis given to their perspectives, and the meanings and meaningful units of the actions or interactions themselves.

3 The Emerging Model: Structural Analysis of Situated Action

The model of human action which emerges from the selective extraction of major themes from this volume can be stated succintly, but its practical implementation is difficult, very complicated and currently of unproven promise.

Human action is situated, temporally and hierarchically structured, and meaningful but modifiably so. The action of interest often is *joint* action, produced by the coordinated activity of two or more people, and not explainable in terms of any one of them. The persons whose situated actions we wish to understand are active agents whose agency is subject to biological and social constraints, and who operate from active perspectives of a continually present interval to reality which is partly specified and partly specifiable. To understand an action, it is necessary to understand the situation of its occurrence, and also to identify the temporal and hierarchical structure of the action – that is, its sequential linkages and its act/action relationships, the meaningful units it contains, and the meanings it carries in the instance of interest. Furthermore, each of these matters – situation, action structure, meanings and units – must be investigated from the active agency perspective of each of the parties involved, including that of the investigator.

To understand the nature of the situation, one must discover the content of each of the interdependent components discussed earlier. Argyle mentions some of the procedures which he and his colleagues are using, and there are other examples as well. The situated identity approach of Alexander and his co-workers (see, for example, Alexander and Scriven 1977) focuses on the evaluative implications of the role demands and performance possibilities in a particular situation. Bem's recent work using a Q-sort procedure characterizes the situation in terms of the various clusters of personality traits it would support or allow (see Bem and Funder 1979; Bem and Lord 1979). In addition to identifying the relevant components, the ease with which each can be modified should be determined. That information is necessary in order to estimate the social constraints which limit the active agency of the actors. Finally, the consequences for the other situational components of a change in any one of them should be assessed, since the situation is conceived as a system of interdependent components, and situations will differ in the extent to which change is transmitted through the system.

The discovery of meanings is a complex issue. The solicitation and even the negotiation of accounts offer one approach, especially if the accounts are used as indicators of the grounds for intelligibility and warrantability of the actions rather than as accurate descriptions of the meanings which the actions had at the time of performance. Observers can be asked to respond affectively to a videotape of an interaction, and then to discuss each of their affective responses; and this can be done with the original interactors as well, who could be asked to view a videotape of their own interaction. Role players can be used in carefully scripted simulations, too (see Geller 1978; Ginsburg 1979c). Scaling techniques, such as the semantic differential, also can be used; but whatever the technique, it must be compatible with the action implication conception of meaning.

The identification of meaningful units of action is another very complex issue, as noted in the previous section and in Collett's chapter. I will not discuss it further here, except to note that the procedures used for identification of units also should be compatible with the implicational conception of meaning.

The explicit use of the active agent perspective for each of the parties to the interaction poses unusual problems. Once an interval of 'specious present' has gone beyond a given action, that action is part of the relatively fixed past and no longer can be contained in an active agency perspective, even on the part of the original agent. Therefore, commentaries about that action, its situational context and its network of meanings will be generated from an *observer* perspective vis-à-vis that action, unless corrective approximations are used. The approximations involve role playing, perhaps in combination with replays of film or videotape taken from the physical perspective of the active agent (again, see Buss 1978; Geller 1978; Ginsburg 1979c; and see Storms 1973; Regan and Totten 1975; Arkin and Duval 1975). With care, such procedures should be quite effective, and it certainly is important to try. The field of social psychology is replete with examples of exclusively observer perspectives being used as models for explaining the actions and experiences of the person. The models of misattribution of emotion illustrate this practice; they all impose an observer perspective on the person and presume that he reflects upon and draws inferences about his own state and its sources, just as a curious observer would do with respect to another person (see Cooper, Fazio and Rhodewalt 1978; Schachter and Singer 1962; Zillman 1978).

The commitment to a model which acknowledges active agency perspectives does not mean a commitment to reportable phenomenology, although neither does it preclude such reports. Also, reports and commentaries about the perspective are not the only sources of data about it. The speech acts of the person during the interaction can be recorded and content analysed for indirect reflections of the meanings from the active perspective of that person. In that case, the problems of the observer perspective and of trying to simulate the active agent perspective do not arise.

This emerging model of situated action and its analysis carries an important methodological and technological implication. Specifically, the structure of situated action is discovered in part by examination of the unfolding of the action in its situational and act/action context over real time. Its emergence and maintenance or modulation is observed and analysed. This means that procedures which allow for relatively permanent records of the episode, such as film and video, will become increasingly common – as already is apparent in published reports. The availability of a permanent record of an episode, thereby allowing for repeated analyses, is essential for structural studies. But it does have certain costs and it does raise an important issue.

The most obvious cost is that of the equipment; but another heavy cost is the immense amount of data which one must analyse (or ignore). This is especially the case in exploratory phases of the research, where the videotape is being examined for patterns. In time, computer-based analyses of video data will become fairly common, but at present neither the necessary hardware nor the software are widely available. Still another cost is the likelihood of selection of episodes and settings that are easily taped or filmed, thus introducing a potential bias into the corpora available for analysis.

A bothersome but intriguing epistemological issue emanates from a commitment to a structural strategy. In structural analyses a completed episode which has been captured on permanent record is analysed over and over again. There is no question about what will happen, since it already has happened. The investigative perspective adopted by the researcher is analytical and retrospective, as opposed to the synthetic and predictive stance common in experimental social psychology. If the structural analyst develops an understanding of the episode, which he may well do after repeated observations of the videotape, that understanding will 'feel good'; it will make sense to him, it will be plausible. This is especially likely to occur if the investigator has an *a priori* belief about the nature of the episode and searches the videotape within the framework of that belief (see Snyder and Uranowitz 1978 for an experimental demonstration). Therefore, it is extremely important for those of us engaged in the structural analysis of situated action to develop cross-validational designs. Furthermore, it is important that we develop *predictive* designs to assess the adequacy of the understandings obtained from our structural studies.

The problems associated with the sceptical evaluation of our understandings and of the serious consideration of alternative interpretations are considerable and deserve extended attention in their own right. However, for purposes of this chapter, it might suffice merely to note that traditional experimental designs can be blended quite easily with structural techniques, so that the process by which the experimental outcome was generated can be examined directly. For example, one could videotape a sample of the experimental participants in each cell of the design (or videotape all and then select a sample of tapes) and structurally analyse those tapes in an effort to discover the processes by which the experimental *outcome* results were generated. Duncan and Fiske (1977) also suggest a comparable approach and gently chide themselves for not having done it with their external variable study. Such a strategy would take advantage of the protections of experimental design, especially the minimization of unknowable bias through randomized assignment of treatments to subjects, and the interpretative benefits deriving from control or baseline comparisons built into the design.

4   *Conclusions and the Future*

This book clearly is part of a growing perspective which is becoming increasingly mature and sure of itself. The exact shape of the science that will be formed by the continued development of this perspective – what I have called the structural analysis of situated action – is not clear yet; but I fully believe it will be more realistic and more useful than most of the knowledge generated by the investigative and scholarly activities of contemporary social psychologists. Several of the chapters in this book will contribute importantly to the advance of the perspective and the field.

References

S. Albert and S. Kessler, 1976, 'Processes for Ending Social Encounters: The Conceptual Archeology of a Temporal Place', *Journal for the Theory of Social Behaviour*, Vol. 6, pp. 147–170

S. Albert and S. Kessler, 1978, 'Ending Social Encounters', *Journal of Experimental Social Psychology*, Vol. 14, pp. 541–553

C. N. Alexander and G. D. Scriven, 1977, 'Role Playing: An Essential Component of Experimentation', *Personality and Social Psychology Bulletin*, Vol. 3, pp. 455–466

W. Apple, L. A. Streeter and R. M. Krauss, 1979, 'Effects of Pitch and Speech Rate on Personal Attributes', *Journal of Personality and Social Psychology*, Vol. 37, pp. 715–727

M. Argyle, 1975, 'Do Personality Traits Exist?', *New Behaviour*, 31 July, pp. 176–179

M. Argyle, 1979, 'Sequences in Social Behaviour as a Function of the Situation', in: G. P. Ginsburg (Ed.), *Emerging Strategies in Social Psychological Research*, Chichester: Wiley

P. Ariès, 1962, *Centuries of Childhood*, New York: Knopf

A. J. Ayer, 1974, *The Origins of Pragmatism*, London: Macmillan

C. W. Backman, 1979, 'Epilogue: A New Paradigm?', in: G. P. Ginsburg (Ed.), *Emerging Strategies in Social Psychological Research*, Chichester: Wiley

J. N. Bassili, 1976, 'Temporal and Spatial Contingencies in the Perception of Social Events', *Journal of Personality and Social Psychology*, Vol. 33, pp. 680–685

D. J. Bem and D. C. Funder, 1978, 'Predicting More of the People More of the Time: Assessing the Personality of Situations', *Psychological Review*, Vol. 85, pp. 485–501

D. J. Bem and C. G. Lord, 1979, 'Template Matching: A Proposal for Probing the Ecological Validity of Experimental Settings in Social Psychology', *Journal of Personality and Social Psychology*, Vol. 37, pp. 833–857

R. C. Bolles, 1972, 'Reinforcement, Expectancy, and Learning', *Psychological Review*, Vol. 79, pp. 394–409

E. G. Boring, 1963, *History, Psychology and Science: Selected Papers*, New York: Wiley

M. Brenner, P. Marsh and M. Brenner (Eds.), 1978, *The Social Contexts of Method*, London: Croom Helm

L. J. Brunner, 1979, 'Smiles Can Be Back Channels', *Journal of Personality and Social Psychology*, Vol. 37, pp. 728–734

A. R. Buss, 1978, 'Causes and Reasons in Attribution Theory: A Conceptual Critique', *Journal of Personality and Social Psychology*, Vol. 36, pp. 1311–1321

D. D. Clarke, 1979, 'The Linguistic Analogy or When is a Speech Act Like a Morpheme?', in: G. P. Ginsburg (Ed.), *Emerging Strategies in Social Psychological Research*, Chichester: Wiley

P. Collett (Ed.), 1977, *Social Rules and Social Behaviour*, Oxford: Blackwell

W. S. Condon and L. W. Sander, 1974, 'Neonate Speech Movement is Synchronized with Adult Speech', *Science*, Vol. 183, pp. 99–101

J. Cooper, R. H. Fazio and F. Rhodewalt, 1978, 'Dissonance and Humor: Evidence for the Undifferentiated Nature of Dissonance Arousal', *Journal of Personality and Social Psychology*, Vol. 36, pp. 280–285

D. Davis and H. J. Martin, 1978, 'When Pleasure Begets Pleasure: Recipient Responsiveness as a Determinant of Physical Pleasuring Between Heterosexual Dating Couples and Strangers', *Journal of Personality and Social Psychology*, Vol. 36, pp. 767–777

D. Davis and W. T. Perkowitz, 1979, 'Consequences of Responsiveness in Dyadic Interaction: Effects of Probability of Response and Proportion of Content-Related Responses on Interpersonal Attraction', *Journal of Personality and Social Psychology*, Vol. 37, pp. 534–550

S. Duncan, Jr., L. J. Brunner and D. W. Fiske, 1979, 'Strategy Signals in Face-to-Face Interaction', *Journal of Personality and Social Psychology*, Vol. 37, pp. 301–313

S. Duncan, Jr. and D. W. Fiske, 1977, *Face-to-Face Interaction: Research, Methods, and Theory*, Hillsdale, N.J.: Lawrence Erlbaum Associates

G. G. Gallup, Jr., 1979, 'Self-Awareness in Primates', *American Scientist*, Vol. 67, pp. 417–421

D. M. Geller, 1978, 'Involvement in Role-Playing Simulations: A Demonstration with Studies on Obedience', *Journal of Personality and Social Psychology*, Vol. 36, pp. 219–235

K. J. Gergen, 1973, 'Social Psychology as History', *Journal of Personality and Social Psychology*, Vol. 26, pp. 309–320

K. J. Gergen, in press, 'Toward Intellectual Audacity in Social Psychology', in: R. Gilmour and S. Duck (Eds.), *The Development of Social Psychology*, Chichester: Wiley

J. J. Gibson, 1963, 'The Useful Dimensions of Sensitivity', *American Psychologist*, Vol. 18, pp. 1–15

J. J. Gibson, 1966, *The Senses Considered as Perceptual Systems*, Boston: Houghton-Mifflin

G. P. Ginsburg, 1978, 'Role Playing and Role Performance in Social Psychological Research', in: M. Brenner, P. Marsh and M. Brenner (Ads.), *The Social Contexts of Method*, London: Croom Helm

G. P. Ginsburg (Ed.), 1979a, *Emerging Strategies in Social Psychological Research*, Chichester: Wiley

G. P. Ginsburg, 1979b, 'Introduction and Overview', in: G. P. Ginsburg (Ed.), *Emerging Strategies in Social Psychological Research*, Chichester: Wiley

G. P. Ginsburg, 1979c, 'The Effective Use of Role-Playing in Social Psychological Research', in: G. P. Ginsburg (Ed.), *Emerging Strategies in Social Psychological Research*, Chichester: Wiley

R. Harré, 1978, 'Accounts, Actions and Meanings – The Practice of Participatory Psychology', in: M. Brenner, P. Marsh and M. Brenner (Eds.), *The Social Contexts of Method*, London: Croom Helm

R. Harré and E. H. Madden, 1975, *Causal Powers: A Theory of Natural Necessity*, Oxford: Blackwell

R. Harré and P. F. Secord, 1972, *The Explanation of Social Behaviour*, Oxford: Blackwell

J. Israel and H. Tajfel (Eds.), 1972, *The Context of Social Psychology: A Critical Assessment*, London: Academic Press

W. James, 1890, *The Principles of Psychology*, New York: Henry Holt

J. Jaffe and S. Feldstein, 1970, *Rhythms of Dialogue*, New York: Academic Press

Journal of Personality and Social Psychology, 1978, Vol. 36, pp. 1310–1360

G. G. Kent, J. D. Davis and D. A. Shapiro, 1978, 'Resources Required in the Construction and Reconstruction of Conversation', *Journal of Personality and Social Psychology*, Vol. 36, pp. 13–22

M. Kreckel, in press, 'Communicative Acts and Shared Knowledge: A Conceptual Framework and Its Empirical Application', in: M. von Cranach and R. Harré (Eds.), *The Organization of Human Action*, Cambridge: Cambridge University Press

E. J. Langer, 1978, 'Rethinking the Role of Thought in Social Interaction', in: J. H. Harvey, W. Ickes and R. F. Kidd (Eds.), *New Directions in Attribution Research*, Vol. 2, Hillsdale, N.J.: Lawrence Erlbaum Associates

P. Marsh, E. Rosser and R. Harré, 1978, *The Rules of Disorder*,

London: Routledge & Kegan Paul

J. J. McDowall, 1978, 'Interactional Synchrony: A Reappraisal', *Journal of Personality and Social Psychology*, Vol. 36, pp. 963–975

C. McPhail and C. Rexroat, 1979, 'Mead vs. Blumer', *American Sociological Review*, Vol. 44, pp. 449–467

G. H. Mead, 1934, *Mind, Self and Society*, Chicago: University of Chicago Press

J. Meddin, 1979, 'Chimpanzees, Symbols, and the Reflective Self', *Social Psychology Quarterly*, Vol. 42, pp. 99–109

R. E. Nisbett and T. D. Wilson, 1977, 'Telling More than We Can Know: Verbal Reports on Mental Processes', *Psychological Review*, Vol. 84, pp. 231–259

S. Schachter and J. Singer, 1962, 'Cognitive, Social and Physiological Determinants of Emotional State', *Psychological Review*, Vol. 65, pp. 121–128

D. J. Shea and R. deCharms, 1976, 'Beyond Attribution Theory: The Human Conception of Motivation and Causality', in: L. H. Strickland, F. E. Aboud and K. J. Gergen (Eds.), *Social Psychology in Transition*, New York: Plenum

M. Snyder and S. W. Uranowitz, 1978, 'Reconstructing the Past: Some Cognitive Consequences of Person Perception', *Journal of Personality and Social Psychology*, Vol. 36, pp. 941–950

Society for the Advancement of Social Psychology Newsletter, October 1979

L. H. Strickland, F. E. Aboud and K. L. Gergen (Eds.), 1976, *Social Psychology in Transition*, New York: Plenum

B. W. Tuchman, 1979, *A Distant Mirror: The Calamitous 14th Century*, New York: Knopf

A. Woodfield, 1976, *Teleology*, Cambridge: Cambridge University Press

D. Zillman, 1978, 'Attributions and Misattributions of Excitatory Reactions', in: J. H. Harvey, W. Ickes and R. F. Kidd (Eds.), *New Directions in Attribution Research*, Vol. 2, Hillsdale, N.J.: Lawrence Erlbaum Associates

Index